An Introduction to Caribbean Francophone Writing

An Introduction to Caribbean Francophone Writing

Guadeloupe and Martinique

Edited by
Sam Haigh

BERG

Oxford • New York

First published in 1999 by
Berg
Editorial offices:
150 Cowley Road, Oxford, OX4 1JJ, UK
70 Washington Square South, New York, NY 10012, USA

Berg is the imprint of Oxford International Publishers Ltd.

Library of Congress Cataloging-in-Publication Data

A catalogue record for this book is available from the Library of Congress.

British Library Cataloguing-in-Publication Data

A catalogue record for this book is available from the British Library.

ISBN 1 85973 293 3 (Cloth)

Typeset by JS Typesetting, Wellingborough, Northants.
Printed in the United Kingdom by WBC Book Manufacturers, Bridgend,
Mid Glamorgan.

Contents

Contents

Acknowledgements

There are a number of friends and colleagues whom I should like to thank for their help with this volume. I am very grateful to Nicki Hitchcott for first suggesting this series as a home for the project; to all the contributors for their participation and hard work; to Richard Burton for his helpful comments on the manuscript; and to Kathryn Earle at Berg. I should also like to thank Bridget Jones for her unfailing support – and her speedy responses to my many questions – as well as Laura Brace, Diana Knight, Christopher Thompson and, most especially, Phil Leonard.

Introduction
Sam Haigh

France and the Caribbean: Historical Context

The Caribbean islands of Guadeloupe and Martinique, with which this volume will principally be concerned, are among France's oldest colonies: they have been French for longer than Calais, Strasbourg or Nice and, as overseas departments (*départements d'outre-mer*, or DOM), they remain French today. These islands of the 'French Antilles' were 'discovered' by Christopher Columbus at the time of his exploration of the Americas – Guadeloupe in 1492 and Martinique in 1502 – along with two other territories which were also to come under French control: the island named Hispaniola by the Spanish in 1492, later Saint-Domingue and now divided into the Dominican Republic and the Republic of Haiti, and the DOM of French Guiana (*la Guyane*) situated on the north-east coast of South America and 'discovered' in 1499.

None of these four territories was settled by the French until the seventeenth century, with that of Guiana proving the most difficult to settle due to the vastness of the area and the hostility of the climate. The plantation system (or, rather, the often smaller 'habitation' system) is, of course, what distinguished France's Caribbean colonies from those it founded later and in different parts of the world. While in Guiana it proved impossible to eradicate the native Carib population, since large numbers of them fled into the inaccessible interior, in Guadeloupe and Martinique the Spanish had already begun what amounted to a campaign of genocide by the time that the French settlers arrived around 1635. Having failed to force the remaining Caribs to work the land, the settlers either exterminated them or drove them out, to neighbouring Dominica, and introduced a system of indentured labour, bringing 'engagés blancs' on three-year contracts from France. It was only when this system failed, a few years later, that the French began to bring African slaves, mainly from the Gulf of Guinea, to Martinique, Guadeloupe and Guiana, thus following the example of the Spanish, who, from 1502, had already begun importing slaves to Hispaniola.

Sam Haigh

In each of the new colonies, slaves soon vastly outnumbered the white plantation owners, and guidelines setting out and sanctioning ways of controlling the slave population soon became necessary. In Guiana in particular, the vastness of the territory once again meant that the settlers' task was more difficult, with *marronnage* (escape) and rebellion much harder to control and put down. Thus in 1685 Louis XIV introduced the infamous *Code Noir*, a statute apparently intended to provide guidelines for plantation owners about the appropriate treatment of slaves, but which in fact reduced the slaves, as Lucien-René Abenon explains, to the status of 'movable property [des biens mobiliers] that the master could use as he wished'.[1] The threat of appalling punishment, even for the most minor of misdeeds, the promise of the rewards of the afterlife through conversion to Catholicism and even the seeds of the infamous colonial policy of assimilation (to which we shall return later) were enshrined in the *Code Noir* as ways of ensuring the lasting subjugation of the growing slave population.

The plantation system continued throughout the rest of the seventeenth century and most of the eighteenth century and, on the eve of the French Revolution, Guadeloupe, Saint Domingue and Martinique were extremely prosperous islands, a fact which explains France's willingness, during the Seven Years' War (1756–63), to trade the majority of its North American colonies with Britain in order to maintain its colonies in the Caribbean. The victory of the French Revolution in 1789, however, and the 'Déclaration des Droits de l'Homme et du Citoyen', marked the beginning of a turning point in France's Caribbean colonies, since the logic of 'liberté, égalité, fraternité' threw into sharp relief the inequalities inherent in the regime of slavery. The revolution in the metropole stirred up anti-slavery feelings on both sides of the Atlantic: abolitionists in France (as elsewhere in Europe) and ever more discontented slaves in the colonies. It was therefore perhaps unsurprising when, in 1793–4, the abolition of slavery was announced. However, it was in this year, too, that Britain, taking advantage of France's disarray during the Revolution, chose to invade its Caribbean colonies and attempt to take control of them. It was thus chiefly because large numbers of extra soldiers were needed at this time if France

---

1. Lucien-René Abenon (1992), *Petite histoire de la Guadeloupe*, Paris: L'Harmattan, p. 51, translation mine. On this, and other aspects of Antillean history, see also Jacques Ziller (1991), *Les DOM-TOM*, Paris: Librairie Générale de Droit, and Jacques Adélaïde-Merlande (1994), *Histoire Générale des Antilles et des Guyanes: Des Précolombiens à nos jours*, Paris: Editions Caribéennes.

was to safeguard its empire, rather than for any purely humanitarian aims, that abolition occurred. It is here, of course, that the history of Saint-Domingue begins to differ radically from that of the other three territories. Indeed, even the history of Guadeloupe and Martinique differs marginally and briefly during this period. In Martinique, the larger and more powerful white planter (*béké*) class colluded with the British in order that the abolition of slavery could be prevented and the old balance of power maintained. Martinique therefore remained under British control until 1802, with slavery very much still in place. In Guadeloupe, however, with its much smaller *béké* population, abolition did take place and the ex-slaves joined the fight to defeat the British. However, with no slaves to work the plantations, the economy began to suffer and, in 1802, Bonaparte ordered the re-establishment of slavery. In Martinique, now French once more, this was a relatively easy task as slavery had never in practice been properly abolished; in Guiana, slavery was reinstated, but the vastness of the territory again made matters more difficult for the French, as relatively large numbers of slaves fled to the deeply forested interior once more. Indeed, it was at this time that Guiana began to revolve less around the economy of the plantation, and to serve much more as a penal colony for France.

In Guadeloupe and Saint-Domingue, however, matters took a different course. In Guadeloupe, led by the now legendary Martinican soldier Louis Delgrès, the black soldiers took up arms and opposed the reinstatement of slavery. Although they were defeated, the famous mass suicide of Delgrès and his army at Fort Matouba, a radical refusal of enslavement, has come to constitute one of the most symbolic moments in Guadeloupean history. In Saint-Domingue, events were even more dramatic and much more successful as, under the leadership of Toussaint Louverture, the much larger numbers of slaves on the island had already rebelled during the early 1790s. Though he had yielded to the French after the 1794 abolition of slavery, he remained powerful and led more rebellions when Bonaparte attempted to reinstate it. While he was himself exiled to France because of these rebellions, and died there in 1803, the French were successfully expelled from the island in 1804 and, under General Dessalines, the island's independence was proclaimed. The Spanish reclaimed the east of the island and then, over the next few decades, and after periods of civil war, the new Republic of Haiti was finally proclaimed in the west, and the Dominican Republic in the east. And it is here that Haiti's history departs definitively from that of the dependent islands. Indeed, as the first independent black state and the first colony to gain independence from

France, Haiti has occupied an iconic position in the Caribbean imagination, despite the violence and instability which have continued to characterize its history. From independence to the present day, civil war, brutal dictatorship, military repression and US occupation have all left their mark on Haiti and its people, and in many ways its future remains as uncertain now as it was in the early nineteenth century.[2]

In the dependent territories, the nineteenth century saw a series of continued struggles for domination between European colonial powers, until France definitively regained control in 1814 – only to be faced with growing internal conflict and unrest. Since the seventeenth century, both Guadeloupe and Martinique had been evolving into three-tier societies divided along class–colour lines, as an 'intermediate class' made up predominantly of mulattos who had managed to free themselves – or be freed – from slavery, gradually established itself. By the early to mid-nineteenth century, these 'free people of colour' ('gens de couleur libres') had become a sizeable force to be reckoned with, and they were beginning to call for rights and recognition. Since the *Code Noir*, French colonial discourses had always expressed aspirations of 'civilization' and acculturation, however minor, and in the nineteenth century France's colonial enterprise began explicitly to be framed as a 'civilizing mission'. Indeed, it was then that what has come to be seen as the distinguishing feature of French colonialism – the policy of assimilation – began to be applied in the Antilles, as France's avowed aim became to export, wholesale, French language and French culture, in order to re-create overseas colonies and their inhabitants in the image of France. In these Caribbean colonies, in which any notion of 'indigenous culture' was, at best, problematic, such a policy was bound to have dramatic effects, and it was of course among the free people of colour that these effects initially became most immediately noticeable.

As the gap between assimilationist rhetoric and actuality became evident – that the act of being freed from slavery by no means guaranteed access to French citizenship, for example – mulatto activists such as Bisette began to take action. During the 1820s, free mulattos campaigned for the right to full French citizenship, and this was finally granted in 1833. It did not mean, however, that this group then became an active force in the

---

2. On Haitian history, see Thomas Madiou (1989), *Histoire d'Haïti (1492–1846)*, 8 vols, Port-au-Prince: Editions Henri Deschamps; Carolyn E. Fick (1990), *The Making of Haiti: The Saint-Domingue Revolution from Below*, Knoxville: University of Tennessee Press; Deirdre McFadyen and Pierre LaRamée, eds (1995), *Haiti: Dangerous Crossroads*, Boston: Southend Press.

fight for abolition and the extension of similar rights to the mass of black slaves. On the contrary, the logic of assimilationist discourses ensured that mulattos were concerned, in their campaign, with distancing themselves as much as possible from the black slaves and presenting themselves as more worthy of citizenship because of their greater assimilation, their greater proximity to the whites at the top of the social hierarchy. The *békés*, in turn, felt their own power and position to be under threat and became ever more racist in their attitude towards both the mulattos and the black slaves. With the abolition of slavery in 1848, and then the extension of voting rights to all black men in 1870, both the *békés'* power and the mulattos' precarious position of upward mobility were felt to be under further threat. And thus the class–colour hierarchy, whose legacy is still evident in the Antilles today, became firmly established, with each group obsessively defining itself in a relationship of superiority to the one below, and with the indentured workers, brought over from India during the aftermath of abolition, positioned at the very bottom.

Thus the three colonies continued through the nineteenth century, and well into the twentieth, under French rule, with Guadeloupe and Martinique in particular remaining relatively prosperous overseas possessions. Not until 1946, with the famous backing of the then Communist mayor of Fort-de-France and Martinican *député* Aimé Césaire, did a change in status finally take place in the form of departmentalization. As France's other colonies throughout the world were beginning to call for independence, Martinique, Guadeloupe, Guiana and the Indian Ocean island colony of Réunion were assimilated ever more into the *mère-patrie*, becoming fully-fledged departments of France, and henceforth to have the same laws and rights applied to their peoples as to all other French citizens.

In practice, the majority of laws and benefits were not extended to the Antilles until well into the 1950s and 1960s, with many not being extended until the 1970s and 1980s. Though certainly well-off in relation to other Caribbean islands who gained their independence from European colonial powers, the French DOM, despite the departmentalist rhetoric of assimilation and equality, are much worse off in relation to France itself. Since the sugar industry began to decline in the 1950s, the once prosperous islands of Martinique and Guadeloupe have seen the virtual disappearance of viable island economies, and have become increasingly dependent upon France instead. The cost of living is high, since most goods are imported from France, the rate of unemployment is approximately double that of mainland France and underemployment is also a significant problem. Despite the growth of the tourist industry, the absence of adequate French government funding for the development of other industries means that unemployment, and the mass emigration to France which began in the 1960s, will continue for the foreseeable future.[3]

This situation of dependence and of an artificial, consumer economy has brought a mixed reaction from Antilleans, especially politically. Many, especially among the older generations, are grateful for France's 'benevolence' and, convinced that the DOM simply could not survive without France's aid, see themselves primarily as French citizens. Others, however, see the islands' relationship with France as one which has remained that of colony to colonial power and have pointed out that, invested as it still is in retaining vestiges of Empire, France may be seen to have deliberately discouraged the implantation of viable local economies in order to foster a culture of passivity and dependence. Indeed, this link between economy and culture in the Antilles is a crucial one. As Richard Burton has pointed out, one of the most damaging effects of the post-departmentalization erosion of the traditional Antillean economy, has been the ensuing erosion of traditional Antillean culture: 'dress, food, family structures, music and, not least, the Creole language itself [have all been] exposed in their different ways to a marked "Europeanization"'.[4] As Burton goes on to argue, this 'decreolization'[5] has to some extent been checked in recent years, as more and more Antilleans have become aware of the threat of 'extinction' faced by Creole culture, and have begun to take steps to save it. Carnival, Creole cuisine, theatre and music have all undergone a measure of revitalization but, as Burton argues, they remain under threat as long as a 'sustaining socioeconomic base' is absent in the Antilles.[6]

These, too, have long been among the arguments of those groups, who, since the 1960s, have been calling for independence for the DOM. Although most active during the 1970s and early 1980s, these groups do

3. Those 'new' industries which have been attempted – based around the production of fruit and vegetables for export – have failed because, since Guadeloupe and Martinique, like the rest of France, have a minimum wage (albeit slightly lower), the goods are not able to be produced at prices sufficiently low to enable competition with those neighbouring countries producing similar products. On these and related political and economic issues in the post-departmentalization Antilles, see Robert Lambotte (1979), 'Les DOM: le sous-développement français', *Options*, 77, pp. 38–42; Jean-Luc Mathieu (1988), *Les DOM-TOM*, Paris: Presses universitaires de France; Richard D.E. Burton and Fred Reno, eds (1994), *French and West Indian: Martinique, Guadeloupe and French Guiana Today*, London: Macmillan.

4. Richard D.E. Burton, 'The French West Indies *à l'heure de l'Europe*: An Overview', in Burton and Reno, eds, *French and West Indian*, p. 5.

5. Ibid., p. 12.

6. Ibid., p. 113.

still have some local support. Indeed, in Martinique, traditionally the least militant of the Caribbean DOM, there is evidence of a slight growth in support in terms of recent voting tendencies, with Alfred Marie-Jeanne of the *Mouvement Indépendantiste Martiniquais* (MIM) having made significant advances in regional and legislative elections throughout the 1990s. It remains doubtful, however, that there will ever be sufficient support, in the foreseeable future, for independence actually to be realized.

The Development of a Literary Tradition

It is against this historical background that the literary and theoretical writing which will be the subject of this volume began to emerge. And this writing, of course – in each of the four territories settled by the French – may be traced back to the work of the priests and missionaries who were first sent to the new colonies in the seventeenth and eighteenth centuries. Père du Tertre's *Histoire générale des Antilles habitées par les Français*, published between 1667 and 1671, and Père Labat's *Nouveaux voyages aux îles d'Amérique*, published in 1722, provide some of the first examples of written 'literature' on and about the Caribbean colonies, literature which consists largely of descriptions of the geography, flora and fauna of the colonies and of the newly established and still developing plantation system. Written very obviously from the perspective of outsiders, temporary residents of the islands, such work was not supplemented by that of Antillean-born writers until well into the eighteenth century, when *békés* began also to write about the experience of living in the colonies.

The white Guadeloupean Nicholas-Germain Léonard, who published three texts – *La Nouvelle Clémentine* (1744), *Idylles morales* (1766) and *Lettre sur un voyage aux Antilles* (1787) – is generally acknowledged as the first Antillean-born writer, although he, like the earlier French writers, spent most of his life in France and based his texts on observations he made as a visitor to the islands.[7] As the eighteenth century drew to a close,

---

7. For further details on these and other texts discussed here, as well as on the development of Antillean literature generally, see Jack Corzani (1978), *La Littérature des Antilles–Guyane françaises*, 6 vols, Fort-de-France: Désormeaux; Roger Toumson (1989), *La Transgression des couleurs: Littérature et langage des Antilles, 18e, 19e, 20e siècles*, 2 vols, Paris: Editions Caribéennes; Patrick Chamoiseau and Raphael Confiant (1991), *Lettres créoles: Tracées antillaises et continentales de la littérature 1635–1975*, Paris: Hatier; A. James Arnold, ed. (1995), *A History of Literature in the Caribbean: Hispanic and Francophone Regions*, Amsterdam and Philadelphia: John Benjamins.

however, the literary history, like the social history, of the dependent and independent territories began irrevocably to change: with its independence in 1804, Haiti began to produce black, racially aware writers long before the dependent territories. Anti-colonial pamphlets, literary journals and poetry by the newly established élite played a major role, throughout the nineteenth century, in establishing a literary scene in Haiti and, by the early twentieth century, the novel had also begun to emerge as an important Haitian genre.

The twentieth century saw the emergence of numerous movements, writers and theories in Haiti, which would eventually have an enormous impact upon writers from the dependent territories: inspired by the work of one of Haiti's greatest intellectuals, Jean Price-Mars, and by nationalist opposition to the US occupation of 1915–34, the *indigénistes* emerged in the 1920s and called for an assertion and celebration of specifically Haitian culture and values. In the 1930s, *indigénisme* gave way to *noirisme*, formulated by a group named *Les Griots*, of which François Duvalier was a member, and whose particular brand of black nationalism entailed an assertion of the 'essential Africanness' of Haitian culture and identity, and a celebration of voodoo mysticism. Although *noirisme* was to become the basis of the Duvalier regime, it gave way intellectually to the Marxism of writers such as Jacques Roumain and, later, to a combination of Marxism, surrealism and magical realism in the work of Roumain, Jacques-Stephen Alexis and René Depestre. With the Duvalier régime, however, came the repression of intellectual life: Depestre was exiled and Alexis murdered, and apart from Frankétienne's *spiralisme*, a late-1960s, anti-authoritarian call to literary experimentation, most Haitian literary and intellectual activity has been exiled – to Montreal, Paris and Dakar. The current climate of political instability means that the future direction of Haitian literature is as uncertain as that of Haiti itself.[8]

Progress towards racially aware black writing in the dependent territories was rather slower, and, throughout the nineteenth century, *béké* texts continued to dominate the literary scene: notably Louis Maynard de Queilhe's *Outre-Mer* (1835), Poiré de Saint-Aurèle's *Les Veillées françaises* (1826) and Jules Levilloux's *Les Créoles, où la vie aux Antilles* (1835). Although the latter may have been a mulatto, and despite the acquisition by mulattos of the right to full French citizenship in 1833, the

---

8. For more detailed and comprehensive studies of Haitian literature see, for example, Raphaël Berrou and Pradel Pompilus, eds (1975), *Histoire de la littérature haïtienne*, 3 vols, Port-au-Prince: Editions Caraïbes; Michael Dash (1981), *Literature and Ideology in Haiti 1915–61*, London: Macmillan; and Joan Dayan (1995), *Haiti, History, and the Gods*, Berkeley and London: University of California Press.

mulatto population produced hardly any writing until the late nineteenth century – and the black population still less. Instead, perceiving their power to be under threat, white Creole writers began to publish ever more racist texts, such as Rosemond de Beauvallon's *Hier! Aujourd'hui! Demain!, ou les Agonies créoles* (1885). As Richard Burton has pointed out, however, the most outstanding text of the late nineteenth century is, in fact, a novel by a Guianese and 'evidently non-white' writer. *Atipa, roman guyanais*, published in Creole in 1885 under the pseudonym of Alfred Parépou, is a text which, according to Burton, 'offers a vivid and mordant picture of colonial society'.[9] The first volume of poetry attributed to a black Antillean was then Eugène Agricole's *Fleurs des Antilles* (1900).

On the whole, however, the early twentieth century saw the publication of several volumes of poetry by white Creole writers, most notably Daniel Thaly's *Lucioles et cantharides* (1900) and *Le Jardin des tropiques* (1911), and the work of Saint-John Perse. At the same time, mulatto poets of the so-called 'regionalist' school, such as Victor Duquesnay (*Les Martiniquaises*, 1903) and Oruno Lara (*Sous le ciel bleu de Guadeloupe*, 1912), also began to write, though, unsurprisingly, in a noticeably 'assimilated' style, derived from that of the white Creole writers, who themselves emulated the work of their 'metropolitan' contemporaries. It was not until the appearance of René Maran's novel *Batouala* (1921), Oruno Lara's *Questions de couleur – noirs et blanches* (1923), Suzanne Lacascade's *Claire-Solange, âme africaine* (1924), Gilbert Gratiant's *Cris d'un jeune* (1926) and Léon-Gontran Damas's collection of poetry, *Pigments* (1937), that a racially aware, Antillean form of writing began finally to develop among the mulatto and black populations of the colonies.

It was with the work of Damas, and particularly his association with Aimé Césaire, that the black Antillean literary tradition continued to emerge in the form of *négritude*. This political, literary and philosophical movement is usually seen to mark the birth of black Antillean resistance to colonialism and to the alienation – both collective and personal – which it entailed. It was founded by a group of black students in Paris – most notably Damas, Césaire and the Senegalese poet Léopold Sédar Senghor, later the President of Senegal – who set up the literary magazine *L'Etudiant noir* in 1935. Although not the first journal to be set up by black students in Paris, its founders felt that it would represent a significant break with predecessors, which they found either to be too imitative of contemporary

---

9. See Richard Burton's extremely useful summary of the development of Antillean literature in his entry on the 'West Indies' in Peter France, ed. (1995), *The New Oxford Companion to Literature in French*, Oxford: Oxford University Press, pp. 851–4.

French writers and poets, or simply too moderate in their claims. They were nevertheless influenced by these predecessors, especially Jacques Roumain's *Revue indigène*, the Nardal sisters' *La Revue du Monde Noir* and Etienne Léro's more radical communist–surrealist magazine *Légitime défense*, which was to have only one issue. In all of these journals, the pioneering work of black writers from Haiti (Price-Mars, Roumain, the *indigénistes* and *noiristes*) and from the USA (Claude McKay, Jean Toomer, Countee Cullen) was published alongside that of newer writers from the Antilles and Africa, who all called for a rejection of European, colonial values and a reassertion instead of the 'essential Africanness' common to all those of the black diaspora, a celebration of blackness and African cultural values.

The ideals of Antillean *négritude*, of a return to African values and a rejection of the ideology of assimilation, were crystallized in Césaire's seminal text *Cahier d'un retour au pays natal*, first published in the Parisian journal *Volontés* in 1939. The journal *Tropiques*, founded in 1940 in Martinique by Suzanne Césaire, Aimé Césaire and René Ménil, then continued, until 1943, to develop and assert these ideas through essays and poems of a broadly surrealist nature. As if demonstrating the central importance of *négritude* in the burgeoning Antillean literary scene, poetry remained the dominant genre throughout the 1940s and into the 1950s. Some novels, however, also began to appear around this time – most notably Joseph Zobel's *La Rue cases-nègres* (1950), which, with the optimism of the newly departmentalized Antilles, describes the Antilleans' struggle against colonialism and injustice as one to be undertaken via the French education by then increasingly available. Other novelists of this period also tended to be from Martinique – Rafaël Tardon, Léopold Sainville and, of course, Mayotte Capécia, whose work became infamous in the wake of Fanon's critique of it in his seminal study of assimilation and its psychological effects, *Peau noire, masques blancs* (1952).

Indeed, Fanon's theoretical critique of assimilation was echoed in much of the poetry of this period, by Edouard Glissant, Guy Tirolien, Paul Niger and Sonny Rupaire, the latter three Guadeloupean and the last two in particular belonging to what might be called the 'protest' tradition of anti-colonial writing. From 1960, however, poetry ceased to be the dominant literary genre in the Antilles, although it has, of course, by no means ceased to be produced: the Guianese poets Élie Stephenson and Serge Patient, in particular, are noteworthy, as are a number of poets who, like the Martinican Joby Bernabé and the Guadeloupeans Rupaire and Hector Poullet, write in Creole. Indeed, their work may be seen as part of a move which has slowly been taking place for some decades in the Antilles: to reassert this language, which developed out of the plantation system and which has always had the secondary status of an oral patois in relation to French as the dominant language of education, administration and social mobility. Examples of Haitian writing in Creole can be found as early as the mid-eighteenth century, and Alfred Parépou's 1885 *Atipa, roman guyanais* was also written in Creole, but apart from the famous nineteenth-century Creole translations of La Fontaine's *Fables*,[10] it was not until the mid-twentieth century, with the work of Gilbert Gratiant (*Fab 'Compè Zicaque*, 1958), that there was significant interest in producing texts in Creole. Indeed, it should come as no surprise that real interest in Creole writing coincided with the pro-independence activities of the late 1960s to the early 1980s, for the promotion of Creole as a national language has been primary among the concerns of some of the pro-independence groups.

It is the francophone novel, however, which has emerged during the last four decades as the dominant genre in the Antilles. The Guianese novelist Bertène Juminer and the Martinican Glissant were both at the forefront of prose fiction writing in the 1960s, and both have continued writing into the 1990s. While the fiction of the 1960s largely followed the realist and broadly optimistic tone of that of the 1950s, a marked change in the tone of prose fiction occurred during the 1970s, with the rather more pessimistic writing of novelists such as the Martinican Vincent Placoly, or the 'magical realism' of Xavier Orville. It was also during the 1970s that two other major changes occurred to the literary scene. First, much more significant numbers of women writers than ever before began to emerge. Writers like Michèle Lacrosil, who had begun writing in the 1960s, began to be joined by others – Jacqueline Manicom, Simone Schwarz-Bart, Maryse Condé, to name but the most well-known. All of these writers, like their male counterparts, used fiction as a means of examining issues relating to Antillean identity, but they also began to explore the ways in which such issues may be further complicated by questions of gender and sexual difference. The second major development in the Antillean literary scene to occur in the 1970s was the emergence of theatre as an important, if never predominant, genre. Although Antillean writers, like Césaire, had been writing plays and producing performances of them during the 1960s, and even before, it was during the 1970s that theatre began to emerge as a vital means of reaching relatively large, and not necessarily book-reading, audiences, often using Creole and certainly drawing upon African and Caribbean traditions of oral storytelling.

10. François Marbot (1976), *Les Bambous. Fables de La Fontaine travesties en patois martiniquais par un vieux commandeur*, Paris: Casterman. Originally published in 1846.

During the 1980s and 1990s, theatrical works have continued to be produced, but the novel remains predominant. Glissant and Placoly have been joined by writers such as Daniel Maximin, Raphaël Confiant and Patrick Chamoiseau. Creole has become more of a force within Antillean writing, either as the main language of expression (the earlier works of Confiant, for example) or in a hybridized Franco-Creole form (Chamoiseau's 1992 Prix Goncourt winner *Texaco*, for example). The East Indian minority has also begun to find a voice, as in the work of Ernest Moutoussamy, and increasing numbers of women writers have also continued to emerge – Schwarz-Bart and Condé being joined by a host of younger, or simply newer, writers such as Sylviane Telchid, Suzanne Dracius-Pinalie, Gisèle Pineau and Lucie Julia.

It is this ever more vibrant and radical contemporary literary scene which is the principal, though by no means only, focus of the present collection of essays, and indeed it is for this reason that more attention has been given above to the earlier period of Antillean writing. Given the ever-increasing volume and range of Caribbean francophone writing, it is inevitable, if unfortunate, that a collection such as this should be selective rather than comprehensive. As has already been made apparent here, this volume deals primarily with writing from those Caribbean island DOM of Guadeloupe and Martinique, whose social and literary history has been the most consistently similar. Though not strictly speaking 'Caribbean', the literature of Guiana is often included in discussions of Antillean writing – the geographical proximity, the shared status of DOM and perhaps especially the fact that Guianese writers like 'Alfred Parépou', Léon-Gontran Damas and René Maran were at the forefront of early attempts at anti-colonial and anti-assimilationist black writing, all combine to encourage such an inclusion. Such inclusion has often led to the marginalization of Guianese writing, as attention has been focused upon the more prolific and better-known writers from the two islands – and in this volume, too, it is unfortunate that, while Guianese writers are mentioned in several of the essays, it proved impossible to include an essay devoted exclusively to Guianese literature.[11]

11. Both Corzani's *La Littérature des Antilles-Guyane françaises* and Toumson's *La Transgression des couleurs*, as well as Arnold's *A History of Literature in the Caribbean*, include studies of the literature of Guiana. In the latter volume, Bridget Jones's chapter, 'French Guiana', usefully discusses the very issue of the way in which Guiana is often 'conveniently' included in discussions of 'the French Caribbean', and points out the important differences which exist between the South American and the island DOM, and (consequently) between their literary output.

A similar decision of inclusion and exclusion has had to be taken, here as elsewhere in Caribbean francophone studies, with regards to the much larger amount of writing from the independent island of Haiti. As we have seen, Haiti initially shared a very similar colonial history with Guadeloupe and Martinique, but, with its early independence and the early development of anti-colonial black writing which resulted, the similarities between the dependent and independent islands have become less marked, and it is for this reason that Haitian literature is not examined in any detail here. However, despite the island's continuing political instability, and the current proliferation of Haitian writing outside Haiti, there has always been much academic interest in Haitian writing, sometimes alongside that of Guadeloupe and Martinique[12] and more frequently as a separate entity.[13] Of course, the links and similarities between the literature of the dependent and independent islands and territories are extremely important – it is vital that artificial separations between geographically and historic-ally similar regions are not made simply on the basis of the divisions created by colonialism. However, as the authors of the 1989 manifesto *Eloge de la Créolité* would undoubtedly agree, the recognition of differ-ence is an equally vital prerequisite to attempts to build links which do not simply repeat that other colonial gesture of considering the other as a homogeneous 'mass'. This volume therefore sets out to examine writing from Guadeloupe and Martinique in some detail, while also, in several of the essays, attempting to widen the debate out further, to consider writing from other Caribbean islands and regions which share similar legacies of colonialism – Haiti, anglophone and hispanophone countries and so on.

As the range of contributors to this collection shows, Caribbean franco-phone writing is an area of literary study which is gaining increasing attention in the anglophone world, and which is being offered at both undergraduate and graduate level on courses in the UK, Ireland, the USA, Canada and Australia, as well as in the anglophone Caribbean. It is therefore hoped that this introduction will prove a useful resource for those studying and teaching such courses, as well as providing the new and more experienced scholar of Antillean writing with a valuable survey of some key issues and with a point of departure for further investigation. Equally, while each chapter may be read on its own, it is hoped that several

12. See, for example, Régis Antoine (1992), *La Littérature franco-antillaise: Haïti, Guadeloupe et Martinique*, Paris: Karthala. A recent publication on women's writing from the francophone Caribbean similarly chooses to include Haiti, while excluding Guiana: Suzanne Rinne and Joëlle Vitiello, eds (1997), *Elles écrivent des Antilles (Haïti, Guade-loupe, Martinique)*, Paris: L'Harmattan.

13. See note 8 above.

more general issues may emerge when the chapters are taken together. For example, a sense of the development of a 'tradition' of writing in the Antilles, in which writers write in relation to those who have come before them rather than in reaction only to France and to the French literary tradition, as may have been the case in the early days of Antillean literature. This is a tradition which may be seen to extend, for example, from the early work of white Creole writers such as Saint-John Perse, whose writing, as Mary Gallagher points out in Chapter 1, has been rather uneasily included as 'Antillean' but who has had an enormous influence on contemporary Antillean writers. And a tradition which really 'takes off' with the work of early black writers like Césaire, a 'pioneer' whose ever-growing *oeuvre* has continued, as Angela Chambers demonstrates in Chapter 2, to be of such central importance that it has been constantly re-evaluated and reassessed throughout the twentieth century. So, too, as Patrick Williams shows in Chapter 3, has that of another seminal figure: Frantz Fanon, whose enormously varied writings and whose work as an anti-colonial theorist and political activist have had influence far beyond his native Martinique or neighbouring Guadeloupe.

Indeed, the inclusion of Fanon in this volume reminds us of the important role played in francophone Caribbean writing by what might be termed 'theory'. Theoretical writing about Antillean identity, culture and history, about issues of class, race, colour and colonialism, as well as about literary production itself, have always been of central importance in the emerging tradition under discussion here. Negritude, of course, was a movement which always concerned itself with 'theoretical' issues, with philosophical and political questions about identity, culture and race. After Fanon, whose work itself often took the form of a reaction to, and critique of, the 'theories' of negritude, has come Edouard Glissant, with his attempts to build upon the work of the negritude writers and especially to broaden their single-minded focus on Africa. Theorizing Martinican and Guadeloupean identity differently, in terms rooted more firmly in the Caribbean itself, Glissant has elaborated the notion of what he calls 'Caribbeanness', or 'antillanité'.

Such is his central importance that Glissant is a figure whose work is discussed by several of the contributors here – by Suzanne Crosta and Beverley Ormerod, for example, but most notably by Celia Britton, who, in Chapter 8, examines the way in which Glissant's theoretical considerations on Antillean identity may be seen to be carried through to his fictional works and the narrative strategies employed there. Indeed, Glissant is not alone in being a writer of both theory and fiction: Fanon is perhaps unusual in that he was a writer 'only' of theory, for the pattern among other Antillean theorists is to explore theoretical concerns also in fictional form.

This is the premise of Lise Morel's exploration, in Chapter 9, of the work of Patrick Chamoiseau and Raphaël Confiant. In their 1989 manifesto *Eloge de la Créolité* (In Praise of Creoleness), written with the linguist Jean Bernabé, these writers put forward theories of Antillean identity, history and culture which form both a response to and a development of the work of their literary 'forefathers', Césaire, Fanon and Glissant. Conceived as a celebration of the diverse cultural elements which make up Antillean culture and identity and as the basis of a form of 'solidarity' with other peoples who have been subjected to colonization, their theory of 'Creoleness' ('créolité') becomes, as Morel points out, a vital element also of Chamoiseau's and Confiant's prize-winning fictional *oeuvres*.

Although the predominance of chapters concerned with discussions of the novel, from various critical perspectives, does reflect the way in which prose fiction has replaced poetry as the predominant Antillean literary form, this volume is not simply a collection of essays on specific Antillean authors. While Britton and Morel focus in detail on the work of Glissant and the *créolistes*, respectively, other contributors provide wide-ranging examinations of the formal and thematic concerns of Caribbean francophone fiction. Suzanne Crosta, for example, in Chapter 10, explores the various ways in which contemporary Antillean writers – Glissant, Chamoiseau, Maryse Condé – both celebrate and problematize the key, Caribbean issue of cultural diversity. Beverley Ormerod, meanwhile, provides us in Chapter 6 with a survey of the ways in which a whole range of Martinican and Guadeloupean writers have chosen to represent Antillean women. Indeed, with reference to archetypal female figures from Caribbean folktales, Ormerod demonstrates how central the representation of women has been to Caribbean francophone literature, perhaps especially that written by men.

The representation of women is also the focus, albeit differently, of Chapters 4 and 11, in which Joan Dayan and Clarisse Zimra, respectively, take up an issue raised in Williams's chapter on Fanon, and begin by re-examining the work of Mayotte Capécia. As the attention she receives in this volume bears witness, this is a writer who has come, since Fanon's vilification of her in *Peau noire, masques blancs*, to represent something of a literary 'foremother' for many Antillean writers, especially women. Indeed, it is Fanon's treatment of Capécia that is the focus of Dayan's chapter, as she explores how Fanon failed to take account of the ways in which the questions he raises about the 'racialization' of identity are necessarily inflected also by gender. Rereading the work of Capécia, Dayan then widens her focus to include an examination also of the younger Haitian writer Marie Chauvet. The complexities of racialized and gendered identities is also examined by Zimra, who similarly takes Fanon's reading of Capécia as a starting-point, this time for a theorization of female identity and the trope of abortion in the work of Michèle Lacrosil, Jacqueline Manicom and Daniel Maximin.

The links between theory and fiction, and the way in which successive generations of Antillean writers are 'haunted' by the work of their predecessors, are thus issues which are central to many of the chapters in this volume – although they are by no means the focus of them all. Jane Brooks, for example, in Chapter 7, is also concerned with the writing of prose fiction, although in this case that fiction is not francophone. As Brooks shows, the development of Creole as a language, primarily spoken but increasingly written, and the emergence of a written literature in Creole, are an increasingly vital aspect of the developing Antillean literary scene, and are part also of attempts to utilize language and literature to redefine identity, history and culture in the 'francophone' Caribbean. So too, argues Bridget Jones in Chapter 5, is Antillean theatre, a vibrant and developing genre, which itself frequently uses Creole rather than, or as well as, French as a means of connecting with an audience increasingly disillusioned with France. Indeed, it is for this reason that theatre, like Creole itself, has often – and perhaps too simplistically, according to Jones – been linked to contemporary forms of anti-colonial resistance and to the movements for independence in Guadeloupe, Martinique and Guiana.

Thus it becomes evident that Caribbean francophone writing takes many and varied forms, and may be seen as a tradition of writing which, though still relatively young, has none the less forged its own identity and can now no longer simply be ignored by or subsumed within French literary studies. What is more, as Régis Antoine demonstrates in Chapter 12, this is a tradition of writing with which links can be made beyond colonial and linguistic frontiers, with the literatures of South and North America, for example, and with those of the rest of the Caribbean. Indeed, Antoine's chapter provides an extremely appropriate finishing-point for this volume, for it reiterates many of the issues discussed elsewhere and, via the connections made with other literatures produced out of colonization, envisages new points of departure for the study of Caribbean francophone writing. Writing which, it is to be hoped, will continue to flourish and expand and to gain increasing international attention and recognition.

–1–

Seminal Praise: The Poetry of Saint-John Perse
Mary Gallagher

The connection between the Caribbean and Saint-John Perse (the literary pseudonym of the Guadeloupean-born poet-diplomat, Alexis Leger 1887–1975) is highly complex. The situation would be entirely different if the poet's *oeuvre* had been limited to his first collection of poems, entitled *Eloges*. Published for the first time in volume form in 1911, these texts unambiguously celebrate the natural and cultural environment of the Caribbean. Written from a position of distance and loss, they also exalt memory, nostalgia and childhood – more specifically, a colonial childhood that was privileged not just socially, but also sensually and imaginatively.

However, whereas *Eloges* is perhaps the highlight, it is neither the sum nor the essence of Saint-John Perse's *oeuvre*. Subsequently, his writing moved through three distinct phases: a transitional stage, coinciding with the poet/diplomat's sojourn in and return from China (*Anabase*, 1924, and *La Gloire des rois*, 1925); the poetry of exile, coinciding with a prolonged period (1940–57) of expatriation in the USA (*Exil*, 1944; *Vents*, 1946; *Amers*, 1956); and finally the works of old age, including *Chronique* (1959) and *Oiseaux* (1962), as well as the last poems, like *Nocturne* (1972) and *Sécheresse* (1974). Although its metaphysical and universalist orientation becomes ever more pronounced, the poetry of these three stages is, one could argue, no less marked by the poet's colonial origins than is *Eloges*; however, its principal inspiration is less Caribbean space than Caribbean history and, in particular, the history of white colonial migration to the 'New World'. Indeed, in so far as it is marked throughout by an atavistic belief in the creative potential of the renewal born of ruptures such as those of exile or migration, all of Saint-John Perse's writing could be seen to spring from a problematic closely related to that of Creole identity. The (white) Creole condition emerged, after all, from the initiative of colonial emigration, even if vexed questions of race and of mixture lurk uneasily behind this problematic of displacement. All too often, the term 'Creole' is used, in French as well as in English, and indeed by Saint-John Perse himself, as though its meaning were transparent. Yet, given its extensive mobilization first to exclude and then to include ethnic groupings other than those of purely white European extraction, such as Alexis Leger (who uses this term to refer to himself or to his family in the exclusive sense), its freight of ambiguity is as confusing as it is illuminating.

It would be perverse, none the less, to claim that the entire poetic *oeuvre* remained as grounded in the Caribbean or in the 'Creole problematic' as are the poems of *Eloges*. Hence, most critics who have sought to claim Saint-John Perse for the Caribbean[1] have understandably concentrated on the poet's first collection. Some, however, have sought to show that the subsequent work is a rewriting of this inaugural text in a variety of keys.[2] Still others have argued that the ever stronger leaning towards exile, mobility and universality, which has sometimes been taken to indicate an abdication from the Caribbean connection, emerges precisely from the poet's identification with his (white) Creole origins.[3] Although these interpretations are all supported by the poetry, this does not alter the fact that the poet's relation to the Caribbean was, from the very outset, a relation of separation and of loss (at the age of twelve, Alexis Leger's family moved back to metropolitan France) and that, subsequently, he would emphatically distance himself from the temptations of return and repetition.

In order to examine the problematic place of Saint-John Perse in relation to Caribbean francophone writing, three areas of exploration would seem particularly appropriate. The first is a reading of *Eloges* and of those parts of the subsequent *oeuvre* which apparently allude to the Caribbean; the second is a study of both the obvious and the subtle ways in which the poet's colonial origins underwrite his entire creative project, informing and motivating every page of his *Oeuvres complètes*; the third is a study of the ways in which other French Caribbean writers have related to the figure and to the writing of Saint-John Perse. This last approach highlights

---

1. Emile Yoyo was the first to make a sustained argument, claiming that the writing of Saint-John Perse was profoundly influenced by Caribbean culture, language and landscape. Yoyo's thesis launched a debate which resonated through the writings of Caribbean writers/ critics, such as Edouard Glissant, Roger Toumson and Georges Desportes, and French critics, such as Jack Corzani and Régis Antoine, with most critics writing after 1970, including Henriette Levillain, Roger Little and Mireille Sacotte, feeling obliged to address the issue (see Emile Yoyo (1969), *Saint-John Perse et le conteur*, Paris: Bordas).

2. One of the best examples of this position is provided by Renée Ventresque's second book on the poet (1995), *Le Songe antillais de Saint-John Perse*, Paris: L'Harmattan.

3. This is my own approach in Mary Gallagher (1998) *La Créolité de Saint-John Perse*, Paris: Gallimard.

a mediated figure and a reflected or diffracted text; it is thus a reading *au deuxième degré*, which informs us as much about the diffracting consciousness as about the object of its critical or creative attention. Since our emphasis here will be on the seminal nature of the poetry, the Caribbean response to Saint-John Perse will be explored briefly in the final part of the chapter.

Poetry Grounded in the Caribbean?

In the definitive version of *Eloges* as it appears in the *Oeuvres complètes*, the three sequences of the collection, entitled 'Images à Crusoé', 'Pour fêter une enfance' and 'Eloges', are preceded by a short poem 'Ecrit sur la porte'. This preliminary text leaves the reader with a strong impression of a disclaimed tension between satisfaction and desire, a dichotomy which vibrates at the end of the poem against the tropical and colonial backdrop of plantation culture (references to plantations of cocoa ('*kako*') and coffee, to the 'white house', to black women receiving orders from a white woman and so on). The poem ends with the following lines:

> I also love my dogs, the call of my finest horse,
> and to see at the end of the straight avenue my cat coming out of the house
> accompanied by the monkey . . .
> all things sufficient to keep me from envying the sails of the sailing ships
> which I see on a level with the tin roof on the sea like a sky.[4]

While the poem gives ultimate importance to this latent friction between, on the one hand, a certain complacency within the limits of the sedentary life of the planter and, on the other, the free, limitless movement promised by the ocean and the ship, a very different tension, subordinated to the primary one, informs the entire discourse of the enunciating subject of the poem: that is, a sense of strain surrounding his identity and, in particular, his racial identity as foregrounded in the poem's opening line: 'I have a skin the colour of mules or of red tobacco.'[5] The evocation here of the speaker's skin colour seems to function primarily as a blurring of racial markers: the common expression 'nègre rouge' ('red nigger') is

4. Saint-John Perse (1956), *Eloges and Other Poems*, trans. Louise Varèse, New York: Pantheon Books, p. 19. (Saint-John Perse (1972), *Oeuvres complètes*, Paris: Gallimard (Pléiade), pp. 7–8.) All quotations from the work of Saint-John Perse will be given in English, but page references to the French versions, collected in *Oeuvres complètes*, will also be given in parentheses.

5. Saint-John Perse, *Eloges and Other Poems*, p. 18. (*Oeuvres complètes*, p. 7.)

replaced by 'red tobacco'; that of 'mulatto' by 'mule'. By suggesting the speaker's skin colour in non-human terms (with reference to vegetation and animals), the poet shrouds in ambiguity the issue of race, making of it that which cannot be named. Indeed, the question of pigmentation is further obscured by references to the speaker's face being muddied and unshaven, references which also compound the reader's sense that the speaker's colour is for him something to be ashamed of, in contrast to that of his daughter:

> My pride is that my daughter should be very-beautiful when she gives orders to the black women.
> my joy, that she reveals a very-white arm among her black hens;
> and that she should not be ashamed of my rough, hairy cheek, when I come home covered with mud.[6]

However enigmatic we might find the poetics of identity in this text, the principal significance of the poem is undoubtedly its subordination of the implicit but insistent question of racial identity to the explicit contrast between fixity and movement and between satisfaction and desire. In this sense, 'Ecrit sur la porte' could be read more appropriately as prefacing the entire *Oeuvres complètes* rather than simply *Eloges*. The single volume of the 'Bibliothèque de la Pléiade' which constitutes the *Oeuvres complètes* of Saint-John Perse is, in fact, entirely underwritten by a dialectic between change and stasis, desire and satisfaction, whereas, although the first three poetic sequences (comprising *Eloges*) do flirt with this question and also with issues of racial and colonial identity, their principal preoccupation lies elsewhere, in the workings of a poetic imagination fired by a very explicit nostalgia.

It is in this nostalgic perspective, from a position of loss and of distance, that the poems of 'Images à Crusoé' celebrate a tropical desert island, contrasting its purity and luxuriance with the decadent, debilitated and degenerate urban setting of Crusoe's true exile or *ex-île*. In addition, these poems exalt the state of exile and separation from which the creative act emerges, for, without that *décalage*, both temporal and spatial, the poem simply would not be. Indeed, the same could be said of the other two poetic sequences of *Eloges*.

In contrast to the poems of 'Images à Crusoé', the six texts of 'Pour fêter une enfance' constitute a paean to an insular space identified both in sociocultural terms as that of the Caribbean plantation or *habitation*

6. Ibid., p. 18. (Ibid., p. 7.)

and in temporal terms as the *temps perdu* of an Edenic childhood. Although the language used to celebrate this circumscribed space and time is often imprecise and unspecific ('I speak of a high condition of old, among men and their daughters, who chewed a certain leaf'[7]), vivid images of the Caribbean do seep out through the text, particularly through precise references to the natural environment and to the colonial world of the *habitation*:

> And a cloud
> yellow and violet, colour of the coco plum, if it stopped suddenly to crown the gold volcano,
> called-by-their-name, out of their cabins,
> the servant women![8]

Much, however, of the poetic power of 'Pour fêter une enfance' inheres in its self-reflexive concentration on the verbal act of celebration itself. The subject as privileged witness rejoices in an act of benediction which restores it to a lost world of plenty or surplus, where beauty and fecundity are almost weighed down by their own overpowering presence: 'O I have cause to praise! O bountiful fable, O table of abundance!'[9]

The metadiscursive dimension of the next sequence of poems, 'Eloges', is even more striking and again serves to underline the poetic productiveness of memories of a Caribbean childhood. To begin with, the poet never seems to tire of referring to the effortless freshness of his own song: 'And the adorable childhood of day, through the trellis of furled canvas, descends along my song'.[10] However, in addition to this constant underlining of his own enunciation, the singer of these poems also dwells upon the 'parole' of the child: 'And the youngest of the travellers, sitting on the taffrail: "I want to tell you about the springs under the sea . . ." (They beg him to tell)'.[11] It is tempting to read this relentless dramatization of the act of speech (and it is worth noting that the entire poetic *oeuvre* of Saint-John Perse is marked by such insistence on the act of saying) as an emphasis on orality, a tendency viewed by many contemporary writers and critics as the essential characteristic of Caribbean culture and texts.

The self-reflexive discourse of *Eloges* is further accentuated in the eighteen-poem cycle (which, confusingly, is also entitled 'Eloges') by

7. Ibid., p.22. (Ibid., p. 23.)
8. Ibid., p. 27. (Ibid., p. 25.)
9. Ibid., p. 31. (Ibid., p. 28.)
10. Ibid., p. 39. (Ibid., p. 37.)
11. Ibid., p. 41. (Ibid., p. 39.)

the very explicit metapoetic programme set for the cycle. For the poet attributes to his dramatized return to an overseas past a clear poetic mission: namely that of showing to others, presumably his readers, the places and the voices which he is revisiting:

> Be a man with calm eyes who laughs,
> [. . .] and from the immobile rim of the lashes he turns back to the things he has seen, borrowing the paths of the fraudulent sea . . . and from the immobile rim of the lashes
> more than one promise has he made us of islands,
> as one who says to someone younger: 'You will see!'[12]

In this dynamics of reviewing and remembering, the poem temporarily repairs the temporal spilt between past and present and, in so doing, reconstructs a lost world, which is brought to life for the reader, who is directly addressed: 'O my friends where are you, whom I do not know? . . . Can't you see this too?'[13]

Apart from the heightening of the self-reflexive or metapoetic dimension of the writing, an obvious difference between 'Pour fêter une enfance' and 'Eloges' is that the former concentrates on the rural and domestic universe of the *habitation*, whereas the latter presents a celebration of the sea and the town. To begin with, the journey of return to childhood space is a maritime one and it seems to be superimposed on childhood memories of family boat trips:

> I have seen many fishes and am taught all their names.
> I have seen many other things that can only be seen far out on the Water; and others that are dead; and others that are make-believe . . . And . . . this bushy fish hoisted aboard to entertain my mother
> who is young and who yawns.[14]

In 'Eloges', the sea is celebrated both as the space in and through which the passage into poetry is effected and as a natural and plenteous habitat, an integral part of the remembered Garden of Eden of childhood. Furthermore, its vivid and boisterous presence also encroaches on the urban space evoked in the second part of the cycle, where it is said to be more noisy than a fishmarket and where it makes itself felt in images of spilt oil and sugar on the quays.

12. Ibid., p. 37. (Ibid., p. 35.)
13. Ibid., p. 51. (Ibid., p. 46.)
14. Ibid., p. 43. (Ibid., p. 40.)

The subsequent poems of Saint-John Perse – particularly *Exil*, *Vents*, *Amers* and *Chronique* – are regularly punctured by allusions not only to the Caribbean, but also to the complex relationship of distance and desire between the poet and his Caribbean cradle: 'O Memory, lodged in the heart of man, of the lost kingdom'.[15] In *Exil*, the poet exclaims: 'Behold, I am restored to my native shore'[16] and, in *Amers*, 'the fair land of birth has to be reconquered, the fair land of the king that he has not seen since childhood, and its defence is in my song'.[17] These allusions resonate all the more vibrantly as echoes in that they recall the generative epigraph (in English) to 'Pour fêter une enfance': 'King Light's Settlements'. Apart from the pun on the word 'light', which translates both 'lumière' and 'léger' (the poem sequence was originally signed Saint-Léger Léger), the epigraph associates with this recollection of childhood those bright vistas of royal supremacy and of colonial territorialism which recur in the later poetry with such nostalgic force. Indeed, most of the allusions to the Caribbean to be found in the later work are simultaneously intertextual echoes of the poetry of the first volume.

Paradoxically, despite the freight of (textual) memory carried by the later works, these are all marked by an explicit determination to eschew retrospection. For example, in the final poem of the cycle *Exil*, 'Poème à l'Etrangère', the poet cries out at the end of the text: 'I proceed, O memory! with my free man's stride, without horde or tribe'.[18] Indeed, in the very long four-movement poem *Vents*, the desire to transcend retrospection and nostalgia takes on a paroxysmal quality: the winds are summoned precisely to protect the poet: 'let them keep a long watch against the renewal of the same things'.[19] The preoccupation with originality and innovation persists in *Amers*: 'Destitution! Destitution! We beg that in sight of the sea promise shall be made to us of new works: of strong and very beautiful works, which are all strength and will and which are all beauty.'[20] In the later poems, such as *Amers* and *Chronique*, although the poet inevitably finds himself awash with vivid and pungent memories belonging to the past, and with the illusions and delusions born of nostalgia, he persistently reiterates his determination not to look back.

15. Saint-John Perse, *Oeuvres complètes*, p. 402. Translation mine.

16. Saint-John Perse (1992), trans. Denis Devlin, in Roger Little, ed., *Translations into English*, Dublin: Dedalus Press, p. 115. (*Oeuvres complètes*, p. 130.)

17. Saint-John Perse (1958), *Amers/Seamarks*, trans. Wallace Fowlie, New York: Pantheon Books, p. 25. (Ibid., p. 268.)

18. Saint-John Perse, *Exil*, p. 133. (Ibid., p. 172.)

19. Saint-John Perse (1953), *Vents/Winds*, trans. Hugh Chisholm, New York: Pantheon Books, p. 161. (Ibid., p. 242.)

20. Saint-John Perse, *Amers/Seamarks* , p. 57. (Ibid., p. 293.)

Mary Gallagher

The Inexorable 'Creoleness' of Saint-John Perse's Creative Identity

As if to underline his belief in the creative necessity of moving on, Saint-John Perse makes much in his published correspondence of his response to Jacqueline Kennedy when she informed him of the destruction of 'La Joséphine', one of the plantations belonging to his mother's family: 'all to the good', he claims to have exclaimed, 'all to the good, all to the good, nothing behind me. May things be always thus, gone with the wind!' The bravura of this boast is somewhat belied by the fact that in the same text, the poet dwells lovingly, even self-indulgently, on his white Creole ancestry. Perhaps, however, the key to this apparent ambivalence lies in the fact that Saint-John Perse, who, during the years preceding his death, himself coordinated his *Oeuvres complètes* in Gallimard's prestigious 'Bibliothèque de la Pléiade' series, had become progressively more and more obsessed with the symbolic and prophetic value of his family origins.[21] He had, indeed, come to credit them with underwriting, or even predetermining, his own creative vocation and destiny. The point of this highly atavistic autobiographical discourse about his forebears' status as 'men of the Atlantic'[22] is to suggest that the creative colonial initiative of these ancestors bequested to the poet his adventurous and enterprising need for ceaseless creative movement. Having striven for much of his life to repudiate any suggestion that he was a regional poet, and having proclaimed at every possible opportunity his pure and absolute Frenchness,[23] the main emphasis of his final creative act, that is, the assembly and harmonization of the *Oeuvres complètes*, was to emphasize the role played

21. Saint-John Perse, *Oeuvres complètes*, p. 1101. Translation mine. Henriette Levillain has written a number of articles which address this question, including (1988), 'La version de la Guadeloupe: L'Amérique', in Henriette Levillain and Mireille Sacotte, eds, *Saint-John Perse: Antillanité et universalité*, Paris: Editions caribéennes, pp. 159–72; (1992), 'Saint-John Perse et l'Atlantique', *Souffle de Perse* 2, pp. 33–8; and (1994), 'L'enfance de Saint-John Perse', in Henriette Levillain, *Guadeloupe 1875–1914*, Paris: Autrement, pp. 190–9.

22. Saint-John Perse, *Oeuvres complètes*, p. XLI. Translation mine.

23. See, for example, Saint-John Perse's comments in a letter to Archibald MacLeish, dated December 1941: 'About France, there is nothing to say. It is myself and all of myself. For me it is something sacred, uniquely so – the only medium through which I can communicate with anything in this world. Even if I were not an essentially French animal, made of essentially French clay (and my last breath, like my first, will be chemically French), the French language would still be for me my only home, the shelter and refuge par excellence, the armour and the arms par excellence, the only "geometrical locus" in the world where I can station myself in order to understand, desire, or renounce anything' (Arthur Knodel, ed. and trans. (1979), *Saint-John Perse, Letters*, New York: Pantheon Books, p. 451).

in his definitive image as poet by his family's colonial past and by his own Caribbean birth and childhood. However, the Creole connection is presented precisely as proof of the authenticity of the poet's quintessential Frenchness.[24] In his composition of an autobiographical preface[25] to the edition of his so-called *Oeuvres complètes,* in the radical revision of selected elements of his correspondence,[26] in the rewriting of several early poems[27] and in the composition of the notes to the *Complete Works*, the poet, who was already in his late seventies when carrying out this ambitious and determined (re-)creation of his definitive literary profile, emphasized very unambiguously the historical or temporal dimension of his Creole (i.e. colonial, Caribbean-born) identity. He brings to bear on this vast project an unambiguous emphasis not just on his metropolitan French and French-Caribbean, or Creole ancestry, but also, and primarily indeed, on the origins of (white) Creole identity – that is, the choices out of which it emerged. He pays particular attention in this context to the dialectic of migration – that is, to the tension between rupture and continuity implicit in the creation of colonial offshoots of old family lines.

Curiously, however, Saint-John Perse never refers to *métissage* or miscegenation in the context of his ethnic origins. Furthermore, he makes it clear that, for him, creolization is simply a process of adaptation to a different environment and has nothing to do with mixing; on the contrary, for him, the process of transplantation paradoxically strengthens the original, genetic identity of a given ethnic group.[28] Interestingly, the poet does, however, mobilize both frequently and pejoratively a rhetoric of

24. See, once again, the letter of December 1941, from Saint-John Perse to Archibald MacLeish: 'the Antilles, even though they steeped my childhood in the animal and plant life of the tropics, are to me of the very oldest French essence' (ibid., p. 451).
25. This so-called 'Biographie' was written by the poet himself and, as its numerous digressions show, it is dedicated to the construction of a poetic rather than a strictly factual identity.
26. See Catherine Mayaux (1994), *Les Lettres d'Asie de Saint-John Perse,* Paris: Gallimard. As Catherine Mayaux demonstrates, most of the 'Lettres d'Asie' which appear in the *Oeuvres complètes*, although signed Alexis Leger and ostensibly dating from the period that the poet/diplomat spent in China, are in reality part of the poet's *oeuvre*, since they were undoubtedly written specially for publication in the *Oeuvres complètes* around the time the poet was assembling this volume.
27. One could cite in particular the rewriting of two early poems, versions of which appear in the correspondence section of the *Oeuvres complètes*. 'Des villes sur trois modes' (*Oeuvres complètes*, pp. 651–4), and 'Cohorte' (ibid., pp. 682–9).
28. See, for example, Perse's letter to his mother, Madame Amédée Saint-Leger Leger, dated 10 January 1917: 'Don't forget the theory I've reminded you about so often, which is taken for granted in genetics and maintains that every living species, whether animal or

miscegenation in his literary commentaries and homages.[29] Transposed on to the level of meta-literary discourse, the charge of mixed identity or of cross-fertilization seems to be for him the ultimate disparagement. It is possible that this displacement, whereby a term of ethnic identity becomes an aspersion cast on stylistic or literary disposition, indicates a deep-seated, but unavowed neurosis, the stakes being too high for the poet to assert explicitly his obsession with racial purity. In the same way, this issue can only be hinted at in 'Ecrit sur la porte', before it is immediately and improbably subordinated to the tension between movement and fixity. The product of his times and upbringing, Saint-John Perse cannot squarely confront the question of race and of colour lurking beneath the Creole question; yet neither can he altogether silence it.

Saint-John Perse and Contemporary Caribbean Writing

For at least two generations of French Caribbean writers, the writing of Saint-John Perse has been an inexorable reference point and, in many cases, a formative influence as well. The generative force of the (early) poetry and indeed of the poet's persona makes itself felt in three principal directions. The first is as a validating mirror: the poet who gained immense universal acclaim, culminating in the Nobel prize for literature in 1960, was not only born in Guadeloupe and brought up there until the age of twelve, but his writing would subsequently draw heavily on his Caribbean origins. The second is as a source of productive tension: for that same poet would always claim that he never again stepped on the soil of Guadeloupe after the rupture of 1899, that his poetry has less to do with the Caribbean than with Africa or the Pacific Ocean,[30] that he is French

---

vegetable, taken outside its native habitat, inevitably reinforces the qualities of its strain by a simple organic defensive reaction against transplanting. And you are fully aware of what our family strain was like, after three centuries of adaptation to the Islands' (Knodel, *Saint-John Perse, Letters,* p. 292).

29. In 1910, the young poet characterized a publication called *La Phalange* as a 'rather shady outfit, very South American, a lower deck loaded with persons of all colours and crawling with mestizos' (ibid., p. 167). In 1961, the mature poet approvingly describes the poet Léon-Paul Fargue as being 'free of all miscegenation' (Perse, *Oeuvres complètes,* p. 511. Translation mine).

30. In a letter to Valery Larbaud, dated December 1911, the poet writes 'Antilleans themselves might think – not about my poems, which are quite simply French, nor about my themes, which I have always lived in the strictest sense – but about my attitude as a human being prior to the dream of life – that this attitude has in it more of the oceanic, Asiatic, or African, or anything else whatever, than it has of the Antillean', (Knodel *Saint-John Perse, Letters*, p. 231).

through and through and that his Caribbean birth simply made him more French than the Metropolitan French themselves.[31] Finally, the poetry is a bank of images and rhythms, to be drawn upon at will.

Although one must recognize the intertextual crescendo of echoes of *Eloges* throughout the past decade of Caribbean writing, Edouard Glissant seems to have been drawn for quite some time towards the layered ambivalence of Saint-John Perse's texts and identity. Indeed, one could say that, of all Caribbean writers, Glissant bears witness in the most consistent and challenging manner to Saint-John Perse. This is partly because of the creative energy which Glissant brings to his own writing, an energy released in particular by the fusion of an intensely critical and speculative mind with a formidable literary creativity. Furthermore, in his theoretical writing, Glissant has attempted to chart the intricate and evolving tenor of his view of Saint-John Perse, the course of which can be reconstructed by a linear reading of his various essays on the poet.[32] To begin with, Glissant acknowledges that Saint-John Perse did not involve himself in the historicity of Caribbean reality:

> It is not surprising that, for those Caribbeans who . . . are attempting to reconcile, despite the chaos caused by colonialism, Caribbean nature and culture, the relation to Saint-John Perse should be ambiguous and reticent. How could we accept him as a Caribbean poet, when he escapes our history and thus denies it?[33]

However, despite the poet's disaffiliation, Glissant is prepared to allow him 'none the less a fragile Caribbeanness, namely, that tendency of ours to move away'.[34]

For Glissant, then, not only is Caribbean nature 'the principal quarry'[35] of Saint-John Perse's poetics, but the centrifugal pull acting on Caribbean consciousness, that openness to the call of the universe, that atavistic migratory yearning is, according to Glissant, shared by Saint-John Perse. Furthermore, on the very first page of his book on William Faulkner, Glissant compares the novelist of the American South with Saint-John Perse, arguing that both are 'auteurs de la Plantation':

31. See notes 23 and 24 above.
32. In essays published in the following works, Edouard Glissant has written about Saint-John Perse: (1969) *L'Intention poétique*, Paris: Seuil; (1981) *Le Discours antillais*, Paris: Seuil; (1990) *Poétique de la relation*, Paris: Seuil; (1995), *Faulkner Mississippi*, Paris: Stock.
33. Glissant, *Le Discours antillais*, p. 430. Translation mine.
34. Ibid.
35. Ibid.

I have so often linked them in my books, using the clichés so often found in such contexts: saying that here are two plantation writers, two men on the margins of a caste soon to disintegrate, two *békés*, but so marginal among their kind, two poets locked into the inexorable question of race.[36]

Glissant is not, of course, alone in seeing in Saint-John Perse a poet of the plantation. An anglophone poet of the same generation as Glissant has also made this connection. It is not surprising that the second Caribbean-born poet to win the Nobel prize for literature should pay tribute to the first; and indeed, in his Nobel acceptance speech, Derek Walcott insists on celebrating Saint-John Perse. He acknowledges, however, that, for some, to do so is to celebrate the old plantation system – 'the plantation rider, verandas and mulatto servants, a white French language in a white pith helmet, to celebrate a rhetoric of patronage and hauteur'.[37] For Walcott, although Saint-John Perse denied his origins ('great writers often have this folly of trying to smother their source'[38]), he cannot be denied by Caribbean writers 'any more than . . . the African Aimé Césaire'. 'This is not accommodation,' he asserts, 'this is the ironic republic that is poetry.'[39] Walcott's feeling, upon recalling the 'fragrant and privileged poetry that Perse composed to celebrate his white childhood',[40] is one of poignant pride. As for the later poetry, he sees there the same 'archaeology of fragments' which he observes everywhere in 'our raucous demotic streets': that is, fragments 'from the broken African kingdoms, from the crevasses of Canton, from Syria and Lebanon'.[41] In other words, in the later poetry of Saint-John Perse, Derek Walcott sees that same post-modern aesthetic, that same openness to the baroque chaos of planetary variations and similarities which Alejo Carpentier has identified as typically 'Creole'[42] (in the inclusive sense of the term, of course).

36. Glissant, *Faulkner Mississippi*, pp. 11–12.
37. Derek Walcott (1992), *The Antilles: Fragments of Epic Memory*, The Nobel Lecture, London: Faber and Faber, p. 21.
38. Ibid.
39. Ibid.
40. Ibid., p. 22.
41. Ibid., p. 23.
42. 'Why is Latin America the chosen land of the baroque? Because all symbiosis, all miscegenation engenders the baroque. The American baroque coincides with creoleness, with the feeling of what it is to be Creole, with the awareness developed by American man, whether he be the son of a white European emigrant, the son of an African Black, or the son of an Indian . . . an awareness of being something different, of being something new, of being a symbiosis, of being Creole; and this is why the Creole spirit is fundamentally baroque' (Alejo Carpentier (1990), *Obras completas de Alejo Carpentier*, Volumen 13, Ensayos, Mexico: Siglo XXI, pp. 182–3. Translation mine).

In the case of a younger generation of Caribbean writers, one could say that their recuperation of Saint-John Perse illustrates and confirms a profound sea change in French Caribbean thought. More specifically, the shift in attitude to Saint-John Perse from one of defensiveness or, at best, grudging acceptance to one of almost unqualified appropriation reflects the general ideological revisionism being promoted by the prolific proponents of the 'Creoleness' movement. While this relatively recent vision of Caribbeanness owes much to the ideology of negritude and even more to the writings of Edouard Glissant on *antillanité* ('Caribbeanness'), its originality undoubtedly lies in its new emphasis on celebration and benediction at the expense of lament. The move away from a preoccupation with the pathology of the divisive colonial inheritance is evident in the very title of the movement's manifesto, *Eloge de la créolité* (*In Praise of Creoleness*), which inevitably calls to mind that of Saint-John Perse's *Eloges*. Furthermore, the poet is one of the few Caribbean-born authors to be singled out for special comment in this short text:

> In literature, the now unanimous recognition of the poet Saint-John Perse by our people as one of the most prestigious sons of Guadeloupe – in spite of his belonging to the béké ethnoclass – is indeed an advance of Creoleness in Caribbean consciousness. It is delighting.[43]

As though to underline and to enact the desire for openness and accommodation which motivates the *créolité* project, the authors of the manifesto echo in Saint-John Perse's own words the latter's euphoric appropriation of the world:

> The Creole literature we are elaborating takes it as a principle that there is nothing petty, poor, useless, vulgar, or unworthy of a literary project in our world. We are part and parcel of our world. We want, thanks to Creoleness, to name each thing in it, and to declare it beautiful.[44]

The intertextual link with *Eloges* is perfectly evident here: 'Naming each thing, I proclaimed that it was great, naming each beast that it was beautiful and good.'[45]

---

43. Jean Bernabé, Patrick Chamoiseau and Raphaël Confiant (1989), *Eloge de la créolité/In Praise of Creoleness* (bilingual edition), trans. M.B. Taleb-Khyar, Paris: Gallimard, pp. 90–1.

44. Ibid., p. 100.

45. Saint-John Perse, *Eloges and Other Poems*, p. 23. (*Oeuvres complètes*, p. 24.)

In their study of the history of Caribbean writing entitled *Lettres créoles*,[46] Patrick Chamoiseau and Raphaël Confiant indulge, at the outset of their chapter on Saint-John Perse, in a prolonged flight of fantasy, which presents itself as first-person reminiscences of the colonial plantation, the white Creole family and the town of Pointe-à-Pitre. Over three to four unashamed pages[47] of overwrought prose, they brew a concoction of direct quotations and pastiches of the poet's writing in an attempt to suggest the vision of plantation culture supposedly entertained by someone who, although born into 'the caste of the white Creole masters',[48] had rapidly declared his hostility to this decadent and dying world.

Chamoiseau and Confiant then proceed to recall how Saint-John Perse was held, until 1969, to have little or nothing to do with Guadeloupean literature until the Martinican philosopher, Emile Yoyo, in a ground-breaking study, provoked much indignation by claiming that the poet's work was entirely underwritten by the Creole language and by Caribbean culture as embodied in the figure of the *conteur*, or storyteller. Chamoiseau and Confiant seem to support Yoyo's thesis, arguing that the poet, whom the rest of the world regarded as 'undecipherable' and whom most Guade-loupeans had regarded as a 'béké', was in reality 'complicitous with us Antilleans'.[49] They claim that, although his poetry is coloured by the ethnic group and class to which he belonged, his sensibility and imagination were devoid of the complexes which mark, for example, Césaire's writing. They argue that, instead of reviling the Creole language, Saint-John Perse accepted it almost as part of the natural environment of his childhood and inheritance. It is on this somewhat dubious and quixotic basis that they then argue that Saint-John Perse fully accepted his Creole identity, pointing to 'this recognition of Creole, and thus this acceptance of self'.[50]

The resentment felt by some Caribbean writers about the complacency of Saint-John Perse's portrait of the passivity of the non-white Creoles is not apparent, then, in the writing of Chamoiseau or of Confiant. Yet they do express a reservation about his refusal to see the Caribbean condition as containing within itself the cultural diversity and universality which he sought outside of himself and beyond the Caribbean. Unlike Edouard

46. Patrick Chamoiseau, Raphaël Confiant (1991), *Lettres créoles, Tracées antillaises et continentales de la littérature 1635–1975*, Paris: Hatier.
47. Ibid., pp. 157–9.
48. Ibid., p. 160. Translation mine.
49. Ibid.
50. Ibid., p. 162.

Glissant, then, they identify the poet's centrifugal or universalist orientation as distancing him from the truth of the Caribbean condition. Other writers, such as Daniel Radford, have expressed much more clearly a certain ambivalence regarding the poetic debt owed to a world-famous literary forebear;[51] Radford's recognition of an important literary influence is, clearly, as pained as it is grateful. A similar complexity of relation is apparent in Daniel Maximin's latest novel, *L'Ile et une nuit*. In a curious move, Maximin has inserted into his novel what the narrator purports to be the text of a letter written by Saint-John Perse about the drama and effects of cyclones on the *habitation*: 'an unpublished letter discovered by the administrator of the Museum at Pointe-à-Pitre'[52] this text certainly confirms Edouard Glissant's view that Saint-John Perse is, above all, a poet of the plantation, and also shows the colonial detachment with which he viewed the 'native land'. Not all readers will recognise in the so-called 'letter' the text of the poet's conversations with Pierre Guerre.[53]

Much more common, of course, in contemporary French Caribbean literature are texts which integrate allusions and even quotations, acknowledged or unacknowledged, of Saint-John Perse's poetry. A clear testimony to the seminal importance of Saint-John Perse in the landscape of contemporary Caribbean writing, the literary texts of at least three prominent authors – Raphaël Confiant, Patrick Chamoiseau and Maryse Condé – yield many examples of such acknowledged and unacknowledged borrowings and *clins d'oeil*. Patrick Chamoiseau's *Antan d'enfance*, for example, a text punctuated by lines of poetry, often provides clear echoes of Saint-John Perse's text and/or tone: 'I remember the coco-plum / Oh, I remember the coco-plum'.[54] Not only does the coco-plum figure in 'Pour fêter une enfance', but so does the repeated construction 'I remember', for example, in: 'I remember the salt, I remember the salt my yellow nurse had to wipe away at the corner of my eyes'.[55]

Similarly, in Raphaël Confiant's *Ravines du devant jour* the final chapter is entitled 'Other than childhood . . .' ('*Sinon l'enfance . . .*'), an unfinished quotation from the text of 'Pour fêter une enfance'. Indeed,

---

51. 'Everyone has his precursors, his elders. Saint-John Perse's *Eloges*, the poem of a Guadeloupean childhood, inspired this story, without in any sense founding it. Far be it from me, therefore, to compare the two works. I shall leave Perse to his heights' (Daniel Radford (1993), *Le Maître-Pièce*, Monaco: Editions du Rocher, p. 10. Translation mine).

52. Daniel Maximin (1995), *L'Ile et une nuit*, Paris: Seuil, pp. 19–21. Translation mine.

53. Pierre Guerre (1990), *Portrait de Saint-John Perse: textes établis, réunis et présentés par Roger Little*, Marseille: Sud.

54. Patrick Chamoiseau (1990), *Antan d'enfance*, Paris: Hatier, p. 161. Translation mine.

55. Perse, *Eloges and Other Poems*, p. 23. (*Oeuvres complètes*, p. 24.)

the reference is made more pointed in the very last words of Confiant's text: 'The Poet said: Other than childhood, what was there in those days that is here no longer?'[56] In the same text, the first sentence of a chapter entitled 'Anges dépeignés' begins 'The Whites [les Grands Blancs] lived separately from the rest of us.' Here the chapter title is borrowed from one of the more enigmatic images of 'Pour fêter une enfance', an image which is interpreted here as referring to the white Creole caste which Confiant regards as rarefied.[57] In a more ironic vein, Confiant again draws on Saint-John Perse's poetry in his irreverent evocation in *Bassin de l'ouragan* of the rapacious predilection of certain Catholic priests for 'tall glistening girls who moved their warm trembling legs near them, thank you Saint-John Perse!'[58] Maryse Condé for her part, when recalling her novel *La Vie scélérate*, explains her pastiche of *Eloges* in that text by the fact that 'Saint-John Perse was never far from my thoughts'.[59]

Even this small sample of contemporary Caribbean writing (a significant proportion of which presents itself as an intertextual, intercultural and interlinguistic mosaic) will suffice to show that, however tense and problematic its relationship might be with the persona and with the poetics of Saint-John Perse, both have proved inspirational. Indeed, the fact that the poet haunts the articulation of contemporary literary consciousness in the Caribbean to the extent that he manifestly does, the fact that his vision

56. Raphaël Confiant (1993), *Ravines du devant-jour*, Paris: Gallimard, p. 208. Translation mine. Cf. Saint-John Perse: 'Other than childhood, what was there in those days that is here no longer?' *Eloges and Other Poems*, p. 25. (*Oeuvres complètes*, p. 25.)

57. Confiant, *Ravines du devant-jour*, p. 98. Cf. Saint-John Perse: 'Reverently, my father's boat brought tall white forms: really, wind-blown angels [des Anges dépeignés], perhaps', *Eloges and Other Poems*, p. 31. (*Oeuvres complètes*, p. 29.)

58. Raphaël Confiant (1994), *Bassin de l'ouragan*, Paris: Mille et une nuits, p. 52. Translation mine. Cf. Saint-John Perse: 'and your mother's maids, tall glistening girls, moved their warm legs near you who trembled', *Eloges and Other Poems*, p. 22 (*Oeuvres Complètes*, p. 23.)

59. Maryse Condé (1995), 'Eloge de Saint-John Perse', *Europe*, 799–800 , p. 22. The most flagrant example of the Saint-John Perse intertext in Condé's work is perhaps to be found in the following quotation: 'Velma was a Negress and smelled of ganja; always I noticed, beneath the great tricoloured scarf she wore tied tightly over her heavy hair, glistening beads of sweat around her midnight black eyes, and her mouth...had the taste of wild guava gathered before noon', Maryse Condé (1987), *La Vie scélérate*, Paris: Seghers, p. 221, translation mine. Cf. Saint-John Perse: 'My nurse was a mestizo and smelled of the castor-bean; always I noticed there were pearls of glistening sweat on her forehead, and around her eyes – and so warm, her mouth had the taste of rose-apples, in the river, before noon', *Eloges and Other Poems*, pp. 27–9. (*Oeuvres complètes*, p. 26.)

of the Caribbean has provoked such diversity and such depth of reaction among Caribbean readers and writers, and finally the fact that it has been addressed with such consistency and subtlety by poets, intellectuals and visionaries of the calibre of Derek Walcott and Edouard Glissant surely testify not just to the seminal nature of his work, but also to its rich and sustained involvement with the Caribbean as place and with the Caribbean condition as problematic.

Critical Approaches to the Literatures of Decolonization: *Aimé Césaire's Cahier d'un retour au pays natal*

Angela Chambers

Aimé Césaire's main literary works were published between 1939 and 1982, a period of profound change in the relationship between colonial powers and their colonies. Césaire and his contemporaries did not merely use literary forms for ideological and political ends, to demand equality and independence, but, through their creative work, participated in the process of decolonization by affirming the existence of new cultures and creating new and different literary voices.

> In a successful process of colonization, the creator of cultural values is the colonizer. And the consumer is the colonized . . . But cultural creation, precisely because it is creation, disturbs this system. It destroys it. Starting with the colonial hierarchy, as it makes the colonized, the consumers, into creators.[1]

It is thus hardly surprising that the interpretation of the literary texts produced both during and after the period of decolonization has posed major problems for authors and critics alike. The critical models which were developed for the national literatures of the colonial powers proved to be totally inappropriate for the study of texts produced in the colonies and former colonies, as they tended to situate the authors and their works in relation to the national literary tradition, thus defining them as marginal and different. From the publication of the first version of the *Cahier d'un retour au pays natal* (*Notebook of a Return to My Native Land*[2]) in 1939

---

1. Aimé Césaire (1959), 'L'homme de culture et ses responsabilités', *Présence Africaine*, XXIV–XXV, p.117. Unless otherwise stated, translations of French prose texts are by the author of this chapter.
2. All references to Césaire's *Cahier d'un retour au pays natal*, which was first published in 1939 in the Parisian journal *Volontés*, will be to the recent bilingual edition:

to the present, readings of the work have varied considerably, providing an excellent illustration of the development of critical approaches more suited to a post-colonial world.[3] Indeed, in the context of post-colonial literatures, the authors of *The Empire Writes Back* list the main new critical models which writers and critics have developed to account for the special character of post-colonial texts:

> First, 'national' or regional models, which emphasize the distinctive features of the particular national or regional culture; second, race-based models which identify certain shared characteristics across various national literatures, such as common racial inheritance in literatures of the African Diaspora addressed by the 'Black writing' model; third, comparative models of varying complexity which seek to account for particular linguistic, historical, and cultural features across two or more postcolonial literatures; fourth, more comprehensive comparative models which argue for features such as hybridity and syncreticity as constitutive elements of all postcolonial literatures (syncretism is the process by which previously distinct linguistic categories, and, by extension, cultural formations, merge into a single new form).[4]

These critical modes did not suddenly emerge in the post-colonial period, but were developed in the preceding decades, as authors and critics struggled to locate new types of literary text. As we shall see, the Caribbean context, in general, and the *Notebook of a Return to My Native Land*, in particular, provide a vivid illustration of how new critical approaches to the works of writers in the colonies and former colonies have emerged in the course of the twentieth century.

The aim of this study is to provide an interpretation of the *Notebook*, not only in terms of the context from which it emerged, but also in the light of the widely different readings of the work which have appeared

---

Aimé Césaire (1995), *Notebook of a Return to My Native Land*, trans. Mireille Rosello with Anne Pritchard, Newcastle Upon Tyne: Bloodaxe Books. The *Cahier* will subsequently be referred to as the *Notebook*.

3. 'Post-colonial' is used here to refer to the period beginning approximately in 1960, when many colonies gained their independence. It is now a problematic term for many writers in those states, partly because it fails to account for their dependence on neocolonial powers, such as the USA and partly because its grouping of a large number of writers from different states in one undifferentiated movement appears increasingly irrelevant to many of them. It is, of course, particularly problematic in the context of the Antilles in general and Césaire's political stance in particular, as he played a leading role in the inclusion of Martinique as a French overseas department in 1946.

4. Bill Ashcroft, Gareth Griffiths and Helen Tiffin (1989), *The Empire Writes Back: Theory and Practice in Post-colonial Literatures*, London: Routledge, p. 15.

since 1939. The aim is not only to assist students and researchers in their understanding of the poem, but also to provide a critical framework within which other studies of this seminal work can be evaluated. The initial focus will be on the interpretation of the *Notebook* provided by Césaire himself, and the analysis of the poem will situate it in the context of readings of the work by writers and critics from different continents and different generations. In commenting on his work, both Césaire and his critics tend to situate it in three major contexts. Firstly, the starting-point of the poet's journey, the island of Martinique, serves as a symbol of the cultural alienation of the colonized. The question arises as to whether the reality of the small island is lost in the grandiose vision of a new cultural identity for the African diaspora emerging in the twentieth century. Indeed, later generations have questioned the relevance of the *Notebook* in the changing contexts of the Antilles and the Caribbean, replacing the emphasis on race with a national or regional model. Secondly, it is not surprising that interpretations of the work throughout the twentieth century have been dominated by the theme of the return to the African heritage and the concept of negritude, which have played a major role in the affirmation of identity by early generations of black writers and also in the development of race-based critical models. Thirdly, Césaire's status as a major poet writing in French has raised the issue of the relationship between his work and that of nineteenth- and twentieth-century French poets. The desire to emphasize the difference of Césaire's writing from the French literary tradition initially led proponents of the black writing or race-based models to see similarities as the result of chance rather than influence. A more appropriate explanation was found in comments by Césaire himself and later critics, which describe these similarities as evidence neither of influence nor of chance, but rather as the appropriation of aspects of the French literary tradition in the new, syncretic context of literature in the period of decolonization.

Césaire's status as a poet in Europe, Africa and, latterly, the USA, has raised the question of the relevance of his work in the context of the Antilles and the Caribbean. It has been pointed out that many of the constituents of Césaire the politician would not be capable of reading and understanding the *Notebook* or the more obscure poems in the later collections.[5] Moreover, throughout his life the poet himself has been eager to emphasize the 'universal' significance of his poetry. In the late 1950s he described the writer's role in the anti-colonial struggle as being of

---

5. Mireille Rosello, Introduction to Césaire, *Notebook of a Return To My Native Land*, p.13.

benefit not only to the colonized peoples but to the whole world, conclud-
ing with the words: 'we shall have contributed to the foundation of a
universal humanism'.[6] More recently, Césaire described himself in an
interview as 'haunted by the universal'.[7] However, despite his claim to
be an African poet[8] and his fascination with the universal relevance of
his works, Césaire has always emphasized that his poetry is firmly situated
in the Antilles: 'I am from the Antilles. I want my poetry to be concrete,
very Antillean, Martinican. I have to name things which are Martinican,
to call them by their name.'[9] The *Notebook* is the first expression of his
struggle to come to terms with the complex reality of the island. In the
early part of the poem, the long evocation of the Antilles and of Fort-de-
France, with its insistent repetition of the name of the islands and obsessive
concentration on the poverty and alienation of the people, forms the
starting-point of the poet's entire literary output. Nowhere else in his poems
or plays is such explicit reference to his own background to be found,
even though the poverty described is an exaggeration of the circumstances
in which the poet himself grew up. It is clear that this poetic expression
of poverty and stagnation is intended to convey the alienation of the
colonized inhabitants of the town and the island.

> At the brink of dawn, the ultimate, deceiving desolate bedsore on the wound
> of the waters; martyrs who will not bear witness; flowers of blood withering
> and scattering in the useless wind like the screeches of prattling parrots;
> an old life's lying smile, its lips opened by disused fears; an old poverty
> rotting under the sun, silently; an old silence bursting with tepid pustules,
> the awful futility of our raison d'être.[10]

Images of wounds, rotting, violence, silence, inability to fulfil any vocation
are accumulated in this evocation of the Antilles. The denunciation of
colonialism is clear, even before one reads the explicit reference to the

---

6. Césaire, 'L'homme de culture et ses responsabilités', p. 122.

7. Charles H. Rowell (1989), 'C'est par le poème que nous affrontons la solitude:
une interview avec Aimé Césaire', *Callaloo*, 12:1, p. 64. For a fuller treatment of Césaire's
views on the universal dimension of his poetry, see Angela Chambers (1997), 'Universal
and culturally specific imagery in the poetry of Aimé Césaire', in Pat Little and Roger
Little, eds, *Black Accents: Writing in French from Africa, Mauritius and the Caribbean*,
London: Grant and Cutler, pp. 31–45.

8. M. a M. Ngal (1975), *Aimé Césaire: un homme à la recherche d'une patrie*, Dakar:
Nouvelles Editions Africaines, p.143.

9. Ibid.

10. Césaire, *Notebook of a Return to My Native Land*, p. 73.

'Empress Joséphine of the French, dreaming high, high above negridom'.[11] Thus, in attempting to express the alienation of his own background and of the inhabitants of a small island in the Caribbean, Césaire immediately gave voice to the concerns of the inhabitants of the African diaspora. This contrast, between the small island on the one hand and the millions of inhabitants of several continents on the other, was to earn the work both praise and criticism from future generations of writers and critics.

It would be misleading to see the opening lines of Césaire's first work solely as the first step in a chronological progression which will ultimately lead him to revolt against this alienation. The images of destruction and reawakening are already here in the opening sequence, once again expressed through the geographical features of the Antilles:

> At the brink of dawn, on the frailest stratum of earth already humiliated and overwhelmed by its grandiose future – the volcanoes will break out, and the naked water will sweep away the ripe stains of the sun and nothing will remain but a tepid bubbling pecked at by sea birds – the beach of dreams and demented awakening.[12]

This coexistence of images of destruction and renewal, present in the poet's earliest writing, will be evident throughout his poetry, giving it its characteristic dynamic and explosive quality. Césaire subsequently defined his poetic intention as the creation of a new literary voice for the Antilles: 'At the beginning we had to destroy everything, to create Antillean literature from nothing. It was violent, cannibalistic.'[13] While this ambition would persist throughout the poet's life, the explicit references to the islands disappear in the later part of the *Notebook* and in the later collections of poems. The actual name of the islands and the town of Fort-de-France are no longer found, but references to islands, to tropical vegetation, volcanoes and other geographical features still evoke the specific reference for readers familiar with the islands and for those familiar with the poet's first work, while at the same time deliberately emphasizing the universal significance of the images. Thus the emphasis on 'Les Antilles' at the start of the poem is replaced by references to 'mon pays', my country, at the end. It is as if the writing of the *Notebook* forms a process of exorcism which will enable the author, both later in the work and in his subsequent collections of poetry, to transform the personal reference into a more

11. Ibid., p. 75.
12. Ibid., p. 73.
13. Ngal, *Aimé Césaire*, p. 64.

universal form. In other words the Antilles are transformed into what Césaire has called his 'géographie imaginaire', the geography of the imagination.[14] Thus in his poetic vision geographical features, animals, plants and the elements combine to express the central themes of destruction and renewal, creating a poetry which is at once evocative of the Antilles and universally relevant, if only to those able to comprehend the complexity of Césaire's writing. It is therefore not surprising that he would quickly come to be seen not only as the progenitor of an authentic literature in the Antilles, but as the poet of decolonization. As we shall see, for critics and writers of later generations, the latter title would threaten the very basis of the former, as the newly discovered Antillean cultural identity risked being immediately dissolved in the immensity of the African diaspora.

Fundamental to the poet's victory over the alienation resulting from the colonial situation was Césaire's discovery of African civilization in the early 1930s, and the *Notebook* can be read as a poetic account of that discovery. By 1931, when Césaire arrived in Paris, a number of writers from Africa, the Caribbean and the USA had begun to publish literary works expressing their revolt against colonialism and racism. The writers of the Harlem Renaissance had been publishing novels and poetry for more than two decades, and Haïtian writers such as Jean Price-Mars,[15] had begun to explore their African past and their suppressed Afro-Haïtian folk culture. As a student at the Ecole Normale Supérieure in Paris, Césaire met other Antillean and African students, most notably Léopold Senghor, and became familiar with works on African civilization by Frobenius, Delafosse and other ethnologists. From that point onwards Africa was to occupy a central position in his works, beginning with the *Notebook*. The evocation of poverty and alienation with which the poem opens leads to a grandiose vision of escape, a desire to represent the suffering of the colonized and the oppressed throughout the world:

> To leave.
> As there are hyena-men and panther-men, I shall be a Jew-man
> a kaffir-man
> a Hindu-from-Calcutta-man
> a man-from-Harlem-who-does-not-vote.[16]

14. Jacqueline Sieger (1961), 'Entretien avec Aimé Césaire', *Afrique*, 5, p. 65.
15. Jean Price-Mars (1928), *Ainsi parla l'oncle*, Compiègne: Bibliothèque haïtienne.
16. Césaire, *Notebook of a Return to My Native Land*, p. 85.

Following this unsuccessful attempt to escape from his own past, the poet turns first to the narrower context of the African diaspora, focusing on the past suffering of his own race by listing geographical locations associated with the slave trade and with racism:

> And I say to myself Bordeaux and Nantes and Liverpool and New York and San Francisco
> not a piece of this world that does not bear my fingerprint
> and my calcaneus on the spines of skyscrapers and my filth
> in the glitter of gems!
> Who can make a better claim?
> Virginia. Tennessee. Georgia. Alabama.[17]

These false attempts to come to terms with his own past and that of his race lead to the ironic denial of the glories of African civilization, which Césaire had discovered during his student years in Paris: 'No, we have never been amazons of the king of Dahomey'.[18] It is only after he fully accepts the humiliation of his ancestry in the incident in the tram and discovers his negritude that the poet can envisage the symbolic destruction of the slave ship and a future in which 'there is room for all at the rendez-vous of conquest'.[19]

Although Léopold Senghor was the author who wrote most extensively on negritude and who was most closely associated with the concept, it was Césaire who coined the term in the *Notebook:*

> my negritude is not a stone, its deafness hurled against the clamour of the day
> my negritude is not an opaque spot of dead water over the dead eye of the earth
> my negritude is neither a tower nor a cathedral
>
> it reaches deep down into the red flesh of the soil
> it reaches deep into the blazing flesh of the sky
> it pierces opaque prostration with its straight patience.[20]

The poet's rediscovery and glorification of his race, with all the suffering and ignominy which it has endured, are based on this concept. Negritude is presented as the poet's discovery of his authentic self, his solution to

17. Ibid., p. 91.
18. Ibid., p. 105.
19. Ibid., p. 127.
20. Ibid., p. 115.

the alienation and loss of identity evoked at the start of the poem. With its triumphant rejection of colonial symbols, the concept was to dominate critical assessment of the *Notebook* for several decades, initially hailed as an expression of revolt against colonialism, but later questioned for its presentation of a common African heritage as a solution to the diverse realities of the diaspora, its dependence on European thinkers and its possible assumption that certain qualities are inherent in certain races.

Both Césaire and Senghor, in developing the concept of negritude, were greatly influenced by the representation of the African past in recent works of European ethnologists, particularly Frobenius. Of particular importance is his subsequently refuted claim that there was one civilization common to the entire African continent. Having defined 'the characteristic style of Africa', Frobenius claims: 'When one comes into contact with it and fully understands it, one realizes that it dominates all of Africa and is the expression of its very being.'[21] It is easy to understand the appeal of this simplified view of Africa for Césaire, Senghor and their contemporaries. These were the first works which they had read which not only admitted the existence of an African cultural heritage, but also treated it with esteem. The emphasis on the African past as a unifying and defining factor for new literary voices emerging throughout the diaspora continued to exert considerable influence not only on Césaire and Senghor, but also on scholars of their work in the 1950s and 1960s, most notably Janheinz Jahn and Lilyan Kesteloot, who used terms such as 'neoafrikanisch'[22] and 'négro-africaine'[23] to group together authors of African origin writing in Africa, the Caribbean and the USA. Despite its undeniable value in the initial affirmation of cultural identity, the continuing insistence on the centrality of Africa was eventually questioned and rejected. It has been pointed out by many critics that Africa was not presented as a reality but rather as a mythical continent in Césaire's poems, since he had never been there when many of them were written, but relied instead on information from African friends and the writings of the ethnologists. To criticize a poet for creating a myth may seem strange, but it is understandable in a context in which the ideas of Césaire and Senghor were presented not only as an affirmation of identity but as the very basis of a critical model for the classification of writers from the African diaspora in the future.

21. Leo Frobenius (1952), *Histoire de la civilisation africaine*, trans. D. Back and D. Ermant, Paris: Gallimard, p. 17.

22. Janheinz Jahn (1966), *Geschichte der neoafrikanischen Literatur*, Düsseldorf, Cologne: Eugen Diederichs Verlag.

23. Lilyan Kesteloot (1967), *Anthologie négro-africaine: panorama critique des prosateurs, poètes et dramaturges noirs du vingtième siècle*, Verviers: Marabout Université.

For later generations of anglophone and francophone writers in Africa and the Caribbean, the European influence at the very heart of negritude was a particular focus of criticism, seen as a paradox in the work of writers who wished to affirm their difference from Europe. The Nigerian writer Wole Soyinka was particularly critical, not of the original concept, but of the continuing insistence on its relevance.

> Negritude proceeded along the route of over-simplification. Its re-entrenchment of black values was not preceded by any profound effort to enter into this African system of values. It extolled the apparent. Its reference points took far too much colouring from European ideas even while its Messiahs pronounced themselves fanatically African. In attempting to refute the evaluation to which black reality had been subjected, Negritude adopted the Manichean tradition of European thought and inflicted it on a culture which is most radically anti-Manichean. It not only accepted the dialectical structure of European ideological confrontations but borrowed from the very components of its racist syllogism.[24]

Soyinka was not the only critic to notice the potentially racist connotations in negritude's innocent affirmation of the specificity of African civilization. It has been pointed out that Senghor's view of that civilization as essentially emotive and intuitive, close to the natural world, unlike Western civilization with its emphasis on reason, can be found in the works of Frobenius.[25] Senghor has defended his claim that negritude is not simply a term which refers to a common historical experience, but also includes an ethnic component,[26] while Césaire has clearly stated that his concept is not in any way race-based: 'I do not think of negritude in terms of biology, but of culture and history.'[27] Arnold points out that, while this comment reflects Césaire's mature views on the subject at the time of the 1969 interview, his earlier views were much closer to Senghor's.[28] Indeed, both Césaire and Senghor were included in Said's critique of the discourse of Africanism, which he defines as 'a systematic language for dealing

24. Wole Soyinka (1976), *Myth, Literature and the African World*, Cambridge: Cambridge University Press, pp. 126–7.

25. A. James Arnold (1981), *Modernism and Negritude: The Poetry and Poetics of Aimé Césaire*, Cambridge, Massachusetts: Harvard University Press, pp. 37–8.

26. Léopold Sédar Senghor (1971), 'Problématique de la Négritude', *Présence Africaine*, 78, p. 15.

27. Lilyan Kesteloot and Barthelemy Kotchy (1973), *Aimé Césaire: l'homme et l'oeuvre*, Paris: Présence Africaine, p. 236.

28. Arnold, *Modernism and Negritude*, p. 38.

with and studying Africa *for* the West'.[29] Both writers later preferred the term 'Africanité',[30] which distanced them from any racist connotations, while at the same time, paradoxically, revealing the increasing irrelevance of the concept in the cultural context of the Caribbean. Younger genera-tions of writers in the Antilles, such as Edouard Glissant, Maryse Condé and, more recently, Patrick Chamoiseau and Raphael Confiant, also rejected negritude, proposing concepts such as 'Caribbeanness' and 'Creoleness' as more pertinent to their own reality. Both Caribbeanness and Creoleness offered alternative ways of widening definitions of Antil-lean reality and identity beyond the exclusive focus on Africa, which was increasingly rejected as the sole point of reference for Antillean and Caribbean reality.[31] The conflict between different critical models is exemplified in the struggle of three generations of writers from the Antilles to create a meta-language which will appropriately define their cultural context. In his later years Césaire was to respond to criticisms of his focus on Africa in a number of ways. Despite the questioning by authors and critics of the relevance of the African context for the Antilles, he has always emphasized its central role in his works. He has also claimed that negritude was never a philosophical concept for him, but simply an affirmation of identity by a race oppressed by colonialism. This controversy has not eased with time, and recent studies, which accept that negritude played a vital role in the 1930s and 1940s, still raise the question of the contempo-rary relevance of the *Notebook* and the danger of 'consigning it to the museum'.[32]

Before proposing an answer to this question, it is important to note that the *Notebook*'s position in twentieth-century literature in French has also played a major role in leading writers and critics to consider a number of major issues. Firstly, Césaire's status as a poet writing in French gives him a prominent place among the large number of francophone African and Caribbean writers whose works have led to a reappraisal of what had previously been unquestioningly accepted as French literature. Secondly, the role of the language of the colonizer in works by colonized writers is itself an important theme in the *Notebook* and has subsequently been the

29. Edward Said (1994), *Culture and Imperialism,* London: Vintage, p. 233.

30. Ngal, *Aimé Césaire,* p. 55.

31. See, for example, Maryse Condé (1974), 'Négritude césairienne, Négritude seng-horienne', *Revue de la Littérature Comparée,* 3, pp. 409–19; Edouard Glissant (1981), *Le Discours antillais,* Paris: Seuil; Jean Bernabé, Patrick Chamoiseau and Raphaël Confiant (1989), *Eloge de la créolité/In Praise of Creoleness* (bilingual edition), trans., M.B. Taleb-Khyar, Paris: Gallimard.

32. Rosello, Introduction to Césaire, *Notebook of a Return to My Native Land* p. 13.

subject of much debate. Césaire's initial attitude to the French literary tradition and to the idea of writing poetry in French was highly ambiguous. His education in the Lycée Schoelcher in Fort-de-France fulfilled two apparently contradictory functions. On the one hand, it developed the critical faculties which enabled him to progress to the highest level of literary education in the Ecole Normale Supérieure in Paris. On the other hand, it increased his alienation by providing him with a quintessentially French education. The choice of the poetic form did not come easily to Césaire, and the period from March 1935 until the publication of the *Notebook* was an extremely difficult one for him.

> The *Notebook* was the first thing which I wrote. I must have worked very slowly on it, in different stages, but I certainly started work on it in about 1936, as a notebook. A notebook because I had given up writing poems. Traditional metre annoyed me a lot, paralysed me. I was unhappy. Then one day I said to myself, 'I'll just give up.' Then I started to write without knowing what would be the result, verse or prose. I had to express what was on my mind. That's why I chose a very neutral title: notebook. In fact it became a poem. In other words, I discovered poetry at the very moment when I turned my back on poetic forms.[33]

The decision to write what would come to be described as poetry in French, as opposed to French poetry, is an early example of the difficulty inherent in creating a new literary context, and the interpretation of this context would prove as problematic for intellectuals in France as for those in Africa and the Antilles.

The first French intellectuals to acclaim the *Notebook* as a masterpiece were clearly attracted to the work because of its revolt against a system which they also fundamentally questioned. Yet their writing was clearly situated within the French system, presenting black literature in French as a subset of French literature, albeit a welcome addition. In his preface to Senghor's anthology, Sartre described contemporary black poetry in French as 'in our times, the sole great revolutionary poetry'.[34] He also analysed negritude from a Eurocentric viewpoint. Having defined the concept as 'l'être-dans-le-monde du Nègre', Sartre proceeded to situate it in a Hegelian dialectic as follows:

33. Ngal, *Aimé Césaire*, p. 143.
34. Jean-Paul Sartre (1963), *Black Orpheus*, trans. Samuel Allen, Paris: Présence Africaine, p. 11. Sartre's essay originally appeared in 1948 as 'Orphée noir', the introduction to Léopold Sédar Senghor, ed., *Anthologie de la nouvelle poésie nègre et malgache*, Paris: Presses Universitaires de France, pp. ix–xliii.

In fact, Negritude appears as the weak stage of a dialectical progression: the theoretical and practical affirmation of white supremacy is the thesis; the position of Negritude as antithetical value is the moment of the negativity. But this negative moment is not sufficient in itself and the blacks who employ it well know it; they know that it serves to prepare the way for the synthesis or the realization of the human society without racism. Thus Negritude is dedicated to its own destruction, it is passage and not objective, means and not the ultimate goal.[35]

Many black writers felt robbed of their cultural identity by this statement, although it proved to be strangely prophetic when African and Antillean writers later rejected the concept as irrelevant to their present reality. Nevertheless, the Eurocentric ideological perspective of Sartre's critique placed it on the margins of the development of new critical models for the study of African and Afro-Caribbean writers. A similar divergence can be observed in Césaire's political life, as he resigned from the French Communist party in 1956, describing it as insensitive to France's colonial problems.[36]

Sartre was not the first French writer to acclaim Césaire as a poet. André Breton, who met Césaire in Fort-de-France in 1941 and wrote the preface to the edition of the *Notebook* published by Présence Africaine in 1956, was particularly attracted by the surrealist aspects of the work, especially by the attack on rationalism. The energy and spontaneity of Césaire's literary expression made him a source of renewal in what was for Breton the otherwise drab environment of contemporary French poetry. From the perspective of the 1990s, his celebration of Césaire as a black writer has a racist tone in that he appears to consider it noteworthy that the poet should surpass his white counterparts, a point noted by Fanon in *Black Skin, White Masks*:

> There is no reason why André Breton should say of Césaire, 'Here is a black man who handles the French language as no white man today can.' And, even though Breton may be stating a fact, I do not see why there should be any paradox, anything to underline.[37]

However, a reading of the preface in its entirety makes it clear that Breton particularly welcomes the poem as an attack on colonialism and racial

---

35. Ibid., pp. 59–60.
36. Aimé Césaire (1956), *Lettre à Maurice Thorez*. Paris: Présence Africaine.
37. Frantz Fanon (1986), *Black Skin, White Masks*, trans. Charles Lam Markmann, London: Pluto, pp. 39–40.

inequality, which he naïvely hopes will disappear as a result of international settlements at the end of the Second World War. Breton's main concern is clearly to welcome Césaire as a great poet in the surrealist sense, and, like Sartre, he approaches the poet's work from the only perspective which he knows for dealing with works written in French, namely that of the French literary tradition.

It is easy to understand why Breton and Sartre had no other ambition than to consider Césaire's work in the context of French poetry. Although they recognized the *Notebook* as innovative and original, they could also observe explicit references to nineteenth-century French poetry and parallels with what were considered to be revolutionary literary and ideological movements in twentieth-century Europe. The line from Baudelaire's 'L'Albatros' is the most obvious direct quotation within the *Notebook*, and is ironically printed in capitals lest the reader miss the reference:

> He was COMICAL AND UGLY.
> COMICAL AND UGLY, for sure.[38]

This and many other echoes of French literature in Césaire's works form an ironic intertext, an explicit reference to the poetic act of appropriating the French language to express a fundamentally different reality. Sartre and Breton, on the other hand, in emphasizing similarities with the European ideologies of Marxism and surrealism, undermine its non-European and anti-colonial nature. It is not surprising that Breton should accept Césaire as a surrealist, while at the same time regarding him as something of a distant cousin in the context of French literature. The *Notebook*'s explicit rejection of reason and its surrealist images are arguably more forceful than anything which the surrealist movement itself had produced. Furthermore, in the journal *Tropiques*, Césaire's contemporaries accepted Surrealism as a weapon in their search for an antidote to the cultural alienation of the Antilles.

> One of the most effective means of achieving this renewal is undoubtedly to be found in surrealism as defined by Breton in his *Manifesto of Surrealism*. The technique, based on the important discoveries of Freud, is to this day the most successful psychological method of bringing to the surface the tendencies, sentiments and reactions suppressed in the Antillean mentality by a most unfortunate psychological phenomenon.[39]

38. Césaire, *Notebook of a Return to My Native Land,* p. 109.
39. René Ménil (1944), 'Situation de la poésie aux Antilles', *Tropiques,* 11, pp. 131–2.

When Césaire wrote the first version of the *Notebook*, he must have been aware that the surrealists were an important literary movement in Paris, but he had no strong interest in their work, and there was certainly no conscious effort on his part to adopt their techniques. Nevertheless, many of the images in the first version can be seen as surrealist, disrupting the rational expectations of the reader by bringing together opposites. The much repeated phrase, 'at the brink [bout] of dawn' is a good example, as the finality of 'bout' undermines the hope implicit in the reference to dawn. However, the more obviously surrealist passages, particularly the rejection of reason, which was added in a later version of the poem, are evidence of what Arnold describes as the gradual surrealization of the work.[40]

> Treasure, let us count:
> the madness that remembers
> the madness that screams
> the madness that sees
> the madness that is unleashed
>
> And you know the rest
>
> That 2 and 2 make 5
> that the forest mews
> that the trees pull the maroons out of the fire
> that the sky smooths its beard
> et cetera et cetera . . .[41]

Such explicit appropriation of the philosophy and techniques of a European literary movement posed a considerable challenge to the proponents of the race-based critical model in their efforts to underline the differences between the poetry of Césaire and that of his European counterparts. Since Breton and Sartre were unwittingly adopting a Eurocentric approach, and were in no way consciously defending it, the race-based approach remained dominant until the late 1970s. In the 1980s a number of studies of the *Notebook* and the later collections freed the work from the limitations of these two approaches. In particular, the collection of studies published to commemorate the poet's seventieth birthday was the first serious effort to show how the *Notebook* had been interpreted in different ways since its publication, depending on the ideological context

---

40. Arnold, *Modernism and Negritude*, passim.
41. Césaire, *Notebook of a Return to My Native Land*, p. 93.

in which it was read.[42] This study also included the first complete publication of the various changes which Césaire introduced in the editions of the *Notebook* between 1939 and 1956, thus giving easy access to students and researchers to material which until then had been more difficult to obtain.[43]

The combination of the increasing international recognition which the *Cahier* has received as a denunciation of colonialism, on the one hand, and the rejection of the race-based critical model, on the other, continues to fuel controversy about the status and relevance of the work in a post-colonial world. In particular, Raphaël Confiant's study of Césaire's continuing attachment to his African roots and his rejection of Creole language and culture attempts to dethrone the poet and politician from the patriarchal position which he has occupied for several decades in the struggle against colonialism. For Confiant, the universality to which Césaire has always aspired is an abstract notion,[44] which serves only to suppress the authentic Creole culture in which he grew up and was active throughout his political life.[45] Although almost all of Confiant's long work is devoted to a strong denunciation of Césaire, he surprises the reader at times by briefly presenting the works in a positive light. The poet's glorification of his denigrated African identity is seen as a tragic expression of the alienation resulting from colonialism[46] and as a necessary first step in the development of a Creole identity.[47] Such positive comments, however, are not given prominence in a work that presents Césaire's cultural and political activities as fundamentally misguided and doomed to failure.

Confiant's study is part of an increasing tendency in the 1980s and 1990s to situate Césaire's work no longer in a pan-African context but rather in the multilingual and multicultural setting of the Caribbean. Jean-Claude Bajeux's *Antilia retrouvée*,[48] a comparative study of the poetry of

42. See, for example, the following chapters: A. James Arnold, 'La réception afro-américaine: un dialogue difficile aux Etats-Unis', pp. 141–61; Thomas A. Hale, 'Césaire dans le monde blanc de l'Amérique du Nord', pp. 109–21; Michel Hausser, 'Césaire à l'école', pp. 203–27; M. a M. Ngal, 'Aimé Césaire devant le grand public africain francophone', pp. 163–202, all in M. a M. Ngal and Martin Steins, eds (1984), *Césaire 70*, Paris: Editions Silex.

43. Liliane Pestre de Almeida, 'Les versions successives du *Cahier d'un retour au pays natal*', in Ngal and Steins, eds, *Césaire 70*, pp. 35–78.

44. Raphaël Confiant (1993), *Aimé Césaire: Traversée paradoxale du siècle*, Paris: Stock, p. 72.

45. Ibid., p. 121.

46. Ibid., p. 91.

47. Ibid., pp. 270–3.

48. Jean-Claude Bajeux (1983), *Antilia retrouvée: Claude McKay, Luis Palés Matos, Aimé Césaire, poètes antillais*, Paris: Editions Caribéennes.

writers from three different linguistic areas, is only accessible to a mono-lingual reader when the poems can all be read in one language. Thus Bajeux includes in his study, alongside a selection of Césaire's poems, a translation in French of thirty poems by Claude McKay and twenty-five by Luis Palés Matos. The Caribbean cultural context is thus created by a combination of the activities of the poets, the researcher and the translator. The African context which so dominated earlier studies of Césaire's works is not criticized, but it is no longer the focus of the study. The relevance of comparative models in the continuing political and cultural complexity of the Caribbean context is clear, and it is understandable that some proponents of such models in the generations of Antillean writers following Césaire have tended to present them as the opposite of the race-based model, consigning it to the museum of history. An accommodation between these conflicting views is perhaps to be found in the more recent accept-ance of hybridity and syncreticity as the background from which writers in colonized countries begin their efforts to create new cultural contexts and new literary voices. In such a context, Césaire's return to his African heritage as an antidote to the alienation of colonialism cannot be inter-preted as the basis of a single new critical model for future generations of writers; nor must it be seen as a false solution to be criticized as inauthentic; nor again need it be considered as a historical moment of little relevance for the present. Its relevance may still be evident in some contexts, absent in others, but it can nevertheless exist alongside 'Caribbeanness', 'Creole-ness' and other concepts as one constitutive element in the development of the literatures of post-colonial countries.

−3−

Frantz Fanon: The Routes of Writing
Patrick Williams

In the world through which I travel, I am endlessly creating myself.

Frantz Fanon, *Black Skin, White Masks*

It has become something of a commonplace of modern literary theory that a text is not the bearer of a single coherent and identifiable meaning determined by the intentions of the author. If as a result it is now unexceptional for literary texts to be the subject of multiple and conflicting interpretations, that is still a rather less common fate for the work of cultural and political commentators, especially, perhaps, for someone whose writing is – apparently – unambiguous, even uncompromising. Fanon, however, seems always to have been, and to continue to be, the subject of a remarkable variety of competing readings and, before examining in detail the directions taken by Fanon's writing, it is worth glancing at some of the directions in which critics currently wish to take him.

For an earlier generation of critics in the 1960s and 1970s, Fanon was fought over largely in terms of his political analysis; currently, his work is a theoretical battleground within the broad field of post-colonial studies.[1] Henry Louis Gates, for example, has written a frequently cited but rather problematic survey of the varied uses and misuses of Fanon in contemporary theory.[2] In a similarly sceptical vein, Benita Parry, in her well-known article 'Problems in current theories of colonial discourse', uses Fanon as the basis for a critique of the post-colonial theorizing of Homi Bhabha, Gayatri Spivak and Abdul JanMohamed, and points out how Bhabha,

---

1. For introductions to the field of post-colonial studies, see, for example, Peter Childs and Patrick Williams (1997), *An Introduction to Post-Colonial Theory*, Hemel Hempstead: Prentice Hall/Harvester Wheatsheaf; Patrick Williams and Laura Chrisman, eds (1993), *Colonial Discourse and Post-Colonial Theory: A Reader*, Hemel Hempstead: Harvester Wheatsheaf; Bill Ashcroft, Gareth Griffiths and Helen Tiffin, eds (1995), *The Post-Colonial Studies Reader*, London: Routledge.

2. Henry Louis Gates (1991), 'Critical Fanonism', *Critical Inquiry*, 17, pp. 457–70.

whose analysis of colonialism is grounded in post-structuralism, 'proffers Fanon as a premature post-structuralist'.[3] Another post-structuralist critic, Robert Young, has more recently suggested that with *The Wretched of the Earth* Fanon could even be seen as inaugurating post-modernism (here understood as cultural crisis and the attempt to decolonize European thought).[4] In particular, Bhabha's reading of Fanon, rather than any gentle 'proffering', appears as a violent appropriation. Claiming that 'Fanon's work will not be possessed by any one political moment or movement',[5] Bhabha proceeds to what many might regard as just such an act of possession, marginalizing Fanon the theorist of nationalism (*The Wretched of the Earth*[6]) in favour of Fanon the theorist of narcissism (*Black Skin, White Masks*[7]), when in fact one of the more important aspects of Fanon's own re-routeing is from the analysis of the politics of psychological states to that of the politics of emergent nation states.

A more 'violent' reading of Fanon is offered by Christopher Miller in his book *Theories of Africans*, a recent work which none the less carries strange echoes of Cold War mentalities. Miller, for instance, claims that Fanon regarded the world of pre-colonial cultures as 'a primitive stage to be transcended, or "liquidated"'.[8] While this is factually inaccurate as a reading of Fanon's work, the choice of 'liquidated' carries definite overtones of murderous Stalinist purges, and, notwithstanding the scare quotes, is not a term used metaphorically or 'under erasure', as it were, since Miller goes on to repeat it in absolutely non-metaphorical ways: 'What is most impressive in reading Fanon is the sheer power of a theoretical *truth* to dictate who shall live and who shall be liquidated.'[9] The generalized potential guilt of Fanon becomes more historically specific, however: Keita Fodeba, dramatist, poet and later Minister of Internal Affairs in independent Guinea, is the only creative writer apart from Césaire on whom Fanon comments at any length in *The Wretched of the Earth*; in 1969, Fodeba was one of many Guineans executed on the orders of President

3. Benita Parry (1987), 'Problems in current theories of colonial discourse', *Oxford Literary Review*, 9:1–2, pp. 27–58.

4. See Robert Young (1990), *White Mythologies*, London: Routledge, Ch. 7.

5. Homi Bhabha (1994) *The Location of Culture*, London: Routledge, p. viii.

6. Frantz Fanon (1967), *The Wretched of the Earth*, trans. Constance Farrington, Harmondsworth: Penguin. Originally published in 1961 as *Les Damnés de la terre*, Paris: Maspero.

7. Frantz Fanon (1986), *Black Skin, White Masks*, trans. Charles Lam Markmann, London: Pluto. Originally published in 1952 as *Peau noire, masques blancs*, Paris: Seuil.

8. Christopher Miller (1990), *Theories of Africans*, Chicago: University of Chicago Press, p. 49.

9. Ibid., pp. 50–1.

Sekou Touré, and Miller contrives to implicate Fanon (who by then had been dead for eight years) on the basis of nothing more than Sekou Touré's fondness for Fanon-style rhetoric.

An example of a critic who does not want to be constrained by interpretations he does not agree with is Patrick Taylor, who says: 'With a mere twist in point of view, one can construe as revolutionary some of the characteristics of Fanon's works identified by the other critics.'[10] While it is by no means certain that 'a mere twist' is sufficient to make a work revolutionary – as Fanon would probably have said, a given text is revolutionary or it is not[11] – this nevertheless serves to indicate something of the ways in which critics still struggle to locate and to interpret Fanon.

If locating Fanon intellectually is a process which is far from complete, the apparently simpler task of locating him geographically is no foregone conclusion either. The assumption of this collection is that Fanon is a Caribbean writer, and there is an obvious logic to that. At the same time, and despite his unquestioned importance as an intellectual, a recent two-volume study, *Intellectuals in the Twentieth Century Caribbean*,[12] makes almost no mention of him whatsoever, since he appears to be regarded as of relevance only to the African situation. While it is difficult to comprehend such an exclusion, it does at least suggest the possibility that Fanon might be better located in other ways. One such is provided by Paul Gilroy's work on the concept of the black Atlantic as an 'outernational and transcultural' strategy for escaping restrictive geographical frameworks, especially those offered by the nation state:

> The history of the black Atlantic since then [the time of Columbus], continually criss-crossed by the movements of black people – not only as commodities but engaged in various struggles towards emancipation, autonomy and citizenship – provides a means to re-examine the problems of nationality, location, identity and historical memory.[13]

Gilroy's stress on the forms of mobility which characterize the black Atlantic is somewhat at odds with other more generally influential positions:

10. Patrick Taylor (1989), *The Narrative of Liberation*, Ithaca and London: Cornell University Press, p. 9.

11. The misquote is from *Black Skin, White Masks*, p. 85, where he says, 'A given society is racist, or it is not.'

12. Alistair Hennessy, ed. (1992), *Intellectuals in the Twentieth-century Caribbean*, London: Macmillan.

13. Paul Gilroy (1992), *The Black Atlantic*, London: Verso, p. 16.

> Marked by its European origins, modern black political culture has always
> been more interested in the relation of identity to roots and rootedness than in
> seeing identity as a process of movement and mediation that is more appro-
> priately approached via the homonym routes.[14]

Although he himself instantiates, rather than explicitly analyses, the 'routes'
dimension, Fanon, as indicated in the epigraph to this chapter, clearly
moves away from the emphasis on identity as 'rooted' (organic, stable,
natural and fixed) towards a more mobile concept.

The journeyings which constitute the 'routes' of the black Atlantic are,
as Gilroy notes, frequently profoundly transformative: 'all these figures
who begin as African–Americans or Caribbean people and are then changed
into something else which evades those specific labels, and with them all
fixed notions of nationality and national identity'.[15] Whether or not one
can count Fanon as someone who gives up ideas of nationality and national
identity altogether, he is undoubtedly one of those 'who begin as . . .
Caribbean . . . and are then changed into something else'. Accordingly,
the rest of this chapter will look at Fanon as a black Atlantic writer,
beginning in the Caribbean but becoming something else in terms of the
routes he follows and his conscious re-routeing of himself and his writing.[16]

Geographically, Fanon's routes are entirely those of the black Atlantic
– from the Caribbean to Europe and then to Africa – linking its three
continents, but also marking a difference from the paths taken by the slaves
(from Africa to the Caribbean, and to Europe if they were lucky). It would,
however, be wrong to see these as simply stages on a seamless journey:
while there are obviously connections between them, in many ways –
politically, culturally, textually – they are disjunctive or divergent, involving upheavals and re-routeings, both voluntary and enforced. In textual
terms, the first route belongs to *Black Skin, White Masks*, the second above
all to *The Wretched of the Earth*.

Having devoted a certain amount of effort to displacing the idea of
Fanon as a Caribbean writer, I would now – slightly perversely, no doubt
– like to insist on the Caribbeanness of *Black Skin, White Masks*. This is
a book which is grounded in the Caribbean, which springs from the
historical circumstances of the Caribbean in the middle of the twentieth

14. Ibid., p. 19.

15. Ibid.

16. Although he does not discuss Fanon, Gilroy does class him as one of 'the two
best-known black Atlantic thinkers' along with C.L.R. James (ibid., p. xi). However, despite
the usefulness of the concept and the insights contained in Gilroy's discussion, it is difficult
to avoid the feeling that the black Atlantic is very much an anglophone conversation.

century, and which is a study of the social psychology of people from the Caribbean (despite its ultimate desire for universal relevance). Although the Caribbean is different, although, as Fanon was to repeat many times, there is no justification for any easy eliding of the Caribbean and Africa, there is nevertheless a sense in which the Caribbean, especially the francophone Caribbean and perhaps Fanon's island of Martinique above all, is representative of a generalized condition which is the result of colonialism.

Colonialism aims to rule as effectively as possible and, while the definition of effectiveness might be historically variable, the co-operation or passivity of the indigenous population was probably always an important element in that. The methods for ensuring a compliant population range from brutal coercion to the gentler approach of hegemony, as defined by Gramsci, where the dominated group in a society is encouraged to consent to its domination and to believe that it is in its best interests. The consent of the dominated – in this case, the colonized population – hinges on their acceptance that the ruling (Western) culture, ideology and practices are the best, or at least superior to their own. Such acceptance is best secured via education as an institution of cultural insemination, and therefore could not normally reach the bulk of the population. In any sphere of colonialism, the educated classes, and above all the intelligentsia, were the most exposed to Western culture and persuasive ideologies. That effect was arguably greater in francophone areas because of the French colonial strategy of assimilation, which worked harder to convince the colonized populations that, in a substantive and meaningful sense, they were French, and arguably greatest of all in areas like the Caribbean, which were told that they were somehow closer to the metropole. The illusion was often sustainable so long as colonized people remained in their own country and, in the phrase to which Fanon returns frequently, 'in their place'.

Black Skin, White Masks is one of the texts from the period of decolonization which registers the traumatic gap between the colonial rhetoric and the facts of life in France (particularly) as a black person.[17] Realization of that gap marks the first and decisive re-routeing for Fanon. Hitherto, his course had (apparently) been clearly set for the heart of the empire, and he himself well on the way towards becoming the favoured colonial subject, the *évolué*: French-educated, French-identified, assimilated to French culture and values, patriotic (Fanon volunteered to fight for the French in the Second World War, and was awarded the Croix de Guerre

---

17. Another, very different, treatment of the same subject is provided by the film *Soleil Ô* (1969), directed by the Mauritanian Med Hondo, which, from its vantage point at the end of the 1960s, also embodies some of the insights of *The Wretched of the Earth*.

in 1945). The insight which accompanies the realization allows Fanon to see that he and all the other Caribbean *évolués* are in fact *aliénés* – alienated, 'self-divided' individuals. This split is registered in the book's title, and is one which it is the book's principal aim to overcome (rather than simply to heal, which would help the individual, but leave the condition itself untouched): 'I believe that the fact of the juxtaposition of the white and black races has created a massive psychoexistential complex. I hope by analysing it to destroy it.'[18]

At this point, there are several important things to register about Fanon's approach to his task. Firstly, the manner in which he presents his findings – 'This book is a clinical study'[19] – reflects the fact that for a time he considered submitting it, rather than the usual, more formal piece, as his thesis when he qualified in psychiatry at Lyons in 1951, as well as pre-empting the criticisms of exaggeration, bias and emotional excess which were bound to greet a work tackling such an emotive subject. Criticisms of this kind are made all the more likely by Fanon's impassioned style, particularly evident in the central chapter 'The fact of blackness', and further heightened in the lyrical, fragmented prose of the Introduction and Conclusion. Secondly, unlike the dominant practice of psychotherapy, Fanon aims for a collective cure. As he says, 'It will be seen that the black man's alienation is not an individual question.'[20] Thirdly, Fanon is strikingly aware of the grounding of psychological states in social conditions, and this is another reason why the problem and its solution are collective, not individual, issues:

> If there is an inferiority complex, it is the outcome of a double process:
> – primarily, economic;
> – subsequently, the internalization – or, better, the epidermalization of this inferiority.[21]

The fact that in view of this Fanon still believes that his analysis – however radical – can destroy something rooted in material circumstances may reflect an overestimation of his own professional sphere; it may also reflect that what he is proposing is very far from psychotherapy as 'the talking cure'.

Although the central chapter of *Black Skin, White Masks* is entitled 'The fact of blackness', much of the analysis is concerned with what we

18. Fanon, *Black Skin, White Masks*, p. 14.
19. Ibid.
20. Ibid., p. 13.
21. Ibid.

might call the meanings of blackness. In the face of white racist stereotyped thinking and black movements such as negritude, both of which would argue that there is an essential, unchanging, black identity (however much they would disagree on the positive or negative content of that identity), Fanon is at pains to establish an anti-essentialist model of blackness: 'The Negro is not. Any more than the white man.'[22] 'My black skin is not the wrapping of specific values.'[23] While his particular interest is the situation of black people, Fanon is opposed to any essentialized constructs in this area: 'There is no white world, there is no white ethic, any more than there is a white intelligence.'[24] If there is no natural, inherent or essential meaning to blackness, then its meaning is a social construct, and Fanon is very clear about just who is doing the constructing: 'White *civilization* and European culture have forced an existential deviation on the Negro. I shall demonstrate elsewhere that what is called the black soul is a white man's artefact.'[25]

Among the points to note here are, firstly, that Fanon's position re-routes him away both from the dominant current of Western culture, in so far as it denigrates black people, and from the most important black cultural movement of the period, negritude, which is also a profoundly Caribbean movement, and secondly that his awareness of how colonialist ideology constructs its meanings through a system of representations prefigures work done from the late 1970s onwards in colonial discourse analysis and post-colonial theory.

In the first case, that Fanon should reject racist Western culture seems obvious, but like other intellectuals of the period he was deeply imbued with that culture, and therefore rejection can be a complex, even unwilling, process. Like his older contemporary, C.L.R. James (though perhaps less vehemently), part of Fanon considered Western culture as an aspect of his inheritance, his roots:

What is this talk of a black people, of a Negro nationality? I am a Frenchman. I am interested in French culture, French *civilization*, the French people. We refuse to remain 'outsiders', we have full part in the French drama.[26]

22. Ibid., p. 231.
23. Ibid., p. 227.
24. Ibid., p. 229.
25. Ibid., p. 16.
26. Ibid., p. 203.

> None the less I am a man, and in this sense the Peloponnesian War is as much mine as the invention of the compass.[27]

The desire, evident in the latter quote, to belong to an undifferentiated humanity, a world, as Fanon puts it, of 'reciprocal recognitions', is what sets him against European racism (which differentiates and denigrates) and negritude (which differentiates and celebrates). The disengagement from negritude is also complicated by Fanon's admiration for one of its key figures, his compatriot and teacher Aimé Césaire. *Black Skin, White Masks* opens with a quote from Césaire; Fanon discusses and praises both *Cahier d'un retour au pays natal* and its author; nevertheless, negritude remains ultimately unsatisfactory for Fanon. As already mentioned, its model of black identity appears too essentialist, and its concept of a black soul far too complicit with Eurocentric notions. In addition, while Fanon agrees with Césaire that an important part of colonialism's *modus operandi* is the devaluation and destruction of indigenous history and culture, and while the rediscovery of black traditions and histories might be temporarily exhilarating, Fanon views an obsession with the past as a trap and a political irrelevance in the context of the brute reality of colonialism in the Caribbean.

> Let us be clearly understood, I am convinced that it would be of the greatest interest to be able to have contact with a Negro literature or architecture of the third century before Christ. I should be very happy to know a correspondence had flourished between some Negro philosopher and Plato. But I can absolutely not see how this fact would change anything in the lives of the eight year old children who labour in the cane fields of Martinique or Guadeloupe.[28]

The second point mentioned above, the question of representation, shows Fanon not so much re-routeing himself as preparing the ground for a major re-routeing in academic work worldwide. The rapid growth of post-colonial studies in the 1980s as a multidisciplinary area of enquiry owes much to the impetus provided by the work of Edward Said. Said's work, especially in the early stages, hinges on analyses of representation (in this case, the way in which the West thought and wrote about other cultures, the images it produced of those cultures). One of the most important aspects of Said's work is his demonstration of the way in which

27. Ibid., p. 225.
28. Ibid., p. 230.

the representations legitimize political, economic or military action against the peoples and cultures who are being represented. Arguably, all of these issues are prefigured in Fanon – although to say this in no way diminishes the importance of Said and others who have followed him.

The focus on representation foregrounds Fanon as reader, rather than writer, of texts, and *Black Skin, White Masks* discusses a wide range of forms, from children's comics to psychoanalytical treatises, paying particular attention to texts written in or about the Caribbean such as Mayotte Capécia's *Je suis Martiniquaise* or Réné Maran's *Un homme pareil aux autres*. In turn, these two serve as the foci for chapters which examine, respectively, the relations between black women and white men, and those between white women and black men. They also reveal one of the weaker areas of Fanon: he is not, it has to be said, a great literary critic. His analyses of representations and the ideologies they purvey are forcefully presented, but not at all subtle or even very accurate. He consistently discusses the central figures in texts (characters or narrator) as if they are the author themselves and, while this may be partly understandable in relation to an autobiographical work like *Je suis Martiniquaise*, it is hardly satisfactory as an approach to fiction. (The fact that Fanon judges Capécia more harshly than Maran may derive from the fact that her book is more 'real' than his, and consequently its pathological representations of black people and their behaviour all the more reprehensible.[29]) Unlike Said's studies, which focus on what colonialist representations enable Europeans to do (colonize, oppress, and so on), Fanon is more concerned with what they cajole black people into doing (assimilate, don 'white masks', live alienated lives) – what we might call their hegemonic effectivity.

In *Black Skin, White Masks*, Fanon sets out to oppose a particular form of representation – the reductive stereotyping of black people – thereby beginning a process which will last for the rest of his life. As Homi Bhabha has pointed out, the stereotype is one of colonial discourse's fundamental modes of representation, but, rather than the stability which other critics have seen in the stereotype, Bhabha's psychoanalytically informed reading sees it – however hard it might aspire to stability – as marked by uncertainty and ambivalence:

29. I am aware that a brief summary of this complex area risks compounding the problems of Fanon's original discussion of Capécia. For a fuller analysis, see Chapters 4, 6 and 11 in this volume.

An important feature of colonial discourse is its dependence on the concept of 'fixity' in the ideological construction of otherness. Fixity, as the sign of cultural, historical or racial difference, in the discourse of colonialism, is a paradoxical mode of representation: it connotes rigidity and an unchanging order as well as disorder, degeneracy and daemonic repetition. Likewise the stereotype, which is its major discursive strategy, is a form of knowledge and identification which vacillates between what is always 'in place', already known, and something which must be anxiously repeated . . . as if the essential duplicity of the Asiatic or the bestial sexual licence of the African that needs no proof, can never really, in discourse, be proved.[30]

Bhabha's is an interesting way of thinking about stereotypes, and has proved influential. However, rather than simply rely on the constitutive ambivalence of colonialist and racist stereotypes to undermine their authority and effectiveness, Fanon sets out actively to combat them by means of historicized and theorized dissections of their nature and ways of operating. This is indispensable, since a lack of coherence, logic or contact with reality has never prevented the repetition of stereotyped 'knowledges' about black people – a fact of which Fanon is also ironically aware. The first area of stereotyping which Fanon tackles is one of the most ancient and most tenacious – the (supposed) excessive sexuality of black people, especially the black male. Fanon cites psychological evidence to show that images of unspeakable black sexuality are closely related to white psychological dysfunction; he cites physiological evidence to show that, for example, black penises are not the monstrous objects of white fantasy; he cites demographic evidence to show that the Japanese and Chinese produce far more children than the 'over-breeding' black population. Nevertheless, he realizes an element of futility in all this:

> But these are facts that persuade no one. The White man is convinced that the Negro is a beast; if it is not the length of the penis, then it is the sexual potency that impresses him. Face to face with this man who is 'different from himself', he needs to defend himself. In other words, to personify The Other. The Other will become the mainstay of his preoccupations and his desires.[31]

Building on insights such as these offered by Fanon, analysts of the ways in which Western discourses represent and construct their black 'Others' have become a central aspect of work in the post-colonial field.

---

30. Homi Bhabha, 'The other question', in Bhabha, *The Location of Culture*, p. 66.
31. Fanon, *Black Skin, White Masks*, p. 170.

After *Black Skin, White Masks*, Fanon did not often return to the Caribbean as a subject for analysis, not least because the following year the next stage of his journey took him to Algeria, which was to be the focus of his life and his writing thereafter. An important transitional discussion, written in 1955, is 'West Indians and Africans' in *Toward the African Revolution*, which addresses a number of themes from the earlier book and, in addition, chronicles the shift in the attitude of West Indians towards Africa and Africans. Once again, Fanon voices his opposition to the concept of a single Negro people: 'There is as great a difference between a West Indian and a Dakarian as between a Brazilian and a Spaniard. The object of lumping all Negroes together under the designation of "Negro people" is to deprive them of any possibility of individual expression.'[32] Despite this, negritude and other pan-African movements have reversed the attitude of superiority, anatomized in *Black Skin, White Masks,* which Caribbean blacks previously held towards Africans. Now, in the post-Second World War period, Caribbean people approach Africa with something like humility, their lighter skins, formerly a source of pride, now a cause of embarrassment. Whatever the problems of pigmentation, however, the post-1945 West Indian is thoroughly African-identified. Ironically, Africans are not necessarily ready to accept these converts, however loudly they sing the praises of the new version of the motherland. In addition, 'It thus seems that the West Indian, after the great white error, is now living in the great black mirage.'[33] In other words, too many for Fanon's liking have simply exchanged the 'error' of an assimilationist stance for the 'mirage' of an uncritical nativism.

Another element of continuity and change in *Toward the African Revolution* is the question of colonialist racist stereotyping, which the article 'The North African Syndrome', written contemporaneously with *Black Skin, White Masks*, extends and transfers to cover the inhabitants of North Africa. Fanon here points out the institutionalized racism of the medical profession, which proceeds on the basis that the colonized are malingerers and liars. In the words of a French medical thesis published just the previous year, 'the powerful sexual appetite that is characteristic of those hot-blooded southerners [male migrant workers from North Africa]' is seen to threaten the bases of normal life. The solutions proposed in the

---

32. Frantz Fanon (1970), *Toward the African Revolution*, trans. Haakon Chevalier, Harmondsworth: Penguin, p. 27. Originally published in 1964 as *Pour la révolution Africaine*, Paris: Maspero.
33. Ibid., p. 37.

thesis are the 'risk' of bringing their families over ('a certain invasion') or providing brothels for them.[34]

The relation between medicine (as the sign of putative Western progress and benevolence) and the attitude of colonized peoples towards it (apparently incapable of comprehending, appreciating or utilizing it) is further explored in *Studies in a Dying Colonialism*. 'Introduced into Algeria at the same time as racialism and humiliation, Western medical science, being part of the oppressive system, has always provoked in the native an ambivalent attitude.'[35] Ill-explained treatments are regarded with suspicion; the doctor is seen as an agent of colonialism (and just how appallingly accurate that perception could be was revealed in the involvement of doctors in the torture of Algerians during the war of independence). The war was also an example of how the meaning of something could be radically altered and, thereby, people's attitudes towards it. In the context of the war, medicine became not an invasive colonialist technology, but an urgent question of keeping people healthy or healing wounded fighters and returning them to the front; it also became 'indigenized', as Algerians were secretly trained in medical techniques. As Fanon concludes, 'The notions about "native psychology" or of the "basic personality" are shown to be vain. The people who take their destiny into their own hands assimilate the most modern forms of technology at an extraordinary rate.'[36] While *Studies in a Dying Colonialism* explodes racist stereotyping of black incapacity to handle technological concepts and practices, *The Wretched of the Earth* does the same with politics, as it demonstrates how, in similar conditions of relevance and urgency, rapid developments in political consciousness, strategy, organizing ability, etc. are not only possible but well within the grasp of 'under-developed' peoples.

Studies in a Dying Colonialism and *The Wretched of the Earth* mark Fanon's most obvious re-routeing, from the academic analyst of the mechanisms of psychological alienation to the theorist of, and participant in, armed insurrection. At one level, this change is real, and Fanon's analysis of – most notoriously – violence in the colonial context can seem a very long way from *Black Skins, White Masks*. At the same time, any route carries traces of where you have been and the way you have come, and there are significant continuities with earlier works in *The Wretched*

34. Ibid., p. 21.

35. Frantz Fanon (1989), *Studies in a Dying Colonialism*, trans. Haakon Chevalier, London: Earthscan, p. 121. Originally published in 1959 as *L'An cinq de la révolution Algérienne*, Paris: Maspero.

36. Ibid., p. 145.

of the Earth. Among such elements are the linked issues of culture, of intellectuals and, yet again, of negritude. The linkage is apparent, for instance, in the way Fanon concentrates on intellectuals in their role as producers of culture, and on 'Negroism' as a particular attitude (intellectual, above all) towards the nature and function of culture.

Running alongside the dissections of colonialist representations of colonized peoples in Fanon's work is the scrutiny of the self-representations of the colonized. Potentially powerfully liberatory, these can also be powerful in their contribution to the maintenance of alienated attitudes (the particular source of Fanon's unhappiness with Mayotte Capécia). In *The Wretched of the Earth*, Fanon is especially interested in the construction of a national culture – self-representation raised to the national level – as a component of the struggle for freedom: 'It is the fight for national existence which sets culture moving and opens to it the doors of creation.'[37] This is particularly true in so far as the arrival of colonialism marks the decline or destruction of indigenous culture. The process does not stop at the national level, however, and Fanon examines Keita Fodeba's poem 'African dawn' as a work with global resonance:

> There is not a single colonized person who will not receive the message that this poem holds . . . this is Sétif in 1945, this is Fort-le-France, this is Saigon, Dakar and Lagos. All those niggers, all those wogs who fought to defend the liberty of France or for British *civilization* recognize themselves in this poem by Keita Fodeba.[38]

In the same way, Fanon's book, though grounded in the experience of the Algerian war and responding to the circumstances of that struggle, aims to speak to colonized people – all the wretched of the earth – everywhere.

Although Fanon sees the desired route as taking him and others beyond the boundaries of the nation state, negritude, despite its impeccable transnational credentials, still does not satisfy him as a possible destination. One reason for this is that, while, in Fanon's view, the national stage may not be sufficient, it is nevertheless indispensable; negritude, however, fails to accord the requisite importance to the national culture. It also fails to recognize the historical specificity which that national culture represents: 'Negro-ism therefore finds its first limitation in the phenomena which take account of the formation of the historical character of men.'[39]

37. Fanon, *The Wretched of the Earth*, p. 197.
38. Ibid., pp. 186–7.
39. Ibid., p. 174.

Unfortunately, even when negritude does focus on historical issues, it does so in ways which lack both the relevance and political urgency which matter so much to Fanon, as well as to the colonized peoples he is writing about: 'Men of African cultures who are still fighting in the name of African-Negro culture and who have called many congresses in the name of the unity of that culture should today realize that all their efforts amount to is to make comparisons between coins and sarcophagi.'[40] At the same time, Fanon is not so rigid as to deny any utility to negritude; on the contrary, he recognizes that colonialism's inability or refusal to differentiate among black people or black cultures logically calls forth resistance which is articulated in the name of all black people. If Fanon's 'coins and sarcophagi' judgement appears harsh, that no doubt reflects the fact that the negritude position is both very attractive and a distraction from more useful political paths. Similarly, the fact that Fanon is still doing battle with it in *The Wretched of the Earth* registers something of his own difficulty in either simply dismissing it or disentangling himself from it.

If Fanon shows himself rather ambivalent towards negritude, he is perhaps only slightly less ambivalent towards those responsible for it – the intellectuals. The question of intellectuals – their position, behaviour, responsibilities and so on – is one which recurs in different guises throughout Fanon's writing. In *Black Skin, White Masks*, the most important groups of intellectuals are writers, philosophers and psychoanalysts. That there is no inherent or essential attitude which belongs to any particular intellectual role is shown by the fact that creative writers can reproduce alienated mentalities (Mayotte Capécia, for instance) or contribute greatly to the overcoming of such mentalities (Aimé Césaire); similarly, psychoanalysts can legitimize colonial domination (Octave Mannoni) or fight for its overthrow (Fanon himself, above all). *Black Skin, White Masks* is in some senses the most 'intellectual' of Fanon's books. It is certainly the one that concentrates the most on intellectuals and their problems – above all, the inferiority complexes and self-alienation which are the result of colonialism, and to which intellectuals are particularly vulnerable because of the cultural and educational channels through which the alienating ideologies are disseminated. This also represents a largely class-specific form of colonial domination (to the extent that it is the middle class who are educated and vulnerable), with a class-specific solution (the literate/'intellectual' work of disalienation embodied in *Black Skin, White Masks*). The domination experienced by members of the working class (plantation workers in the

40. Ibid., p. 188.

Caribbean, for instance) and the appropriate means of their liberation are fundamentally different.

In *The Wretched of the Earth,* intellectuals are positioned differently and understood differently. While they are still producers of culture and purveyors of concepts, these activities are framed very much by the politics of decolonization, the armed struggle, the needs of the emergent nation, the attendant snares of neocolonialism, rather than the (seemingly) more individualized concerns portrayed in earlier books. The situation is now more highly charged, more is immediately at stake in terms of the anti-colonial struggle, and what intellectuals do matters more. As a result, they are subject both to suspicious scrutiny and political exhortation. On the face of it, not much is to be expected from them as members of the colonized middle class. In Fanon's pithy expression, 'the bourgeois phase in the history of under-developed countries is a completely useless phase'.[41] Nevertheless, Fanon recognizes that there will be 'a small number of honest intellectuals', not politicized but well-intentioned, who can be of use to the progressive forces, especially to the extent that they distance themselves from the middle class and take the side of 'the people'.

The chapter 'On national culture' in *The Wretched of the Earth* is Fanon's lengthiest analysis of colonial and post-colonial intellectuals, and contains his famous three-part model of the typical route they follow. 'In the first phase, the native intellectual gives proof that he has assimilated the culture of the occupying power.'[42] For centuries, the only way in which many black people could hope to convince Europeans of their fully human status was by desperately competing on European terms and according to European standards in cultural and intellectual production. While that particular invidious cultural game is still far from being over, it is one which a number of intellectuals refuse, at a certain point, to play any longer.

'In the second phase, we find the native is disturbed; he decides to remember what he is.'[43] This first major re-routeing for the intellectuals corresponds in Fanon's case to the moment of *Black Skin, White Masks.* Although the phrase 'remember what he is' suggests the recovery of a pre-existing identity, already constituted but forgotten, this hardly fits with what we have seen of Fanon's views so far, and points instead to a desire for a 'return to the source', a rediscovery of the historical forms and practices of the intellectuals' own culture rather than the one to which they are so relentlessly exposed. Many intellectuals immerse themselves

41. Ibid., p. 142.
42. Ibid., p. 178.
43. Ibid., p. 179.

in the cultural past and never re-emerge, and this is the equivalent at the level of national culture of the seductive, entrapping power of negritude. An additional problem for intellectuals is that, as a result of their previous orientation towards Western culture, they are, to a greater or lesser degree, alienated from their own people, and therefore their attempts to write about them in this phase often have an artificial, 'external' quality. The difficulty of connecting with their own culture as it exists now makes it more comfortable for intellectuals to dwell on the cultural past. A further difficulty which Fanon identifies is recurrent in debates surrounding post-colonial cultural production:

> At the very moment when the native is anxiously trying to create a cultural work, he fails to realize that he is utilising techniques and language which are borrowed from the stranger in his country. He contents himself with stamping these instruments with a hallmark which he wishes to be national, but which is strangely reminiscent of exoticism.[44]

Questions raised here of cultural relevance and authenticity and of the Eurocentric ideologies which may be perpetuated (even unwittingly) by a continued use of Western forms and languages have been important since the period of decolonization and continue to divide numbers of post-colonial writers and critics.

'Finally, in the third phase, which is called the fighting phase, the native, after having tried to lose himself in the people and with the people, will on the contrary shake the people.'[45] This is an even more important re-routeing for the intellectuals. Especially in the first phase, what they write is addressed outwards, abroad, to a Western audience. The second phase turns them more towards their own people, but it is only in the final phase that they produce works which really speak to the people, which rouse and mobilize them via a 'literature of combat' that draws on the struggles of the emergent nation. This is a view of writing as rooted in the reality of people's lives and returns us yet again to the issue of the relevance of what intellectuals do.

In spite of such an uplifting scenario, however, the fact remains, as Fanon was all too aware, that not all intellectuals are prepared for such a change of direction. Many remain alienated; many have such an investment in the colonial status quo or in its neocolonial black élite replacement that a change of this sort is unimaginable. As they remain loyal to the worst aspects of their class origins and formation, they exhibit the negative

44. Ibid., p. 180.
45. Ibid., p. 179.

face of intellectual potentiality: 'Spoilt children of yesterday's colonialism and today's national governments, they organize the loot of whatever national resources exist. Without pity they use today's national distress as a means of getting on through scheming and legal robbery, by import–export combines, limited liability companies, gambling on the stock exchange or unfair promotion.'[46] The last hope in such a situation is that the (transformed) ordinary people, the 'new men' created by decolonization, will not tolerate this kind of state for long.

This last point, the creation of new men, is an important one, which takes us both back to the chapter's epigraph and forward into an uncharted future. As we have seen, Fanon is aware of how identities are not pre-given, but are formed by particular histories in particular contexts. In this way, what can be seen as almost primordial oppositions – the colonizer and the colonized, the settler and the 'native', the white man and the 'nigger' – are for Fanon relations constituted by the circumstances of colonialism and its racist ideologies, and as such are destined to be dissolved away in the struggle for decolonization. Although these relations have an apparent symmetry, they are obviously not equal, nor are they born of any process of mutual recognition. On the contrary, the lesser or negative term is very much an enforced or imposed identity. As Fanon says, it is the settler who brought the 'native' (as an identity which connotes lazy, deceitful, oversexed, or underdeveloped) into existence, and who maintains that existence. The creation of identities is not unidirectional, however (although again the relation is unequal), and, if Europe obliges the colonized world to be what it is, then in a sense the colonies enable Europe to be what it desires to be. This allows Fanon to assert that 'Europe is literally the creation of the Third World'.[47] In other words, continued European economic exploitation of its colonies creates the wealth that permits the adoption of an identity which assumes civilization, advancement, superiority and the like. These historically constituted identities are being reconstituted through the process of decolonization: 'Decolonization is the veritable creation of new men. But this creation owes nothing of its legitimacy to any supernatural power; the "thing" which has been colonized becomes man during the same process by which it frees itself.'[48] It is important to note that what reconstitutes identities is what people do – they are not mere passive objects moulded by historical forces, but agents interacting with those forces.

46. Ibid., p. 37.
47. Ibid., p. 81.
48. Ibid., p. 28.

At the same time, although decolonization certainly sets in motion the reconstitution of identities, and although it embodies the destruction of the historical relation responsible for the dehumanizing ideologies, it is clearly not a process that can be rapidly accomplished. Indeed, to the extent that colonialism affected more or less the whole of the world, then what is involved is the remaking of identities on a global scale – remaking humankind almost. It is on this level that Fanon's final words, the Conclusion to *The Wretched of the Earth*, written in the days before his death from leukaemia, frame the task. As such, the distance travelled, from the individualized self-fashioning of the end of *Black Skin, White Masks* (as in the epigraph) to the necessary collective reworking now envisaged, is enormous. 'For Europe, for ourselves and for humanity, comrades, we must turn over a new leaf, we must work out new concepts, and try to set afoot a new man.'[49] Although Fanon knew it was not a journey he himself was going to make, the sketching out of a tentative new route is altogether typical. While with the benefit of hindsight it may be (all too) easy to dismiss this as the dream of a dying revolutionary, it is equally a 'dream' grounded in an assessment both of the possibilities of the historical moment and of the changes embodied in the routes Fanon and his generation had travelled.

49. Ibid., p. 255. The original French for 'turn over a new leaf' is 'faire peau neuve'. In the context of what we have seen, the importance of envisaging the remaking of humanity as involving a shedding of skin hardly needs stating.

−4−

Women, History and the Gods: Reflections on Mayotte Capécia and Marie Chauvet

Joan Dayan

In 1930s Paris, when Aimé Césaire, Léon Damas and Léopold Senghor crafted their image for voice regained in the word 'négritude', Josephine Baker, fêted in Paris as 'Black Venus', appeared in Marc Allégret's film *Zou Zou*. Zou Zou makes her musical debut wearing nothing but feathers. She swings in a gilded cage and sings 'Who will give me back my Haiti?' Such poignant lyricism in a black body locked in a golden frame was welcomed by the Western consumer. Trapped in the 'beautiful cage' that she laments is 'nothing but a jail', Zou Zou sings to the white audience who can assure her success.

Whether Senghor's 'femme noire', Césaire's 'pauvre folle' or Allégret's icon of pathos, woman bears the burden of being representative. In his 1948 *Orphée noir* (Black Orpheus), Sartre defined negritude as the descent of the black man into the hell of his soul to retrieve his Eurydice. More a love song between two apparent opponents – the élite black writer and his cultivated white reader – than a means of change, the required plunge into the depths remained a male endeavour – the woman mere passage to his song. It was he, *l'homme de culture*, who knew how to gain strength from a particular representation of woman. Negritude not only encased the black in the castle of his skin, but its call to transcendence, with the iconic black woman in tow, condemned women in the Caribbean to a crushing loss of presence.

Placed outside the call to recollection and retrieval, the muse of the writer in search of his voice, she remained unrecognized, unvoiced, part of someone else's history, someone else's celebration. Her status replayed in an uncanny way the experience of the colonized, fighting to speak. Though central to the black man's construction of his identity, she was appropriated and metaphorized out of existence. Even now, in our heady atmosphere of 'Creoleness', 'multiculturalism' and 'nomadism', writers who perpetuate the spectacle of 'womanhood' are published, translated and reviewed.

As Caribbean studies becomes fashionable in the global academy, writers like Maryse Condé and Simone Schwarz-Bart are celebrated and taught, while Mayotte Capécia and Marie Chauvet remain untranslated and out of print. I am not arguing for an agon between the respective strengths of one set of writers and the other, but, rather, I want to turn to what we might investigate as the politics of the underread: an examination of what remains so threatening about Capécia and Chauvet's visions of colour, class and sexuality that makes these works inaccessible or resistant to easy accommodation in the liberal compact of cultural, feminist or African-American studies.

Both Capécia and Chauvet depend on a series of hauntings: whether the male 'heroes' of standard national histories, or the African and New World gods, or shape-shifting spirits. Most upsetting to those who celebrate an ideology of something called 'blackness' or that much-touted 'female identity' is the insistence of both writers that their characters shuttle between extremes, inhabiting an equivocal and indeterminate world. Fanon's scathing indictment of Capécia's *Je suis Martiniquaise* in *Black Skin, White Masks*, as 'cut-rate merchandise, a sermon in praise of corruption'[1] is a response to the demand that sexuality, belief and colour be clearly defined, that those of us who inhabit a particular space called 'black' or 'white' must, especially if we are women, be clear about our alliances, be serious about our geneological inheritance and place ourselves carefully in proper and uncontaminated categories.

Capécia's *Je suis Martinquaise*, like Chauvet's *Amour, Colère et Folie*, tells a story of forced intimacies that is nothing less than a retrieval of colonial and post-colonial history and its legacy of mimicry, contamination and violation. For contemporary academics in quest of the lyrical compromise, so fitting to the dehistoricized arena of the race, class and gender trinity, the reconstruction of what could be deemed embarrassing stereotypes of colour and servitude forces readers into a past unalleviated by a redemptive spiritual vision. While Chauvet, especially, is reticent about representing the unrepresented, Simone Schwarz-Bart in *Pluie et vent sur*

---

1. Frantz Fanon (1967), *Black Skin, White Masks*, trans. Charles Lam Markmann, London: Pluto, p. 42.

2. Simone Schwarz-Bart (1972), *Pluie et vent sur Télumée miracle*, Paris: Seuil, trans. Barbara Bray (1974), *The Bridge of Beyond*, London, Kingston and Port-of-Spain: Heinemann.

Telumée miracle[2] appeals more easily to general readers accustomed to the relics of exoticism. Endorsing the claims of ancestral landscape, matriarchy and blackness, Schwarz-Bart presents the rural surround as a repository of enduring value. To celebrate, as she does, 'the permanence of Antillean being' (the vicissitudes of history notwithstanding) threatens to turn the particulars of society into the ideals of folklore.

The pain and recognition experienced in reading Capécia and Chauvet result from their narrative compulsion to inhabit their place, to circumscribe themselves as demonic underbelly to metropolitan culture. Writing their versions of Caribbean Gothic, they force readers to confront the implications of being a *mulâtresse*, to know what it means to bear the curse of being caught between two kinds of racialism, 'poisoned', as Derek Walcott puts it in 'A Far Cry from Africa', with 'the blood of both'.[3] And the claims of colour are themselves shifting and pernicious, summoning unexpected scenes of conquest and possession.

Capécia's Cult of Colour

Four years after the publication of Jacques Roumain's classic novel of peasant life and political romance, *Gouverneurs de la rosée* (1944), Mayotte Capécia published *Je suis Martinquaise*.[4] Roumain's work remains with us: translated into many languages, it marks an extraordinary turn to the possibilities of collective production and stresses what the facts of history make of language and religion. Capécia's novel is out of print and, indeed, as Clarisse Zimra has argued, we only know of it, perhaps, because of Fanon's scathing indictment of the author and her text in *Black Skin, White Masks*.

Fanon condemns *Je suis Martiniquaise* as the most blatant example of the assimilated *bourgeoise* who wants nothing more than to adapt – physically and spiritually – to the colonial system: 'Mayotte loves a white man to whom she submits in everything. He is her lord. She asks nothing, demands nothing, except a bit of whiteness in her life.'[5] Rather than a

---

3. Derek Walcott (1986), 'A Far Cry from Africa', in *Collected Poems: 1948–1984*, New York: Farrar, Straus & Giroux, p. 18.

4. Jacques Roumain (1944), *Gouverneurs de la rosée*, Fort-de-France: Désormeaux (reprinted 1988, Paris: Editions Messidor), trans. Langston Hughes and Mercer Cook (1978), *Masters of the Dew*, Oxford: Heinemann; Mayotte Capécia (1948), *Je suis Martinquaise*, Paris: Correa. *Je suis Martiniquaise* won the Grand Prix des Antilles in 1948, and in 1950 Capécia published *La Négresse blanche*, Paris: Correa.

5. Capécia, *Je suis Martiniquaise*, p. 42. All translations mine.

celebration of whitening love, what Fanon calls 'lactification', however, Capécia's story offers a cruel analytic of 'love' in Vichy Martinique. If the sublime is a production of excess in the minds of men, dependent for its force on the split between what can be allowed and what must be forbidden, Capécia will interrogate and repeat the processes of idealization.

It is startling how much Fanon oversimplifies the complexities of *Je suis Martiniquaise*, how blind he is to Capécia's irony and self-consciousness. Capécia is above all a writer. And, like any good Gothic memorialist who makes perceived sin the source of fiction, Mayotte, as a character in her own narrative of compulsion, begins by asking: 'Why have I begun writing?' But Fanon has another agenda, and it has to do with another kind of domination. 'The person I love will strengthen me by endorsing my assumption of my manhood,'[6] he begins 'The woman of colour and the white man', the chapter that includes his attack on Capécia, not as writer but as a certain kind of cursed woman. And if Mayotte is neither muse nor support, she must be scorned – a vanishing ritual Fanon commits to a footnote: 'In fact, there is an aura of malediction surrounding Mayotte Capécia . . . Depart in peace, mudslinging storyteller'[7] Obviously, a woman in the late 1940s in Paris could not make the same assumptions about identity as her male compatriots, especially when the ideology of negritude, like that of some Marxist 'civilisation universelle', left women out of the game. At the same time that Joséphine Baker and Katherine Dunham performed in Paris, when *Présence Africaine* and its writers celebrated Black Africa, the 'Black Soul' and 'Black Orpheus', where could one place 'a woman of colour'?

Je suis Martiniquaise is Capécia's questioning of her ability to say 'I am', her ironization of the very possibility of speaking for or as a nation. What does it mean for a woman of colour to say 'I am'? What is a 'Martiniquaise' in an island bewitched by the competing claims of sex and colour? Capécia's desire for whitening is inseparable from her recognition of the power of the spirits and the persistence of Creole, which makes its way into her story at crucial moments. In this atmosphere of multiple bewitchings and the contradictions of colour, her love object André comes off as nothing more than a husk of colour, an icon of civilization cast in terms of whiteness. Even as the novel ends, as Mayotte completes her

---

6. Ibid., p. 41.
7. Fanon, *Black Skin, White Masks*, p. 53. Note that the French version is far more chilling: 'Il y a en effet une malediction qui flotte autour de Mayotte Capécia...Partez en paix, ô éclaboussante romancière' (Fanon (1952), *Peau noire, masques blancs*, Paris: Seuil, p. 42).

manuscript in Paris, she is haunted by her dead ancestors and places herself in an ever-present lineage of belief: 'It is true that for *us* the dead are never dead. I have often felt when writing these pages that they continued to prowl around me.'[8]

Most crucial is Capécia's questioning (for she can never totally assimilate or fully reject anything) of the most valued assumptions of metropolitan culture. Although the novel appears to be cast as capitulation to the metropole – as Mayotte abandons Martinique for Paris, it actually allows her to return to the place where she was born. Constructing her character as a two-selved being – indeed, there seem to be two Mayottes – she shakes up all fixed binary oppositions: for example, the categorical or unequivocal assertion of the meaning of such terms as masculine and feminine, black and white, spirit and body. She writes out of an unsettling place, where alternative possibilities coexist: sanctified dichotomies, such as *la métropole* or *le pays natal* are revealed to be problematic rather than known or assured. Fanon's much discussed assertion – 'To speak means . . . to assume a culture, to support the weight of a civilization'[9] – Capécia demonstrates to be not at all certain. Mayotte has two languages – the Creole of the majority, and the official language of the élites – and she cannot assume 'mastery' of either. That is not her concern.

Oppressed ultimately by two constructs not of her own making – the white foreigner and the black nationalist – Capécia also suffers separation from other women. If male writers felt themselves torn between their native land and the *métropole* – words from France taming their heart from Senegal, to paraphrase the words of the Haitian poet Léon Laleau[10] – women writing not only experienced Gallic conventions (French as a literary language) as a wedge between two worlds, but they also had to confront their position outside all forms of production, whether literary or popular. For Capécia would not be read by the women of her class, and she could not be read by the Martinican peasant or working-class women.

The pain and recognition experienced in reading Capécia results from her narrative compulsion to write her version of Caribbean Gothic, forcing her readers to know the implications of being or being told to be 'pure

8. Capécia, *Je suis Martiniquaise*, p. 202.

9. Fanon, *Black Skin, White Masks*, pp. 17–18.

10. Léon Laleau (1931), 'Trahison', in *Musique nègre*, Port-au-Prince: Collection Indigène: 'And that despair – the most intense of all – / Of using words from France to tame and train / This heart of mine that came from Senegal,' trans. Norman R. Shapiro (1970), in *Négritude: Black Poetry from Africa and the Caribbean*, New York: October House, p. 93.

11. Capécia, *Je suis Martiniquaise*, p. 98.

and without stain'.[11] Capécia repeats and questions the processes of idealization; indeed, she out-idealizes the idealizing propensities of her male admirer. André, her Fascist lover, is so blatantly spiritualized that we must wonder how Fanon missed her satire on men touting love, talking politics and calling on God. But perhaps he got the point. Mayotte is not supporting any man's assumption of his manhood. In assuming her womanhood, 'Je me croyais déjà femme', she, a Creole Emma Bovary, enters a realm of phantoms and illusions: 'I laughed less, I became sentimental . . . I fell in love with the moon, I filled my heart with its light, which seemed purer and more stirring than the sun'.[12] Yet Mayotte's construction of what she calls 'independence' or 'liberty' – surrounded by hostile blacks and scornful whites – bears some consideration. Her memories of André and her recounting of their 'spiritual' love, in the course of her recollections, becomes deeply unsettling. He turns her into a *courtisane*, warning her about her 'wild prancing about' ('trémoussements sauvages'), but, as she talks to herself in Creole, André begins to matter less than her thoughts about him. Analysing the processes of idealization and its effects, she exaggerates the tropes of masculinized conquest and feminized submission, overturning her society's stereotypes even as she adopts them.

Writing out of her marginality as 'concubine' and 'exile', Capécia meditates on language, society and race in the intimacy of her reminiscences. But her analysis of ruling-class greed (whether mulatto or white) and the colonial compromise is effective because she so fully inhabits her bourgeois world, it narcissism and delusions. Years before her supposed surrender to whiteness, Mayotte poured a bottle of ink over the head of a student who treated her without respect. 'It was my way of changing whites into blacks.'[13] It is the first of her transformations. As her story unfolds, she reveals her fascination for varying disguises, inventing scenes for mortification, excess and illusion. But she locates these imaginings in a factual context that we are not allowed to forget. After her transgressive blackening of the white student, she reflects:

> Of course, I was punished. And not only for these kinds of things. Arithmetic, grammar, history appeared to me great enemies. I resisted them, I refused to overwork myself for them. In short, I didn't worry about them, I had something else on my mind. I, whose ancestors had been slaves, I had decided to be independent.[14]

12. Ibid., p. 87.
13. Ibid., p. 19.
14. Ibid.

When she later defies the French civilizing mission, she continues to refer to her heritage, a conceit of servitude that remains for her the motive underlying her story.

We cannot read Capécia and appreciate the ambiguities of her writing unless we recognize how deeply she is inhabited by the gods. Whether she is in Didier, the well-to-do area of Fort-de-France (where you don't have to be racially pure to be called white), or in Paris, her history relates to and supports the demands of a religious experience that cannot be contained in or erased by her Catholic education. Her desire for whiteness, to be lifted up into the sanctity of her envisioned pink and white angels, is criss-crossed with the sighting of the *zombi*, the call of the *djablesse* (she-devil) and her dealings with the sorcerer or *quimboiseur* even as she prepares to leave for Paris, cursing in Creole: 'My *quimbois* is stronger than yours. It gave me the power to charm men. Yes, I charmed my lover and I'm afraid of nothing.'[15]

Capécia seems acutely aware of the perils of assimilation: the more you read, the less you hear the voice of the gods, or, more precisely, the beliefs and legends of the black majority. The codes and trappings of the European enlightenment contributed to how the spirits of Africa would be received, comprehended and sustained in the New World. In his striking appendix to *Life in a Haitian Valley*, Melville Herskovits refers to the accommodation or 'adjustment' to disjunction, to the tension between Europe and Africa. He describes 'the two ancestral elements' that 'have never been completely merged' as 'socialized ambivalence', and thereby explains the 'vacillation' in the Haitians' behaviour, the oscillation between traditions polarized as either sacred or demonic. Capécia's articulation of ritual belief, whether describing the Church or *Quimbois*, exemplifies the syncretism, the processes of association and interpenetration that Herskovits described as 'selection', 'working over', 'revamping and recombining the elements of contributing cultures'.[16]

While casting herself as yielding to things French, Capécia remains obsessed by what it means to be Martinican, to be between irreconcilables, writing out of the interstices. The superstitions, demons and witches of pre-Reformation Europe, transported to the island by provinical priests, became part of new rituals, appreciated for their spiritual or symbolic force, but also for their practicality. Capécia demonstrates the two-way

15. Ibid., p. 168.
16. Melville Herskovits (1972), *Life in a Haitian Valley* (with introduction by Edward Brathwaite), New York: Doubleday, pp. 299, 301.

configuration of magic and materialism, what we might call a 'Creole Catholicism'.

If colour is destiny, then sexuality is sin. Mayotte's effective internalization of Catholic notions of purity is exemplified when she experiences 'this pure physical love' with Horace, 'a most beautiful Martinican type'. After her sexual surrender, she rides into the forest, her horse jumps and she sees 'A black dog, enormous' that blocks her path. Flames leap from its eyes and its open mouth, before the 'horrible creature' disappears. Mayotte makes the connection between sex and the unnatural *zombi* spirit herself: 'in a single night I had known love and seen the *zombi*'.[17] Her relation with André is nothing but the culmination of Mayotte's zombification, what René Depestre in *Bonjour et adieu à la négritude* defines as 'this absolute reification . . . the pure and simple project of assimilation of the colonized, the annihilation of his psychological being'.[18] Whether offered feminizing love or sexualized religiosity, Mayotte's options are limited. As first her mother and then her friend Loulouze had warned her: 'Life is difficult for a woman, especially for a woman of colour.'[19]

Capécia's *Je suis Martiniquaise* brings back the ghosts of colonial Martinique. The stereotype of the luxurious *mulâtresse*, a necessary prop in colonial fantasies of the French islands, operated as a dream of whiteness superimposed on the fact of blackness. As icon of what every white man most wanted and every white woman most feared, she ran the gamut of idealization and denigration. A surfeit of representation alternated with systematic debasement. For whether adored or condemned, the *mulâtresse* or *femme de couleur* became a metaphor for 'luxury', 'excess' and 'seductiveness'. What purpose did this stereotype serve? The necessity to separate materially the double categories – slave and free, black and white, even as they mixed and became ever more indistinct, meant that the very idea of 'free' and 'white' had to be qualified and transformed. The increase in the light-skinned products of colonial mixing and the freedom that attended that procreative spectacle resulted in strategic denigration. The project of certifying place, position and rank in a chaos of contradictions became a

17. Capécia, *Je suis Martiniquaise*, pp. 106–7. In Guadeloupe and Martinique, *zombi* usually means evil spirit, but in Haiti the *zombi* undergoes a double incarnation, meaning both spirit and, more specifically, the animated dead, a body without mind or, as the Jamaican novelist Erna Brodber has so aptly put it, 'flesh that takes directions from someone' (Brodber, *Myal*, London: New Beacon Books, 1988, p. 108).

18. René Depestre (1980), *Bonjour et adieu à la négritude*. Paris: Robert Laffont, pp. 97–8.

19. Capécia, *Je suis Martiniquaise*, pp. 20, 58.

colonial obsession. Systems of classification, backed up by repressive laws, became more urgent as the visible economic and traditional proofs of distinction vanished.[20]

The cultural work of 'blackness' for francophone intellectuals depended on the retrieval of 'black essence', with the accompanying binary oppositions heralded in the dialectic of negritude. As Fanon wrote: 'I am White, that is to say that I possess beauty and virtue, which have never been Black . . . I am Black: I am the incarnation of a complete fusion with the world, an intuitive understanding of the earth.' [21] In a sense, the work of *Présence Africaine* recuperated a necessary definition of the human as being black, much as Jean-Jacques Dessalines, founder of the Haitian Republic in 1804, declared in his Constitution of 1805 that henceforth Haitians, whatever their colour, would be known as blacks, referred to by 'only the generic word *black*' (Article 14). Since the most problematic division in the new Haiti was that between *anciens libres* (the former freedmen, who were mostly *gens de couleur*, mulattos and their offspring) and *nouveaux libres* (the newly free, who were mostly black), Dessalines attempted by linguistic means and by law to defuse the colour issue.[22]

In a startling passage of *Orphée noir*, Sartre expressed his momentary desire to rip off his white tights. The 'camouflage' of blackness becomes crucial to this proposed disclosure. For, in Sartre's hands, negritude becomes ultimately a 'nudity without colour'. In this world, which he describes as 'white over black', a 'secret whiteness of the black' and 'a secret blackness of the white', ontological 'convertibility' is open to all men.[23] There are no women in this flickering world of being and non-being.

Capécia, while invoking this duplicity of colour or doubling of black and white, retrieves the facts that undergird such a complex of colour: the conflation of loving, buying and selling in the colonies. Risking the recuperation of what might first seem sensational or tasteless categories and stereotypes, Capécia enquires into this textured and complex past.

20. See my extended discussion of 'Taxonomies of enlightenment' and the colour codes of Moreau de Saint-Méry in Joan Dayan (1995), *Haiti, History, and the Gods,* Berkeley and London: University of California Press, pp. 219–37.

21. Fanon, *Black Skin, White Masks,* p. 45.

22. For a full discussion of Dessalines's radical response to colour and class distinctions in colonial Haiti, see Dayan, *Haiti, History, and the Gods,* pp. 24–6.

23. Jean-Paul Sartre (1948), 'Orphée noir', Preface to Léopold Sédar Senghor, ed., *Anthologie de la nouvelle poésie nègre et malgache de langue française,* Paris: Presses Universitaires de France, trans. Samuel Allen (1963), *Black Orpheus,* Paris: Présence Africaine, pp. 62–3.

And her enquiry depends for its power on her recognition of the duplicities of colour: 'every nuance, from African black to white, ranging from yellow, red and all the series of browns'.[24] As opposed to the dichotomies of Fanon or Sartre, she endorses a language of amalgamation, a shuttling between extremes, in order to disclose the curious misalliances in what is normally seen as a theatre of opposition. In her metaphors of whitening, laundering and purifying, she captures the task of enlightenment, as well as the inventive recolouring of *gens de couleur*.

Chauvet's Colonial Fantasies

If Capécia, at the end of *Je suis Martiniquaise*, leaves her readers in a locale of empty, but privileged, forms, nothing more than the detritus of colonial fantasy – a snow-covered Paris and a son named François – Chauvet asks two fundamental questions in everything she writes. First, what happens to words such as 'power', 'purity', 'love' or 'dirt' when, as an anonymous planter from Saint-Domingue put it, you've 'tasted the pleasures of a nearly absolute domination'? And, second, what is a woman to do when she reads her continued servitude, this time expressed by the men in her midst, who idealized something called 'the national soul', while converting women into nothing more than property?

In all of her fiction, Chauvet literalizes the idealized Haitian history of heroes and martyrs through the bodies of women. Chauvet moves from the eve of the revolution in Saint-Domingue, in *Danse sur le volcan* (1957), to the memory of the bloody week of Tonton Nord Alexis (who ruled Haiti from 1902 to 1908), in her radical ethnographic narrative *Fonds des nègres* (1960), to the bitter black nationalism of the mulatto Sténio Vincent, in *Amour*, treated by Chauvet as precursor to her allegory of the apocalyptic terror of Duvalier's regime in *Colère* and *Folie*.[25] In these works Chauvet scrutinizes the idiom of colour, historicized and codified

24. Capécia, *Je suis Martiniquaise*, p. 10.

25. Marie Vieux Chauvet's first published work, written for the stage under the pseudonym Colibri, was (1950), *La Légende des fleurs*, Port-au-Prince: Deschamps. *Fille d'Haïti* (Paris: Fasquelle, 1954) won the *Prix de l'Alliance française* in Haiti; *La Danse sur le volcan* (Paris: Librairie Plon, 1957) was translated into English by Salvator Attanasio as *Dance on the Volcano* (New York: William Sloan, 1959); and *Fonds des nègres* (Port-au-Prince: Editions Deschamps, 1960) won the *Prix France-Antilles* in Paris. *Amour, Colère et Folie* (Paris: Gallimard, 1968), once published, caused a scandal in Port-au-Prince, and Chauvet was forced into exile in New York. There she wrote *Les Rapaces* (1986), published posthumously by Editions Deschamps in Port-au-Prince, Haiti.

as social hierarchy. The claims of sex are never far from the mechanics of power and submission motivated by this epidermic fatality.[26]

As in Capécia's writing, Chauvet's stories force readers into a purgatory of non-acceptability, as she risks the recuperation of what might first seem sensational or tasteless categories and stereotypes. Until 1968, when Gallimard published *Amour, Colère et Folie*, Chauvet occupied a privileged position as a light-skinned member of the Port-au-Prince bourgeoisie. But the publication of this analysis of Duvalier's dictatorship – and, more particularly, of women's place in a society crippled by the 'calamity' or 'curse' of colour – caused a scandal. In *Folie* (the climax of her trilogy), the story of four 'mad' poets, who have locked themselves in a stinking room to hide from the *tontons macoutes* (called 'the devils'), the mulatto René tries to define his identity by his skin: 'What am I, born of a father so mulatto that he seemed white? Skin of saffron, skin of mahogany, skin of sapodilla. No, skin of a rotten coconut. "Colour of a fart," as my mother said.'[27]

The trilogy, once printed, remained in warehouses for twelve years, 'blocked by the "conciliabules" between the Haitian and French bourgeoisie'. Dany Lafferrière, among other Haitian critics, has discussed how *Amour, Colère et Folie* was deliberately ignored or mocked in the major papers in Port-au-Prince.[28] Madeleine Gardiner, one of Haiti's few women literary critics, has asked: 'But why this voluntary omission of the writings of a woman whose whole life has been a long quest for justice, liberty and brotherhood, all those things that seem meanwhile to be the dream of all our men of action, poets, writers or political men?'[29]

Chauvet's work is a complex answer to Fanon's condemnation of Capécia; indeed, she writes *Amour, Colère et Folie* in order to examine how the force of epidermal criteria determines women's status in ways

26. Chauvet is crucial to my investigation of fiction, history and ethnography in *Haiti, History, and the Gods* (see the chapter entitled 'Fictions of Haiti', pp. 77–139). For an in-depth analysis of *Amour*, see Joan Dayan (1991), 'Reading women in the Caribbean: Marie Chauvet's *Amour, Colère et Folie*', in Nancy Miller and Joan DeJean, eds, *Displacements: Women, Tradition, Literatures in French*, Baltimore: Johns Hopkins, pp. 228–53.

27. Chauvet, *Folie*, p. 340. All translations mine.

28. Dany Lafferrière (1983), 'Marie Chauvet: *Amour, Colère, Folie*,' in Jean Jonassaint, ed. *Littérature haïtienne*, special issue of *Mot pour Mot*, 11, pp. 7–10.

29. Madeleine Gardiner (1981), *Visages de femmes: Portraits d'écrivains*, Port-au-Prince: Editions Deschamps, pp. 11–111. See also Pierre-Raymond Dumas (1985), 'Chauvet: "Amour, Colère et Folie"', *Conjonction*, 167, pp. 17–19; Franck Laraque (1975), 'Violence et sexualité dans *Amour, Colère et Folie*', *Présence Haïtienne*, 2, pp. 53–6; 'Marie Chauvet (1916–1973): Notice biographique et littéraire', *La Nouvelle Haïti Tribune* (New York), 16–23 June 1982.

Fanon could not have imagined, oppressed by both the 'civilizing' and the 'barbarian' men in their midsts. For Chauvet in post-independence Haiti, women were still the bodies across which political power was confirmed. In the remarkable *Colère*, the mulatto daughter Rose plays the game of submission to the death, by giving herself to the embodiment of the new political dispensation in Haiti, the black thug Chauvet calls 'the gorilla'. All that ultimately remains of Rose is a heap of dead flesh that testifies to the efficacy of state tyranny. Her brother, at first unaware of her death, binds the reader to the specificity of her degradation in words that end the novel: 'Used up, they've used her up, her also.'[30]

Perhaps the greatest horror of colonization and slavery was the conversion of persons into property. Dominion over the black was extended to the bed, and the taking of black women by white men was nothing less than a ritual re-enactment of the daily pattern of dominance and duress. *Colère* begins with the appropriation of land. Duvalier's racial theories justified an authoritarian populism by claiming it was particularly suitable for those of African descent. The 'men in black' stake their claim to the land owned by the Normils, who are identified as the 'petite-bourgeoisie' of Turgeau, an 'ultra chic' neighbourhood in Port-au-Prince.

Chauvet analyses the duplicitous force of this tyranny: the conversion of colour into commodity under the sign of property. Identities are construed and histories made, but the antagonisms only perpetuate the ruses of colonialism. When the Normil house is quarantined, the inhabitants are isolated and circumscribed. The 'devils' drive stakes into the ground to encircle the house, post a placard forbidding anyone to enter and then build a wall to separate the Normils from their land. Land becomes the site for the performance of male power, but this fable of dispossession can be enacted only when that land is annexed to a woman's body, the place that can be entered. The desired body is Rose, the mulatto daughter. The virgin Rose assumes 'martyrdom' by undergoing excruciating daily sex with the man known as 'the gorilla', who confesses: 'I can only be a man with these beautiful saintly heads of your kind, the beautiful head of a conquered martyr.'[31]

Those who claim blackness, invade the earth and penetrate women play a game of power in which the prizes include money and sex. Rose offers herself in exchange for land: 'I will risk everything in order to save our land.'[32] She meets with the gorilla every night for one month. The

30. Chauvet, *Colère*, p. 330.
31. Ibid., p. 284.
32. Ibid., p. 285.

exchange both repeats and inverts the metaphoric process involved in the legend of Haitian national origins, where the submission of a mythic Rose produces the 'native land'. Here, however, the land precedes the lady. Chauvet's Rose is not an origin or source, but a kind of secondary benefit.

The chapter that describes her violation remains one of the most disturbing memoirs by a woman in all of Caribbean fiction. Her brother Paul, obsessed with her 'error and concupiscence', reduces the once adored body to something vile and rotten, mere stench: 'The odour of death is already on Rose.' Yet Rose's monologue breaks out of a masculine agenda of possession, in that she turns an object of consumption – rotten merchandise – into a speaking subject. Opened by the gorilla's fist, reflected in the mirrors of his bedroom, her sex sucked bloodless by her 'vampire', she admits, 'My complicity has no limits.' She wonders about the reductive, masculine fables of purity and impurity: 'Is my fate really so terrible? Surely many husbands must behave in love like this man. Vices sanctified by the marriage sacrament.'[33]

Let the gorilla call her virgin, Rose will claim 'nothing astonished me in love'. She speaks of her 'nauseating docility' and questions her previous celibacy: 'Docile, too docile for a virgin. Am I virgin? Accomplice? Am I not getting used to him, looking to him for my pleasure?' If she could be free of the genteel constraints of her class, she thinks, with more than a hint of pride in her sexuality, 'If I were liberated, he would surely find in me a partner worthy of him.' Her thoughts end in a conversion ritual, with both partners turning into the 'bestial couple', in which traditional sexual polarities are reversed: the gorilla becomes 'a poor dog in search of tenderness', and the virgin a 'lascivious and insatiable panther!'[34] Rose's revelation of 'savagery', even though marked by guilt, takes us back to the white man's most deviously manipulated fear: that of virginal white ladies mounted by dark Calibans. Chauvet spares neither Rose nor the gorilla: both are victims of what they have internalized as a racial and sexual myth.

Given that myths make meaning, symbols help establish order and metaphors overdetermine, how do these elements construe artifices of identity? Fecundity and the sweet smell of rot, exaltation and sacrifice, the sexualization of the tropics: metaphoric notions of abundance and decay typify both the language deployed in the description of the *tristes tropiques* and the women in them. The binaries fundamental in much of Western thought, and those compelling oppositions (virgin/whore, peasant/

33. Ibid., pp. 289–90.
34. Ibid., pp. 292–3.

lady, beauty/hag) embedded in the lexicon, are difficult to break out of, especially for writers representing those places least known but most appropriated as symbols. Like Capécia before her, Chauvet complicates these oppositions, as she responds to the contingencies of history and gives flesh to the de-idealized putrid body, the failed icon, the dirty ideal. Once littered with the remnants of the colonial past in the present, her fiction questions the making of heroes – or heroines – and the ideal of love.

–5–

Theatre and Resistance?
An Introduction to some
French Caribbean Plays
Bridget Jones

By its nature, theatre is more elusive than fiction or film, as no fixed 'text' can serve as a reference for the overall experience. However, the immediacy of a live event, in which play, performers and audience come together, also makes theatre a form that can reflect a community very directly, demonstrating what values, concerns and means of expression are shared by the group. The dramatic heritage of the French Caribbean is complex: these are small-scale societies where the oral traditions associated with African survivals remain important, whereas the educational system requires respect for French classical drama and its written texts. In Guadeloupe particularly, ritual practices from the Indian subcontinent also survive; in Guiana, small groups descended from the original Amerindian inhabitants of the region, as well as maroon communities,[1] continue to practise traditional arts. Moreover, as Overseas Departments (*départements d'outre-mer* (DOM)), the parameters within which the theatre functions are ultimately set by French political and administrative decisions. Directly and indirectly, most budgets are funded from France. The theatre thus becomes a privileged arena, a site where the paradoxical strains of dependency and difference can be enacted. The dominance of the French language can be contested in Creole, agony danced to a drumbeat as well as explored in alexandrines. Even the unpretentious farces that appeal to

---

1. In Surinam and French Guiana, the deep forest allowed escaped slaves to set up free communities, which have retained distinctive cultural traits: see Jean Hurault (1970), *Africains de Guyane. La Vie matérielle et l'art des noirs réfugiés de Guyane*, Paris and The Hague: Mouton; Richard and Sally Price (1980), *African-American Arts in the Surinam Rainforest*, Berkeley: University of California Press, especially 'Performance in maroon life', pp. 167–87; Richard Price (1983), *First-Time: The Historical Vision of an Afro-American People*, Baltimore: John Hopkins.

the widest public often stage a clash of cultures and stress the resilient distinctiveness of Caribbean societies.[2]

Before looking at a few plays in more detail, however, it may be useful to set the scene by looking back over the general development of French Caribbean theatre in recent times, and considering the context in which the plays are produced.[3] In the circumstances of deprivation and traumatic loss imposed by slavery, the survival of the human spirit depended on reaffirming values: funeral rites and wakes to testify that a person was more than a beast of burden, bought and sold like cloth or salted meat; dances to rejoice and revive the weary body; storytelling which could transcend bondage by empowering the imagination. A strong and continuing paradigm for Caribbean drama is the art of the storyteller who gives voice to the group, recomposing a collective memory and spirit.[4] Through expressive gestures, songs, refrains, calls and responses (for example, the key formula: 'Yé Cric?!' – 'Yé Crac!'), a dynamic interaction with the audience is established. Carnival also continues some of the traditions of masking, the distinctive rhythms and the subversive approach to power and gender characteristic of African festivals, even if its pre-Lenten season and many of its disguises can be traced to Europe. Music and movement, a liberated virtuosity of the spoken word, the assertion of an identity distinct from French, these are central to the performing arts for the majority.

However, since black *da* (nurses) cared for the fair-skinned children of the masters, and many of the poor whites came from the rural provinces of western France with their own oral traditions, there could be no rigid divide in practice. In the folktales, Ti Jean from Brittany and Compère Lapin from the African savannahs play interchangeable roles as the puny trickster defying the powerful. Nevertheless, the values of the dominant

2. *Moun Koubari*, for example, a rollicking farce of village life by José Jernidier (Guadeloupe), turns on the quarrel and eventual reconciliation of two brothers, one a policeman, speaking a pretentious French full of adverbs in '-ment', the other a country postman, too fond of the rum bottle, but serving as a nostalgic image of rural Caribbean values. First performed in Pointe-à-Pitre in 1991, the play is as yet unpublished.

3. The situation in Haiti, with a small but well-established corpus of dramatic literature in French, popular theatre for the Creole-speaking majority and several thriving overseas groups, is not dealt with here. Useful references may be found in Gary Victor (1996), 'Haiti (Overview)', in Don Rubin, ed., *World Encyclopedia of Contemporary Theatre*, London and New York: Routledge, pp. 297–303; Robert Cornevin (1973), *Le Théâtre haïtien*. Ottawa: Leméac; Vèvè Clark (1992), 'When womb waters break: the emergence of Haitian new theater (1953–1987)', *Callaloo*, 15, pp. 778–86.

4. See Patrick Chamoiseau and Raphaël Confiant (1991), *Lettres créoles: Tracées antillaises et continentales de la littéature 1635–1975*, Paris: Hatier, pp. 62–4.

culture were those of the French élite, prizing French education for their children, in drama represented by the texts of the seventeenth century, often historical tragedies couched in elevated rhetoric. As life became more settled and prosperous, leisure pursuits extended to imitate French ways, and theatre performances took place. The old capital of Martinique, Saint Pierre, boasted an elegant theatre building (1786), a reduced-scale version of the neoclassical Grand Théâtre in Bordeaux. Even before the creation of dedicated stages, visiting companies had brought theatre to the main urban centres, and all through the nineteenth century imported operas and operettas, melodramas and vaudevilles attracted audiences, still, of course, racially segregated. Only a handful of local authors can be identified, with almost nothing to distinguish their plays from those by their Parisian colleagues, even when using colonial settings. De Mallian and Pinel Dumanoir[5] were wholly assimilated into the attitudes and subjects of the French boulevard, which continued, as late as the postwar tours of the Jean Gosselin company,[6] to supply undemanding entertainment for colonial outposts.

From the somewhat tentative regionalism of the cultural renaissance between the two world wars, a few dramatists have survived, especially Gilbert de Chambertrand (Guadeloupe) and Constantin Verderosa (Guiana). Ideologically they too accept a scale of values which gives unquestioned superiority to France, the *mère-patrie*, but, by choosing dialogue in Creole, and staging, even in comic mode, the concerns and behaviour of local characters (Chambertrand's deaf servant in *Les Méfaits d'Athénaïse* (1918),[7] Verderosa's Maman Cénéline in *Céphise* (1947))[8], they observe and re-create a different and specific community. Both worked in educational contexts, and doubtless school drama consisted both of French plays on the syllabus and of skits and sketches modelled on local reality. The revue put on by the girls' high school (Pensionnat Colonial) in Fort-de-France to mark the tricentenary of French colonization in 1935 was something of a watershed, undoubtedly celebrating attachment to France but, to the consternation of some patriots, also reminding the audience that Martinique

5. On these nineteenth-century dramatists, see Jack Corzani (1978), *La Littérature des Antilles-Guyane françaises*, Fort-de-France: Désormeaux, Vol. 1, pp. 154–65, and Jack Corzani (1992), *Dictionnaire encylopédique Désormeaux*, Fort-de-France: Désormeaux.

6. For a personal account and list of plays performed, Jean Gosselin (1984), 'Paris – Antilles – Guyane', *Bulletin d'information du CENADDOM*, 73, pp. 25–33. Gosselin's classical matinées gave many schoolchildren their first taste of professional theatre.

7. Gilbert de Chambertrand (1976), *Théâtre d'expression créole*, Basse-Terre: Editions Jeunes Antilles.

8. Constantin Verderosa (1994), *Scènes créoles*, Paris/Schoelcher: L'Harmattan/GEREC.

had a past in which African slaves worked for white masters to produce cheap sugar for France and Caribs were massacred.

However, the contemporary history of theatre in Martinique and Guadeloupe really takes shape in the 1970s. This is the period when a political theatre expresses most openly resistance to French colonization. There was increasing disillusionment, especially among young people and organized labour, with the results of departmentalization. Closer union with France might have brought improved education and a measure of social security to the most deprived, but the new politicians had to compromise with the old ruling class, and dependency seemed increasingly humiliating at the time of revolution in Cuba, as well as independence for Algeria and most of France's African colonies. Riots, put down brutally by police and riot police (*compagnie républicaine de sécurité* (CRS)), most flagrantly in Fort-de-France in 1959 and in Pointe-à-Pitre in 1967, supplied images of confrontation and hardened the resolve of activists to use drama as a tool to raise awareness and campaign for independence. Some of the most radical plays were first produced in Paris by student groups, Boukman's *Les Négriers*,[9] the collective creation *Kimafoutiésa*,[10] but often subsequently toured the islands to bring their ideas to audiences in market squares and engage in debate.[11]

Official reactions illustrated a typical twofold strategy: repressive gestures, banning, enforced residence or cutting off funds, putting individuals under surveillance, and on the other hand moves to channel energy into French-controlled cultural activity. One example of these subsidized facilities[12] is the Centre Martiniquais d'Action Culturelle (CMAC), which was constituted in 1974, and has regularly sponsored 'Rencontres théâtrales' as a showcase for visiting companies from France and the Caribbean region, and an opportunity for cultural exchange. On the other hand, the Service Municipal d'Action Culturelle (SERMAC) was founded by Aimé Césaire as Mayor of Fort-de-France to develop the creative expression of a distinctive Martinican identity. Links with African liberation and the black diaspora, with the wider Caribbean, have been stressed, and the

---

9. Daniel Boukman (pseudonym of Blérald) (1971), *Les Négriers*, Honfleur: P.J. Oswald. Republished by L'Harmattan in 1978.

10. *Kimafoutiésa* was published anonymously, accompanied by striking black and white prints (Paris: 1975).

11. Quite a full and candid account of these performances, by a participant and observer, may be found in Max Jeanne (1980), 'Sociologie du théâtre antillais', *CARÉ*, 6, pp. 7–43.

12. See Sonia Zobda-Quitman in the Alizés-Karthala dossier: Jean Blaise, Laurent Farrugia, Claude Trébos, Sonia Zobda-Quitman, eds (1981), *Culture et politique en Guadeloupe et Martinique*, Paris: Alizés-Karthala.

French influences were from radical theatre practitioners, such as Jean-Marie Serreau and Ariane Mnouchkine. From 1972 in summer festivals, and then through a permanent organization on a large central site, SERMAC has offered training in the visual and performing arts, and has given a start to many gifted individuals of slender means. In Guadeloupe and Guiana, a similar tendency can be noted, especially in the 1970s, towards a polarization of theatre activity between militantly independent groups, often of younger people, and established official organizations, each pursuing in different ways a highly politicized agenda.

The most recent French decision to have an impact on theatre in the DOM was the 1982 decentralization measures put in place by the Mitterrand government. Each department became simultaneously a 'region' (although proposals for an *assemblée unique* have so far proved too controversial), hence also equipped with a budget disbursed by a regional office for cultural development (Direction Régionale d'Action Culturelle (DRAC) or Action Régionale de Développement Culturelle (ARDEC)). Subsequently the developing professionalism of the theatre in Martinique was consolidated by the creation of a Centre Dramatique Régional (CDR), and there is now a national stage, 'L'Artchipel', in Basse-Terre, as well as at the CMAC in Fort-de-France, a focus for collaborative productions where performers and technical personnel can train on state-of-the-art equipment. The impressive infrastructure in theatre, especially now that many larger towns and several neighbourhoods of Fort-de-France have well-equipped cultural centres, allows more of the population to take an active part, with workshops for young people, the unemployed, the elderly. Good for recreation and personal development, but not necessarily fostering a competitive climate of excellence, and certainly not halting the drain of talent towards France.[13]

The plays selected as illustration here are intended to demonstrate the constant negotiation to give dramatic form to specific Caribbean concerns in the face of so powerful a French presence – today also expressed massively through the electronic media. In an outspokenly satirical text, *Les Négriers*, Daniel Boukman uses historical parallels to attack French policies and attitudes. His medium is the caricature, carnivalesque masking, he agitates the puppet figures of anti-colonial propaganda. More

---

13. After the international success of Euzhan Palcy's film, *La rue Cases-Nègres* (1983), a showcase of Antillean theatrical talent, hopes for a thriving local industry have not been altogether fulfilled. Some excellent performers (Robert Liensol, Greg Germain, Jenny Alpha, Mariann Mathéus, for example) work mainly in France. Caribbean writers and actors are present both in French commercial television and in initiatives to promote knowledge of Caribbean literature and Creole lore in schools and communities.

subtly, in *Agénor Cacoul*,[14] Georges Mauvois re-creates on the basis of observation the linguistic power play between French and Creole, his critique of the political status quo made more powerful by its humour and authenticity. Simone Schwarz-Bart in *Ton beau capitaine*[15] illustrates the strength of women's writing in Guadeloupe. She is sensitive to the privileged status of the DOM today from the perspective of migrants from poorer parts of the Caribbean. Her poignant short play on love and separation uses a telling fusion of theatrical expressivity: dance, gesture and song. These plays exist as published texts, but their production history and reception are often also instructive.

However, it is impossible to discuss these dramatists without first pointing out the importance of Aimé Césaire's influence. His *Cahier d'un retour au pays natal* is already a powerfully 'charged utterance',[16] and in the 1960s Césaire deliberately turned to drama as a medium that would transmit his vision and summons to black achievement more clearly to a wide audience. As in so much of his poetry, he addresses psychological as well as economic or political dependence. The best known of his four dramatic works is based on the life of Henri Christophe (1767–1820), *La Tragédie du roi Christophe*,[17] outstanding both in its literary quality and, increasingly, in its appeal to audiences. Set in the aftermath of the Haitian revolution, it debates issues of kingship and governance and enacts decolonization with a quite post-modern reluctance to locate a centre. The inspiring rhetoric of black pride and nation-building has often been extracted from a much more complex and tragic play of self-immolation. However, whether as self-consciously theatrical rite, chronicle of failure, critique of tyranny, celebration of new nationhood or, better, all of these, the play unfolds with the dignity and superlative word-power characteristic of all Césaire's work. Very many younger playwrights, such as Boukman

14. Georges Mauvois (1988), *Agénor Cacoul* (with *Misyé Molina*), 2nd edn, Schoelcher/ Paris: Presses Universitaires Créoles/GEREC/L'Harmattan.

15. Simone Schwarz-Bart (1987), *Ton beau capitaine*, Paris: Seuil.

16. Abiola Irele, ed. (1994), *Aimé Césaire: Cahier d'un retour au pays natal*, Ibadan: New Horn Press, p. lxvi.

17. Aimé Césaire (1963), *La Tragédie du roi Christophe*, Paris: Présence Africaine. There are several valuable studies of this play and of other works by Césaire, including Régis Antoine (1984), *La Tragédie du roi Christophe de Aimé Césaire*, Paris: Bordas 'Lectoguide'; Marianne Wichmann Bailey (1992), *The Ritual Theater of Aimé Césaire*, Tübingen: Narr; Suzanne Brichaux-Houyoux (1993), *Quand Césaire écrit, Lumumba parle: Edition commentée de 'Une saison au Congo'*, Paris: L'Harmattan; Anne-Marie Nisbet and Beverley Ormerod (1982), *Négritude et Antillanité: Etude d'Une tempête d'Aimé Césaire*, Kensington: New South Wales University Press.

or Jocelyn Régina,[18] have begun so spellbound by his language that they only gradually liberate themselves and find a personal voice.

Moreover, Caribbean history as a dramatic subject plays an extremely significant part in the assertion of an independent identity. For a long time, it was a bitter standing joke that black primary-school children, like their peers in France, had to recite that their ancestors were Gauls with blonde hair and long moustaches. Resistance to French brainwashing of this kind obviously demanded the rehabilitation of Caribbean heroes and heroines, and restaging of historical feats like slave rebellions and workers' strikes. Haitian history has fascinated many Caribbean minds: Edouard Glissant's only published play deals with Toussaint Louverture,[19] and Vincent Placoly's *Dessalines* was mounted in 1994.[20] A particular concern has been to make local history powerfully alive by setting a commemorative play in its original location, as when José Alpha's play *1902*,[21] on the eruption of the volcano, Mont Pelée (when the death toll was so high because the authorities forced voters to stay), used as backdrop the steps of the ruined theatre in Saint Pierre. Maryse Condé's script, *An tan revolisyon* (1991),[22] on the lines of Mnouchkine's *1789*, dramatized the heroism of the Guadeloupean people in the setting of a French fort. Placoly with Alpha devised several plays and commemorative pageants:[23] restaging events such as the arrival of Columbus, retelling the childhood of the white Creole girl who became Empress Joséphine. Mobilizing large numbers of extras, the research for these productions often involves an oral history project and provokes a new historical awareness in all concerned.

Césaire's plays deal with emblematic figures of black revolt and liberation: Lumumba, Caliban, as well as King Christophe, but never sited within

18. Although best known as author and performer of topical skits and Creole comedies, Régina has written two full-length poetic dramas: *Le Clin d'oeil du sang* (1990) and *S'il n'en reste qu'un* (1993), where the influence of Césaire's *Et les chiens se taisaient* is perceptible. Both plays were self-published by Régina in 1993.

19. Edouard Glissant (1961), *Monsieur Toussaint*, Paris, Seuil. A later version, revised for the stage, was published by Acoma in 1978.

20. Vincent Placoly (1983), *Dessalines ou la Passion de l'indépendance,* Havana: Casa de las Américas. A typographically corrected edition was published in Case-Pilote by L'Autre mer in 1994.

21. José Alpha (1983), *1902. La Catastrophe de Saint-Pierre*, Fort-de-France: Hatier-Martinique.

22. Maryse Condé (1991), *An tan revolisyon ou Elle court, elle court la liberté*, Basse-Terre: Conseil régional.

23. A bibliography of Placoly's work appears in the special commemorative number of *Révolution Socialiste*, 727 (11 January 1992).

a realistic Caribbean context. In contrast, the 1966 comedy by Georges Mauvois, *Agénor Cacoul*, is a brilliant study of the abuse of power, satirically heightened but suggesting close personal observation. Apparently focused on the petty tyrannies of local authority figures, his 'well-made' plays implicitly call in question the whole power structure of Martinique. French political and economic power is mediated through Governors (after full departmentalization, Prefects), French political parties and local capitalists. In the 1960s, these were still mainly the *béké* owners of sugar factories, but these families now more often grow bananas and pineapples, or own supermarket chains, property development companies and so on. Local politicians must constantly negotiate between a restive electorate and these forces.

Mauvois, born in 1922, began as a Post Office worker and came into conflict with the French administration over his activities as a trade-unionist and militant in the Parti Communiste Martiniquais. He refused a disciplinary posting to France in 1962 and lost his job. Subsequently qualifying as a lawyer and practising at the Bar in Fort-de-France, Mauvois has enjoyed a successful late career as dramatic author, since, until the 1990s, his plays had not been performed (apart from a student production in Paris of *Agénor Cacoul* in 1967, directed by Vincent Placoly). His intention to 'shed light on some dirty deeds',[24] observed in the course of a long career of political activism, gives a backbone of seriousness to action which is often hilarious (in this, his work can be compared to that of the Jamaican playwright, Trevor Rhone). In particular, his dialogue, in its apposite code-switching between French and Creole, adds excitement and tension to many scenes, and shows a virtuosity and invention not always obvious in younger dramatists, who have grown up in the modified linguistic continuum of today's urbanized Martinique.[25]

Structured in three acts, *Agénor Cacoul* deals with a strike on a sugar plantation. It begins and ends in the mayor's parlour in the town hall, shifting to contrast this sleazy context with a dignified group of field-workers, talking together in a rough shelter lit with a petrol lamp. As Act

24. 'Eclairer quelques turpitudes' (telephone interview with Bridget Jones, 25 July 1995). Unless otherwise stated, translations are my own. The prose sketches by Mauvois (1982) in *Case-navire: Choses et gens de naguère*, Fort-de-France: Désormeaux, include a chilling portrait of mayor Romain Gontier.

25. Since the publication of Jean Bernabé's fundamental 1983 study *Fondal-natal* (3 vols, Paris: L'Harmattan), research has suggested that a less rigorous separation of French and Creole characterizes the language of many speakers, e.g. Christian March (1996), *Le Discours des mères martiniquaises. Diglossie et créolité: un point de vue sociolinguistique*, Paris: L'Harmattan.

One opens, Cacoul is on the telephone to the Governor, assuring him he that can deal with the strike, obsequiously respectful but, as an aside confirms, well aware that he is only an expendable pawn in a bigger game. The act centres on a long verbal duel between Merius, the leading representative of the sugar workers, and the mayor. Merius has come for a paper authorizing free medical treatment for his only child, a three-year-old boy who has a bad fever. Cacoul exults in his power, encapsulated in the bland refrain, 'I am the Mayor, my friend.' He knows all about Merius, and exploits to the hilt his dominant position. In defiance of any democratic principle or republican Rights of Man, he gloats: 'I am the law. I decide what your rights are' ('Le droit c'est moi. C'est moi qui décide quel est votre droit').[26] Mauvois has created here a chilling but captivatingly theatrical monster. Reinforced by plausible motivation, Cacoul is utterly unscrupulous in manipulating the system. When wrangling with his secretary and mistress, Jeanne, some of the spoils of office are revealed: jobs found for relatives, housing allocations, the petty corruption of misappropriated bags of cement. Later, Cacoul is ready to falsify council minutes or condone trumped-up charges to bully the disaffected workers. A visit by the Brigadier (of police) to introduce his new second-in-command, freshly landed from Marseilles, promotes further revealing comments on Cacoul's rise, how he works his electorate, how he connives to intimidate, and all this 'in the service of France'. As he goes off to marry a couple, scions of two *béké* ruling families, sugar-factory owners, he spares a thought for how proud his father would be. Like a Balzac *arriviste*, Cacoul convincingly incarnates the gleeful revenge of a have-not who, by sheer will-power, hard work and lack of any moral scruple, has acquired power and wealth.

Act Two explores with sympathy but little sentimentality the dilemma of the estate workers, desperate for better wages but well aware that their collective bargaining power is at the mercy of the well-armed and trigger-happy security forces. The mayor has already explained to the new 'adjoint' that strikes begin with a carnivalesque excitement and end in blood. These are the men whose blood will be shed. The range of topics and shifts in tone show the author's imaginative identification with the world of the sugar workers: at first elegiac, as an old man, Papa Coq, discusses with another the death of Merius's son, holding the mayor morally responsible, but knowing no charges could stick; then celebratory, when some fish, caught in a local stream Riviè-d'or (Golden river), are brought in. But

---

26. Mauvois, *Agénor Cacoul*, p. 30. The echo of the absolutist Louis XIV's famed declaration, 'L'état c'est moi', is worth noting.

the core third scene centres on the strike, the workers' right to the fruits of their labour, rising in tension as they consider strategy. As they tally the sections prepared to refuse to cut cane, Néné speaks for the *casés*, the families housed by the estate, the most intimately vulnerable and dependent on the owner (their situation a clearly intended metaphor for the whole state of DOM dependency). Knowing the importance of a general stoppage, not just a partial protest by the fieldworkers, they want to involve the technical staff in the factory. Papa Coq begins to sing, reliving the heroics of past rebellion, and mobilizing the group to the beat of a bel-air (*bélé*) drum: 'Mister Dubarry oh / The people have risen up oh / The strike has broken out' ('Missié Dibari ô / Manmaille-la lévé ô / La grève-la pété').[27]

The final act returns to the mayor's parlour, introducing the secretary to the council, Mousse, in a flirtatious dialogue with Jeanne. In ironic contrast to the urgency of the workers' basic needs, they are arguing over borrowing the official car, a prestigious German vehicle. When Cacoul comes in, worried at the extent of the stoppage, he discusses the complex interplay with French political allegiances. Outside, the first clashes between workers and police are signalled by gunshots. In the space for suspense as to the next stage of the conflict – we know police reinforcements are expected – Mauvois develops, rather too lengthily, his candid critique of democracy, Martinican style. The mayor discusses election tactics with Mousse. For Cacoul it is the presiding clerk who can intimidate voters by sheer force of personality, whereas Mousse is very proud of his skill in compiling voter lists: he has a supplementary list of 968 voters 'dead, disappeared, gone away, etc.',[28] all duly registered with identity cards. Mauvois has chosen to centre his portrait on the abuse of municipal power. The confrontation takes place off-stage; we imagine the bloodshed and grief as a critical counterpoint to the corruption. Duparquet, the local policeman, rushes in, a grotesque messenger figure with his pedantically formal French. Shots are heard. Mousse reports on a confrontation between seven and eight coachloads of police reinforcements and the desperate strikers. A number of them lie dead and wounded by police carbines. Meanwhile, the cynical Cacoul is more concerned about his amorous assignation: the champagne is ready iced for young Marcelle. The play's closing scene is given to Duparquet (ironically named after one of the earliest French governors of Martinique), the unashamed scrounger of scraps from the mayor's lines of official credit, most abject example of corrupting dependency. However, to open out a bitter and pessimistic

27. Ibid., p. 49.
28. Ibid., p. 61.

ending, Mauvois intercuts Duparquet's gloating with a defiant Creole chant from the audience, foreshadowing a new people's movement arising, a force for resistance.

Thematically, this play builds up a dense and detailed portrait of the actors on the wider stage of Martinican politics, communicating both Mauvois's sympathy for plantation labour, still locked in a trap of poverty, eating salt fish, not meat, and his appalled fascination with those like Cacoul, who have turned departmentalization to their own corrupt advantage, a caricature of Césaire's hope in democracy. It is to be noted that this play has been much less often produced than the social comedies *Man Chomil* (about a tyrannical postmistress) or *Misyé Molina* (the comeuppance of a social-climbing parent), less savage in their political critique.

The interest of this play is also in its use of Creole/French diglossia, a feature that is emphasized in the preface to the 1988 edition by the Creole linguist Jean Bernabé, noting that the earlier edition was hailed more for its satirical content. He stresses how Mauvois's virtuosity in manipulating both languages gives authentic voice to social situations too often falsely reduced to an expression in French (Césaire's Haitian peasants use a kind of all-purpose rustic vernacular of French). With perfect naturalness, in Act Two, the workers converse in Creole, forceful over injustice, lyrical in speaking of rivers, at times sardonically interpolating phrases in French when acknowledging the mayor's power. A scene deserving very close study is Act One, Scene Three, where Cacoul deploys his command of both languages against Merius, fluent only in Creole – reiterating in French his official position and power, yet manoeuvring in Creole to extract information, to bully or mock. In a striking exchange, Cacoul expresses candidly in Creole his hostile view of the workers' insatiable demands for a better deal, only to revert to French when Mérius taxes him with betraying his Socialist rhetoric. Another brilliantly convincing scene of code-switching occurs when the mayor's secretary Jeanne drops her mask of decorous formal French for a torrent of recrimination in Creole over his interest in her younger rival.[29] The mayor dominates the play with his virtuosity in both codes, but it is significant that Mauvois focuses in the closing scene on Duparquet, a minor functionary alienated to the point of claiming to have no other voice than a formal French, ludicrous when spoken. It is in Creole that the people's representative invades the stage at the end.

Mauvois did not emerge as a dramatist until the 1990s, but the more prominent role given to the Creole language in cultural production through

---

29. Ibid., p. 33.

the efforts of the Groupe de Recherches et d'Etudes en Espace Créolo-phone (GEREC) has encouraged him to write more. With his lucid appraisal of contemporary manners and skill in creating satirical portraits, his work offers good opportunities to local groups and reaches a wide audience. Indeed, the centrality of the linguistic question, expressing as it does the will to cultural autonomy (although the ballot-box does not reflect a majority vote for political independence[30]), is also shown in the evolution of the younger playwright, Daniel Boukman. He began as a militant anti-colonial dramatist more than twenty years ago, influenced by Fanon and the Algerian war of independence, and writing much more directly against French domination. In recent years, he has responded to the shift away from international Marxist activism, composing poetry in Creole and a play dealing with paternalism and oppression through the prism of a family, *Delivrans,* [31] where an overbearing (Creole-speaking) father imposes the French language on his whole household, even the maid and the parrot.

Boukman's best-known and most widely produced play is a typical product of the early 1970s; indeed, the text is dated summer 1968. As the title suggests, *Les Négriers* puts on stage the slave-traders plying from Africa to Martinique. However, in a device sustained throughout the play, the seventeenth- and eighteenth-century traffic in black labour to work the cane plantations parallels the economically driven migration back across the Atlantic during the postwar reconstruction of France. Workers were recruited in Martinique through an official French government agency, BUMIDOM (Bureau de Migration des Départements d'Outre-Mer), to fill jobs in France, especially as domestics, ward-maids, postmen, minor functionaries. Within his framework of a critical restaging of the middle passage, Boukman offers a rapid sequence of sketches, explicit and grotesque enough for his message to reach the most naïve or unin-formed public.

The play opens on a parody of the electoral process: a ballot-box filled by the votes of those (planters, traders, teachers, etc.) who prosper under French protection, while bundles of banknotes descend on the happy *député* as soon as he is elected. Four main figures will provide continuity for the action of the play: the politician, the social worker, the priest and the employers' representative, shifting (masks, hats or other accessories can be used) into their historical counterparts: an African potentate, a

---

30. Alfred Marie-Jeanne, leader of the Mouvement Indépendantiste Martiniquais (MIM), was elected *député* for the south of Martinique in 1997. Commentators differ on how significant his role can be.

31. Daniel Boukman (1996), *Delivrans*, Paris: L'Harmattan.

do-gooding lady (inspecting the slaves like cattle), the priest again, a trader, while over them presides the figure of Death, somewhat ambiguously seeming to stand for both France and international capitalism. Antillean history is recapitulated, and then the figures regain their modern guises to devise the publicity campaign that will best lure the islanders to migrate. Boukman aims to arouse indignation by their crudely patronizing and racist images, suggesting, for example, that the Folies Bergères and snow are what the 'natives' long for.[32] A group resembling the Frères Jacques sings and mimes, with appropriate sound effects (the trade union steamer's siren), and a family of migrants are contrasted with a sulky, unemployed youth who resists the call. By creating a collage of sound and interweaving past and present, the voyage is dextrously suggested, and, once in France, racism and discrimination are enacted with a telling concision – the prejudiced concierges, the colour bar operated over rented accommodation, the crude sterotypes (black virility, smelly cooking) founded on ignorance: material which, even twenty-five years later, has not lost its relevance to the daily experience of black workers in Europe. This first act closes with the oppressors, once more modern capitalists, planning to flood the island with tourists in place of the migrants gone to rebuild France (at rates of pay undercutting unionized labour).

By this point, Boukman has set out his positions unmistakably, and, rather than developing dramatic action, he continues to accumulate further illustrations. The main enrichment comes from a contrastive appeal to traditional values and call to revolt, embodied in a shadowy ancestral figure. The publicity for migration ('DUBIDON' thinly disguising 'BUMIDOM') continues with a game show – 'Guess the famous monuments' (including Senghor), and the politician (no doubt intended for Césaire, whom Boukman attacked very savagely and explicitly in his earlier dramatic poem, *Orphée nègre*, dedicated to Fanon). Proof of the good life in France lies in caustic caricatures of Caribbean celebrities: a boxer, an operatic soprano, writer Edouard (Glissant), the Guianese President of the Senate Gaston (Monnerville). A new dogged but disillusioned procession of migrants forms, and the 'slave trade' resumes to the refrain: 'Raise the sails! Fresh cargo for sale! / Strong arms!'[33] Boukman imagines a scenic effect with modern migrants crossing the stage dejectedly as a line of slaves is projected moving in the opposite direction, and the silhouette of the ancestor laments Mother Africa and the ceaseless journeying with no return. As if inspired by his words, a new group comes forward, rebellious

32. Boukman, *Les Négriers*, p. 12.
33. Ibid., p. 31.

slaves crushed by Napoleonic rigour, who are then updated as modern militant youth facing French lawcourts. In a rather ill-judged development of the idea of 'génocide par substitution', Boukman has a sequence involving test-tubes of different liquids, parodying a chemistry class held by Death for her managers. The ship's siren/train whistle leitmotif heralds a film widening the scope – Africans as well as West Indian 'guest workers' in other European countries, with a voice off pursuing the history lesson. To close this 'act', more snapshots of the reception in the host society – exploiting, manipulating, and the disillusionment of the 'exiles from the land of the sun',[34] who dance to a melancholy clarinet.

The first sequence of the last 'act' parodies the ceremonial visit of a 'général François' (manifestly intended as General de Gaulle, but represented as a carnival 'boiboi' (bwa-bwa, a giant puppet in papier mâché), schoolchildren waving little flags, singing hymns of welcome. Fade to the slave-traders and a sarcastic scene of tourist paradise – sand, sun, sex, drugs, casinos, even a tame poet reciting for a few coins (Césaire pilloried again) – degenerating into a more sombre orgiastic scene. Back to the slavers, dissolving one company to found another and now pursuing their policies with repression, not persuasion. News of posters calling for independence, protest demonstrations heightens the tension. Now in the guise of judges, the slavers pass prison sentences. Death orders the utmost repression – 'Meetings . . . FORBIDDEN! . . . Suspects arrested? TORTURE THEM!'[35] – until the revolutionary uprising is crushed. Having represented genuinely radical opposition brutally put down, Boukman parodies the interchangeable claims of the moderate 'assimilationistes' and 'légalistes', and the politician dreams of becoming a puppet king. Unable to resist yet another history lesson, Boukman brings on again the African ancestor and the maroons, the rebel slaves who have broken their chains. A roll-call of Caribbean resistance, maroons, rebel slaves, leaders and fighters, is called, and the end of slavery is retraced, not as bestowed by French abolitionists but as fought for in a long series of revolts and uprisings, events usually censored in the colonial history books. The maroons disappear but not before the ancestor has solemnly passed on his machete to an echoing summons for remembrance. The board meeting can regain its confidence and the sentimental anthem of the brainwashed assimilationists, 'Paris, c'est une blonde', shifts into a military march and a climax of gunshots and explosions.

---

34. Ibid., p. 46.
35. Ibid., p. 61.

A hopelessly overlong and overloaded play, then, swivelling constantly to attack almost every possible target, and yet held together by its parallel time structure, which can be scenically expressed as a *chassé croisé* on an upper and lower deck (Med Hondo's film version used a boat setting with three acting levels). Simple props, reinforcement by an imaginative sound track of songs, music and effects, together with scenes in snappy rhythmical dialogue, gave the work a strong appeal to student and non-professional groups, especially in the post-May 1968 period. It was put on in Paris by Med Hondo's Griot-shango group of black actors and students, and in the Caribbean it was adopted into the repertoire of the keen agitprop groups of the 1970s, such as the Poulbwa, who aimed to arouse popular awareness of French domination and exploitation. It can stand for a very much larger repertoire, which relied heavily on the same thematic material: migration, repression of popular protest, the history of slavery and *marronage*.[36] Most of these scripts have not been published, although *Kimafoutiésa*, something of a collective Creole reworking of *Les Négriers* by Joby Bernabé and friends, Auguste Macouba's *Eïa! Man-maille là!*, *Siklòn* and *Nuit blanch* by the Guadeloupean Théâtre du Cyclone did get into print.[37] Boukman's other plays continued in the same vein, though dealing with a global picture rather than Martinique. *Les Négriers* was written in French: Boukman, having refused to be con-scripted in 1961, worked as teacher, journalist and activist in Algeria, and only later left North Africa to work in Paris on the pro-independence Radio Mango, and reconvert himself into a Creole poet. It is useful to bear in mind that the generations of activists who preceded the 'Creoleness' militants[38] took advantage of the French language to exchange ideas within an international decolonizing movement: the Maghreb, black Africa, Indo-China. The great advantage of a play script, particularly with experienced performers, is that its language can be modified to suit a particular audience and the text is only one component in the total communication process.

The plays considered so far have tackled political issues boldly, staging debate at the level of the fundamental power struggles that determine the

36. Note Richard D.E. Burton's provocative rereading of the myth of the maroon: (1997), *Le Roman marron: Etudes sur la littérature martiniquaise contemporaine*, Paris: L'Harmattan.

37. Auguste Macouba (pseudonym of Armet) (1968), *Eïa! Man-maille là!* Honfleur: P.J. Oswald; Théâtre du Cyclone (1975), *Nuit blanch, Siklòn*, Pointe-à-Pitre: Imprimerie guadeloupéenne des éditions sociales.

38. For example, Jean Bernabé, Patrick Chamoiseau and Raphaël Confiant. For a more detailed study of the work of these writers, see Chapter 9 in this volume, and on the issue of Creolophone writing, see Chapter 7.

quality of daily life, but also implicitly interrogating the future for a society caught in the ambiguities of status as a DOM. They express in distinctive ways unease at the state of society in the tense and troubled 1960s and 1970s. On the other hand, the perspective of a woman writer, Simone Schwarz-Bart, reflects the 1980s, when the DOM enjoyed a level of material prosperity envied by their independent neighbours. Like Ina Césaire in *Mémoires d'isles*,[39] role-playing based on the life experience of two elderly women, or 'Rosanie Soleil'[40] (three women reflect upon the 1871 'Insurrection du Sud'), Maryse Condé in *Pension les alizés*[41] and Gerty Dambury in 'Bâton maréchal',[42] she explores public issues sensitively and specifically through their impact on private lives. The short play, *Ton beau capitaine*, is less dogmatic and self-righteous than the anti-colonial protest plays, looking sympathetically at outsiders much less privileged. Her protagonist is a Haitian husband who has had to leave his wife behind and seek work as an agricultural labourer in Guadeloupe. Both illiterate, they communicate by audio cassettes, and the story which unfolds is a humble tragedy. Marie-Ange has reluctantly been unfaithful to Wilnor and is expecting a baby by a treacherous emissary who carried his gifts. The play traces the gradual revelation, his anger and sorrow and eventual fortitude in coming to terms with betrayal. An apparently slender dramatic thread, but representing a vital and significant mental event in the life of this couple.

The play is a poignant portrait of exile, touching on the constant wanderings in search of a livelihood: 'isn't there any country then where we Haitians can find work and send a bit of money home?'[43] and mentioning other sufferers: Petrus, whose raft sank with thirty other desperate souls, the husband who went to pick oranges in Florida and finished up begging at the crossroads. Wilnor is 'shrunk', physically and mentally reduced by isolation and the self-denial needed to remain faithful and send almost all his earnings home. In an indignant rite of self-mortification and sacrifice, he burns the banknotes saved, the only token which grounds him in this alien land.

---

39. Ina Césaire (1985), *Mémoires d'isles. Maman N. et Maman F.*, Paris: Editions Caribéennes.

40. Ina Césaire, 'Rosanie Soleil' unpublished, first produced 1992.

41. Maryse Condé (1988), *Pension les alizés*, Paris: Mercure de France. Like Schwarz-Bart, Condé here also puts on stage a Haitian exile, a doctor, aided by a Guadeloupean woman.

42. Gerty Dambury's 'Bâton maréchal' (unpublished) explores daily life during the Vichy occupation of Guadeloupe through the experiences of four women.

43. Schwarz-Bart, *Ton beau capitaine*, p. 19.

The play is in one act but divided into four sections: an opening, when Wilnor comes wearily home but shares through the recorded voice in the life and vitality of family and home community. Hints of an undisclosed problem add suspense, and the second tableau traces Wilnor's mounting horror and fury at the confession of infidelity. With a violence of feeling expressed as much through body language and distorted sound as in wounded sarcastic words, Schwarz-Bart imagines a quadrille, normally a joyous social dance, reworked as an image of exclusion and pain. Wilnor's own confessions of weakness and ritualistic gestures in the fourth scene bring a new mood of forgiveness, but the final repetitions of 'Your handsome captain' insist on an interrogative note; there are no easy re/solutions.

Performances of this play have dealt variously with the opportunities offered by the text; in particular, the disembodied voice on the cassette is sometimes accompanied by the presence of Marie-Ange, behind a screen or singing and dancing in a removed area of scenic space.[44] Schwarz-Bart is concerned to create a concentrated work of 'total theatre', in which movement, sometimes drawing on the significant gestures of voodoo ritual, music, using traditional song and dance with modern synthesized discords, combine with text and the visual elements of set, costume and accessories. The first production had a Haitian director, Syto Cavé, and actor, Max Kénol, and it is likely that the hints of the spirit-haunted world of voodoo were reinforced by them; the setting of Wilnor's sparsely furnished hut was dominated by a 'poteau mitan', the centre pole focusing worship and joining human and spirit worlds. The metaphors of travelling by water are enriched by visual allusions to Agoué, loa of the sea, for example, while Erzulie Freda Dahomey, goddess of love, is propitiated in the gifts of perfumed soap, and Wilnor identifies with Ogun to gain courage. The richness of Haitian lore, the permeable frontiers between spirit possession and the actor identifying with his role, make this fund of symbolic ritual a constant reference point for Caribbean drama. However, the subtle mental spaces of Noh theatre and Chekhov's ability to convey pain with reticence also influenced Schwarz-Bart's work.

In dramatizing universal emotions of loneliness, jealousy, love and separation, Schwarz-Bart uses mainly a very pared-down French style, resonant and lyrical in its simplicity and plausible for her peasant characters. In this, as in some of the allusions, the play leads us back to

44. See Alvina Ruprecht (1995), 'Performance transculturelle: Une poétique de l'inter-théâtralité chez Simone Schwarz-Bart', in Pierre Laurette and Hans-George Ruprecht, eds, *Poétiques et imaginaires: Francopolyphonie littéraire des Amériques*, Paris: L'Harmattan. pp. 313–23.

Roumain's classic novel of the Haitian countryside, *Gouverneurs de la rosée*, which has been dramatized several times for stage and screen. Her poignant and lyrical play deals with injustice without bombast or preaching, and it is to be hoped that Schwarz-Bart will continue writing for the stage.[45]

It should be clear that the plays we have considered are only a handful of works among a much larger number which seek to frame and communicate in dramatic terms some fragment of the complex history and cultural heritage of the French Caribbean. The anomalies of departmental status, the small scale and personal nature of debate lend themselves to a theatrical heightening of political issues, often mediated through historical analogies. Very many plays, including those of Césaire, approach the audience in the guise of a storyteller, tapping into this most resilient and characteristic of Caribbean narrative pacts in order to teach, preach and entertain. A tradition of expressive ritual, both festively carnivalesque and more solemnly realized in folk religion, also offers a rich formal resource. Increasingly, play scripts in French or Creole, or reflecting the diglossia and using both, are coming into print. In a time of political stalemate, the theatre is likely to see some of the most original and creative expressions of these paradoxical societies.

45. Simone Schwarz-Bart's *Ti Jean L'horizon* (Paris: Seuil, 1979), a novel inspired by the Caribbean folktale hero, has generated a number of dramatic adaptations and reworkings. Patrick Chamoiseau adapted André Schwarz-Bart's novel *La mulâtresse Solitude* (Paris: Seuil, 1972), and the joint Schwarz-Bart work *Un plat de porc aux bananes vertes* (Paris: Seuil, 1967) has also been staged. See Bridget Jones and Sita Dickson Littlewood (1997), *Paradoxes of French Caribbean Theatre. An Annotated Checklist of Dramatic Works (Guadeloupe, Guyane, Martinique) from 1900*, London: Roehampton Insititute.

–6–

The Representation of Women in French Caribbean Fiction
Beverley Ormerod

It is tempting, when considering the representation of women in French Caribbean fiction, to recall the archetypal figures of Caribbean folklore, which sometimes seem to anticipate the female condition as it is shown by novelists.[1] In traditional tales, the old woman may be a witch (*Dame Kéléman,* Mistress Magic), a powerful spirit who can sing headless, the terrifying counterpart of the good grandmother. *Man Tigre,* the tiger's domineering wife, fierce in defence of her young and her property, is the precursor of the hardy, resilient working woman whom the male novelists of the 'Creoleness' school celebrate as the *femme matador.*[2] Swift in her response to threat or oppression, she may function – like the witch – as an image of resistance. In a different register, pretty Princess *Bèbelle* (whose name, suggestive of *bêbête,* simpleton, is an ironic glimpse into Caribbean class conflict) is a symbol of privilege, but she depends on her father to choose her husband. She might be viewed as the passive forerunner of the privileged, but more adventurous, fictional girls who reject middle-class parental values but face difficult choices among the shifting social and racial signposts of the contemporary world. The peasant's daughter, on the contrary, may represent the discreet sensuality and unwavering fidelity that are highlighted in the tale of *Mari-Baleine,* the

1. For folktales with female characters from the Ti-Jean cycle, see Ina Césaire (1987), *L'Enfant des passages, ou la geste de Ti-Jean,* Paris: Editions Caribéennes, pp. 8, 12, 29–33, 35–43, 97–109; for examples from funeral wake stories, see Ina Césaire and Joëlle Laurent (1976), *Contes de mort et de vie aux Antilles,* Paris: Nubia, pp. 24–37, 50–61, 84–94, 216–18.
2. The Creole term *matadò* has a number of meanings: the one frequently invoked by novelists is that of the West Indian woman who boldly confronts life's trials. See Ralph Ludwig, Danièle Montbrand, Henri Poullet and Sylviane Telchid (1990), *Dictionnaire Créole–Français,* Paris: Servedit/Editions Jasor, p. 224.

magic sea creature, whose beloved sings back to her from distant oceans and dies of grief when it is killed.[3]

Many of the well-known female protagonists in French Caribbean narratives are old: matriarchs, witches, healers. They are often symbolic in a way that involves physical unattractiveness: cane-field workers with bent backs and gnarled fingers; loud-voiced proletarians who mete out blows and truculently weather the ups and downs of life. But a traditional prestige attaches to the grandmother as substitute mother, offering care, protectiveness and a stability that the birth mother may not be able to provide.[4] She symbolizes the strength of the matrifocal household that was born of the shattering of African family patterns during slavery. There may also be some overlap between the grandmother, possessor of wisdom, and the witch. In the West Indian social context, the witch's magic is not necessarily perceived as evil, since African herbal healing is traditionally practised by women, more sinister magic being commonly regarded as the province of men.[5] In literature, the theoretically opposite types of good grandmother and repulsive witch may be juxtaposed or even blended within the same narrative. Young women, however, are assigned different functions. They may be images of alienation, obsessed with the idea of racial inferiority, or bent upon a search for cultural identity that leads them to reject the idea of integration within a Caribbean lifestyle and landscape. Love and fidelity often elude them: several novels present a female narrator betrayed by the illusion of identity that was held out by some foreign liaison. The openly sensual female is a comparatively minor figure in this body of fiction, and is generally to be found in the work of male novelists.

There are powerful prototypes of the grandmother in two classic Caribbean novels: Joseph Zobel's *La Rue Cases-Nègres* (1950) and Simone Schwarz-Bart's *Pluie et vent sur Télumée miracle* (1972). Both works portray a rural society in the early twentieth century and, in both, a grandmother is seen through the eyes of a child narrator whose intensely close relationship with her is based on love or fear. Zobel's M'man Tine is shown entirely through the eyes of her grandson José, who is five years old at the start of the narrative. His vision of her is charged with an ambivalence that sometimes recalls the negative elements of the witch, the old hag who stands between the hero and his true mother. But this

3. Césaire and Laurent, *Contes de mort et de vie*, pp. 116–26.
4. On grandmother households, see Edith Clarke (1966), *My Mother who Fathered Me*, 2nd edn, London: Allen and Unwin, pp. 133–9, 178–81.
5. Simonne Henry-Valmore (1988), *Dieux en exil*, Paris: Gallimard, p. 216.

dour, exhausted cane-field worker, struggling to ensure that her grandson will have a better life than her own, is also an icon of female endurance. The loosely autobiographical novel is recounted from two points of view: that of the inexperienced child, and that of the man looking back and reinterpreting the phenomena which were once observed only in relation to the preoccupations of childhood. Thus M'man Tine's manifestations of pain, fatigue and ill temper, once taken as signs of her displeasure at his misdeeds, are seen by the adult José as evidence of the miserable conditions in which she toils.

The figure of the old woman operates here at a number of levels. Her situation encapsulates many standard features of the destiny of female labourers in the century after the abolition of slavery, and points to the failure of emancipation to bring radical improvement to their lives. Her immediate function is to represent all those descendants of slaves who, for want of money and education, were driven to become ill-paid field-workers in the very plantation milieu which inevitably recalled the forced expatriation and ultimate death of their ancestors. At the level of gender, she is woman as victim: her rape in early adolescence by the overseer of the children's team is a reminder of the sexual helplessness of the female slave, who was forced to be a breeding machine for the plantation. As José's grandmother-carer, she heads the standard West Indian matriarchal household. She is never shown in relation to an emotional or sexual partner. She is personalized only by the character traits which the child narrator emphasizes: her fierce respectability and independence, her merciless punishments and her infrequent moments of tenderness.

Although M'man Tine plays a maternal role in his life, there is no hint of feminine gentleness in the narrator's unflattering physical assessment of her. Her skin is withered, her feet are cracked, her hardened hands are ever ready to clout him and her misshapen body is hidden within a grotesque collection of rags, whose sole function is to protect her from being scratched by the sharp-edged cane leaves. Thus she recalls the witch of folklore, with her toothless gums and sunken chest, a creature devoid both of sexual appeal and of maternal attributes.[6] This negative presentation is counterbalanced by two factors. One is a traditional Caribbean theme within the narrative proper: her struggle to get José educated and her immense pride in his scholastic success. Stoical and undemonstrative, she is none the less driven by her determination to save him from the cane fields. The other factor is her symbolic importance as a victim of the plantation system. Through her angry reminiscences of her days as an

---

6. See Césaire and Laurent, *Contes de mort et de vie*, pp. 84, 88.

unwanted orphan, forced to work in the children's gang on a sugar estate, financially exploited by her uncle and sexually abused by the overseer, giving birth to a daughter who is doomed to repeat the cycle of exploitation and pregnancy, she bears witness to the brutal historical truths of slavery.

Interestingly, however, Zobel does not choose to represent M'man Tine as José's principal mentor. Despite her railing against the injustice of the system, she offers no alternative vision of black destiny; while she does not go to the extreme of linking her race with inferiority and sin,[7] she is conditioned to accept the deference of black to white. The role of cultural sage is reserved for the ancient, solitary Médouze, who plays traditional riddle games with the child and speaks to him of the slaves' homeland, ancestral Guinea. By the glow of Médouze's cooking fire, his wretched loincloth-clad body is transformed into a 'handsome, masculine' form, while his half-closed eyes, red-streaked hair and wild beard give him the appearance of an archaic mask. In African tradition, it is the old man, not the old woman, who holds the magic secrets of the race and hands them on to his male successors – a pattern reflected, for instance, in Edouard Glissant's *Le Quatrième Siècle* (1964), where old Papa Longoué instructs the young protagonist Mathieu about the African-Caribbean past. After his death, Médouze still basks in the prestige that the male gaze reserves for illustrious elders, while the adolescent José's view of his grandmother declines from awe and apprehension into impatience and guilt.

Because of this ambivalence on the part of the narrator, Zobel's M'man Tine is not entirely an exemplary figure. A more complex portrayal of the elderly woman is offered in Simone Schwarz-Bart's *Pluie et vent sur Télumée miracle*.Télumée, the female narrator, expresses love and admiration not only for her grandmother, the heroic Reine Sans Nom, but also for Reine's friend Man Cia, the village witch reputed to have transparent eyes, grooved claws for nails and breasts that serve as wings. Here the witch is positively valued as foster-mother and friend, healer, interpreter of dreams and custodian of the memory of slavery. Man Cia's lessons to Télumée hold no nostalgia for an unattainable Guinea, but dynamically reinforce the moral teaching of Reine Sans Nom concerning human ability to transcend a seemingly intolerable existence. Both old women are exceptional survivors in a milieu emotionally damaged by the racial bias of the white plantocracy. Reine Sans Nom's teaching is concerned with female strategies for personal survival, tempered with compassion for

---

7. Contrast Amboise's grandmother and the village gossips in Simone Schwarz-Bart (1972), *Pluie et vent sur Télumée miracle*, Paris: Seuil, and Man Louise in André and Simone Schwarz-Bart (1967), *Un plat de porc aux bananes vertes*, Paris: Seuil.

others and an understanding of the psychological vulnerability that is slavery's legacy. An image of stability, she functions as the perfect model for Télumée's less than perfect life.

Man Cia's doctrine has more of a cutting edge: she is an image of resistance, the voice within the narrative that speaks of slavery with the most bitter and unforgiving sarcasm. She is more directly concerned with treachery and injustice, and less benevolent towards her fellow men. But, following African tradition, she imparts the ancient herbal lore that will enable Télumée to become a healer in her turn. The positive presentation of female ageing is enhanced by the portrait of Télumée herself as an independent old woman, happy in spite of past loss and betrayal. Underlying the narrative is her instinctive sense of the historic wrongs that have bred insecurity and resentment in a disadvantaged peasant community. This awareness informs her relationships with her two partners (and with her enemy Médard), which are marked by a willingness to understand that largely protects her against bitterness; like the girl in *Mari-Baleine*, she represents loving sensuality and fidelity, but unlike the folktale heroine, she is too strong to die of sorrow.[8] In her capacity to withstand setbacks and misfortune, there is also something of the *femme matador*'s stubborn refusal to be browbeaten. Despite the negative depiction of women's attitudes in general within Télumée's community, the novel takes an unusually positive approach to the representation of individual female experience in the Caribbean.

Of the many fictional autobiographies created by West Indian women novelists, *Télumée miracle* is certainly the least troubled by the issue of cultural identity. Perhaps more confidently than her female mentors, whose birth took place nearer to the era of slavery, Télumée can assert at the start of her narrative: 'I've never found my country too small ... if I could choose it's here in Guadeloupe that I'd be born again, suffer and die.'[9] This total commitment of a peasant girl to her national and racial origins is in contrast to the impulse to reject a racial and cultural identity associated with slavery, a motif which frequently occurs in fiction by Caribbean women.

An early example of this type of fiction is Mayotte Capécia's first novel, *Je suis Martiniquaise* (1948), which was made notorious by Frantz Fanon's

8. For further discussion of Télumée's attitude to love and personal identity, see Beverley Ormerod (1985), *An Introduction to the French Caribbean Novel*, London: Heinemann, pp. 113–15, 121–8.

9. Schwarz-Bart, *Pluie et vent sur Télumée miracle*, trans. Barbara Bray (1974) as *The Bridge of Beyond*, London: Heinemann, p. 2.

denunciation of the author for her racial prejudice.[10] Capécia's use of a first-person narrator bearing her own name, and the fact that her heroine's actions and values are never questioned in the narrative, encouraged Fanon to treat the text as a demonstration of Capécia's own alienation. Thus he explains the fictional Mayotte's decision to become a laundress as over-compensation for the fact that she cannot bleach her own skin, while her preference for a white God and angels is taken as evidence of a neurotic desire to negate her blackness.

Hopefully setting off for France with her illegitimate blue-eyed child at the end of the novel, Mayotte seems almost an archaic figure, a leftover from a time before the emergence of negritude. Yet it is interesting to reconsider Capécia's text as a social document of the colonial French era. *Je suis Martiniquaise* describes a semi-rural, pre-Second World War society, less than a century away from the abolition of slavery, in which the superiority of the white race is still taken for granted. The epitome of male good looks is the blond country curate, basking in the reflected prestige of more remote white deities, such as the Empress Joséphine. The light-skinned *chabines* so admired in Mayotte's schoolyard, with their tight blond curls and green eyes, have, in fact, remained a symbol of sexual desirability right up to the late twentieth-century fiction of the 'Creoleness' school (Patrick Chamoiseau, Raphaël Confiant, etc.). As a child, Mayotte is taught to be proud of her white grandmother and to consider black men (like her promiscuous, spendthrift father) as unreliable partners. Given her upbringing and milieu, her ambition to acquire a white lover appears inevitable. She romanticizes her liaison with a French naval officer, but the narrative also realistically depicts the drawbacks to such a relationship in those days. Mayotte lives with impermanency and hostility: her lover's black maid is insolent to her, the *béké* population will not receive her and the resident French offer her, at best, a tolerant condescension. In the end, her lover sails off without her and the local population is resentful of her pale-skinned baby.

The presentation of Mayotte's opinions and behaviour involves much evidence of racial alienation, of which the first-person narrator appears unaware. She pays lip-service to the myth of the exotic, sensual woman: 'Martinican girls, daughters of the sun and love, are (as everyone knows) the most beautiful of West Indian women.'[11] But her actions and attitudes

---

10. See Chapter 2 of Frantz Fanon (1952), *Peau noire, masques blancs*, Paris: Seuil, trans. Charles Lam Markmann (1986) as *Black Skin, White Masks*, London: Pluto.

11. Mayotte Capécia (1948), *Je suis Martiniquaise*, Paris: Correa, p. 169. Translation mine.

indicate a low sense of self-worth. She attributes her social ineptitude to her non-white upbringing, and looks to her lover for intellectual and artistic education. Even when he abandons her and she is spurned by white society, she remains emotionally dependent on the idea of whiteness. Despite changed attitudes in Martinique towards race and civil rights in the aftermath of the Second World War, she still hopes for marriage to a Frenchman, while sadly maintaining that 'a coloured woman is never quite respectable in the eyes of a white'.[12] There is an unresolved contradiction between this belief and the proud proclamation of the novel's title.

In its unthinking acceptance of derogatory racial stereotypes, there can be no doubt that Capécia's novel is a faithful reflection of attitudes that were extremely widespread in colonial times. From plantation days onward, West Indian life had demonstrated the social and financial advantages of being white or light-skinned, and women had traditionally sought to gain a measure of power for themselves or their children by acquiring a pale-skinned partner. Apart from the question of power, society had internalized the idea of a divinely ordained racial hierarchy that placed the white race at the top. Women were conditioned to seek out partners that were socially acceptable, that is, not too reminiscent through appearance or occupation of the 'disgrace' of slavery that had somehow contaminated the descendants of slaves rather than of slave-owners. Jacqueline Manicom's *Mon examen de blanc* (1972) shows the continuing importance of France as a point of reference for the Caribbean woman through its depiction of a mixed-race (Indian/black) woman doctor, whose heart and physical passion are given to a fellow Guadeloupean, but whose confidant and artistic mentor is a male colleague from France.

The colour neurosis and cultural cringe that marked Caribbean society even in the years following the Second World War have remained a fertile inspiration for later novelists. Michèle Lacrosil's early fiction (*Sapotille et le serin d'argile*, 1960; *Cajou*, 1961) is built around the destructive effects of racial prejudice upon West Indian women. As with Capécia's Mayotte, Lacrosil's Guadeloupean protagonists identify France as the home of the ideal other; as with Mayotte, they cherish the presence of white blood in their veins. Sapotille, a *câpresse* (daughter of a mulatto woman and a black man), is victimized by French nuns because she is the darkest child in their school, and then finds her romantic desires frustrated because her first love is a light-skinned man. Later on, her black husband takes out on her the humiliations he endured in a Nazi prisoner-of-war camp. Cajou, a mulatto and a successful research scientist, is admired by

12. Ibid., p. 202.

her French fiancé but emotionally crippled by her obsession with her mother's unattainable whiteness. Her sense of inferiority is represented in a way that contrasts with the naïve optimism of Mayotte. The latter is never shown as fully conscious of the personal repercussions of her beliefs about race, nor does she experience self-destructive urges. She is in many ways a shrewd survivor, while Lacrosil's characters are continually racked by the memory of racial insults and perceived unworthiness, to the point where they must flee their existing identity through physical departure from their island, or by suicide.

In a novel written much later, but set in 1943, Michèle Maillet's *L'Etoile noire* (1990), there are certain initial similarities to the work of Capécia and Lacrosil. The narrator, Sidonie, a young Martinican woman living in France, is of mixed race and has a romantic view of her white ancestry. The novel largely concerns the transformation in her attitude towards her ethnic origins and national identity. Although she is abandoned by her French lover when she becomes pregnant, this does not alter her initial attitude to race, which is geared towards the notion of white superiority – an orientation symbolized by the gesture with which her French foster-mother replaces Sidonie's real mother's gift of a gold slave chain with a string of pearls. However, during the Nazi occupation of France, she is rounded up with a train load of Jews and deported with her young twins to a concentration camp. Surrounded by evidence of white inhumanity, she invents an African god, Agénor, to sustain her new sense of pride in black identity. In Ravensbrück, she is struck by the parallels between Nazi victims and the black slaves of history: deportation, branding, physical abuse and death. After the loss of her children, she clings to the mythical Agénor, now more West Indian than African: victorious slave, free maroon, symbol of black revolt. With more insight than Mayotte or Cajou, and perhaps unusually for the era depicted, she transcends a self-defeating belief in white cultural superiority and chooses solidarity with the African and black American prisoners, who reinforce her sense of Caribbean identity.

This group of writers uses the framework of autobiographical fiction to present France-orientated protagonists who are conditioned by the colour hierarchies of the mid-twentieth-century Caribbean. Maillet's narrator moves beyond a state of dependency to challenge positions on race that remain undisputed in Capécia's and Lacrosil's narratives. But all three writers show the intensity of French cultural influence in the Caribbean woman's attempt to define her identity. Cajou and Sidonie are caught in predicaments ascribable to their race, and, although they are portrayed as in some ways misguided, they are figures too tragic to be assimilated to the Princess *Bèbelle* tradition. However, several of the protagonists of Maryse Condé may be regarded as sophisticated, ironic variations on the *Bèbelle* motif.

The underlying theme of many of Condé's novels is a search for identity, which involves not cultural identification with Europe, but the emotional importance of Africa for the educated woman from the black diaspora. The protagonist of her first novel, *Heremakhonon* (1976), a university graduate from a privileged background, rebels against black middle-class norms by falling in love with men outside her circle: the light-skinned rich boy in Guadeloupe, the Frenchman who picks her up in a Paris street. To the black bourgeoisie of her native island, 'with its talk of glorifying the Race and its terrified conviction of its inferiority',[13] the ultimate outsider is the African. Véronica, on a teaching contract in an African capital, readily embarks upon a liaison with Ibrahima Sory, the government minister within whose portfolio, as she later discovers, lies the systematic repression of all who militate against the regime. She has arrived in Africa fiercely determined not to be led astray by any superficial exoticism. Yet she is drawn to Sory because of his aristocratic background – the antithesis of the branded Caribbean slave, who has lost his lineage – as much as because of the dynamic attraction of his wealth and power.

The story is presented in autobiographical mode, but the constant use of irony forestalls any emotional involvement between protagonist and reader. Condé also creates an effect of distance between narrator and author through Véronica's self-awareness and her unflattering insights into her own compromises with self-respect. Despite her interest in ancestral Africa, Véronica is more objective about her lover's country than are other, France-directed heroines; indeed, her view of the African male is rather different from negritude's uncritical exaltation of black sexual energy. She is irritated by Sory's casual assumption of her compliance and by his refusal to relate to her in other than sexual terms; but, above all, she is shocked by his ruthlessness. Condé's female protagonists, unlike those examined earlier, are significantly politicized; here Véronica's infatuation and subsequent disillusionment undercut her initially hopeful view of Africa, while her dream of acquiring a sense of authentic racial and cultural identity through an African liaison is ultimately perceived as a tragic mistake.

Condé's second novel, *Une saison à Rihata* (1981), uses multiple points of view to present another Guadeloupean woman's inability to be integrated

---

13. Maryse Condé (1976), *Heremakhonon*, Paris: Union Générale, translated by Richard Philcox (1982) as *Heremakhonon*, Washington: Three Continents Press, p. 52.

within African society. The narrative underlines the persistence of Caribbean attitudes in this expatriate wife, whose relationship with Africa, compounded of lethargy and disappointment, echoes the disillusionment of a nation that is presented as both cynical and without hope. Yet Condé's view of an African/Caribbean marriage, for all its disenchantment, is less negative than that of Myriam Warner-Vieyra in her *Juletane* (1982). Like Condé's protagonists, Juletane has come to Africa expecting that her ancestry will ensure her a sense of belonging. But her cultural integration proves impossible, owing to her rejection of Islam, her failure to bear children and her refusal to participate in her husband's polygamous arrangements. Her former identity is lost, along with her name: she is known to all as 'the madwoman'. Comfortless in an alien culture, she is a victim in a way that Condé's more dynamic protagonists are not, despite their frequent sense of personal failure.

In her prolific career, Condé has invented characters to illustrate many aspects of female experience: the West Indian-born slave of *Moi, Tituba, sorcière noire de Salem* (1986), defying Puritan North America with her African customs, doomed to be treated as a sexual possession and a heretic; the unhappy, dependent women of the Guadeloupean country village in *Traversée de la mangrove* (1989), unable to see their way out of centuries-old male domination; the black American college teacher in *Les Derniers Rois Mages* (1992), who marries an unemployed French West Indian, a painter of mediocre water-colours, having invested him with glamour because of his family's alleged descent from the African king Béhanzin.[14] Many of Condé's central themes concerning female attitudes to race and identity are exemplified by Thécla in *La Vie scélérate* (1987). The only child of besotted parents in a newly rich black household, Thécla is an embodiment of confusion and contradiction, a social climber with Marxist leanings, a racial snob who dreams of black liberation. When she has an illegitimate child by a light-skinned West Indian who considers her too black to marry, she is obliged to confront the ugly realities of a colour prejudice from which money and education had cushioned her. Her bitter response is one of the strongest statements about race to be found in Condé's fiction: 'For no one ever talked about my colour, which was the real problem. People don't talk about colour, even if it's there staring you in the face: that just isn't done! Colour is dirtier than the green diarrhoea

---

14. The romanticizing of African identity may also be pursued by a Caribbean protagonist in France, as occurs in Suzanne Dracius-Pinalie (1989), *L'Autre qui danse*, Paris: Seghers.

of amoebic dysentery or the sulphur-yellow piss of incontinence!'[15] Divided in her heart between Europe and the Third World, Thécla's chase after elusive political and racial goals is resolved only at second hand, when her daughter Claude, long relegated to a French foster-mother, at last discovers her Guadeloupean identity.

The woman in search of personal or cultural identity may be used as a symbol of the national quest for identity. Edouard Glissant represents his major female character, Marie Celat (Mycéa), in this light. Glissant, often cited for a particular, compassionate passage about the female condition in *Malemort* (1975) – 'But the woman, who thinks of the woman, the beast destined to endure, the gentle, dazed creature'[16] – in fact depicts few such acquiescent victims in his work. His historical characters – militant Louise, imperious Stéfanise, visionary Liberté, short-tempered Ephraïse and a number of others – are all survivors in their different ways; Mycéa and her mother Cinna Chimène are active, independent and resolute women. Glissant's portrait of Mycéa is slowly developed across several novels. She first occurs as an adolescent in *La Lézarde* (1958), where she is an emblem of integrity and revolutionary ardour. Seen through the eyes of a young male narrator, she is an idealized, abstract figure, proud and reserved, in contrast to the more sensual girls around her. Not until *La Case du commandeur* (1981) is the reader afforded a glimpse of a more human, everyday Mycéa, the scholarship-winning child of illiterate peasants, a secretive and wilful girl who must shoulder, from the age of ten, the burden of looking after her father and his household.

In *La Lézarde*, Glissant announces a symbolic role for Mycéa. She stands for the Caribbean landscape, pregnant with half-lost memories that hint at Martinique's unrealized need for self-discovery: 'I am the call. Truly, the earth. The black earth. Earth now gone. Where? When?'[17] It is she who represents the last descendants of the maroon family that Glissant chronicles in *Le Quatrième Siècle* (1964), although she figures only briefly in that narrative and, in her role of realist as opposed to her lover Mathieu's dreamer, fights against what Glissant calls elsewhere the vertigo of time.[18] Years later, Glissant uses the estrangement of Mathieu and Marie Celat as the backdrop to *La Case du commandeur*. This is the only novel in which she is not presented primarily through the gaze of her male admirers,

15. Maryse Condé (1987), *La Vie scélérate*, Paris: Seghers, p. 275. Translation mine.

16. Edouard Glissant (1975), *Malemort*, Paris: Seuil, p. 56. Translation mine.

17. Edouard Glissant (1958), *La Lézarde*, Paris: Seuil, trans. Michael Dash (1985) as *The Ripening*, London: Heinemann, p. 115.

18. Edouard Glissant (1981), *Le Discours antillais*, Paris: Seuil, p. 435.

but through personal relationships with her father, her sons and daughter, her psychiatrist and a fellow patient. The focal point of the narrative is her frustrating search for traces of her ancestors, whose lives, like those of other slaves, were unrecorded, but are here disclosed by a semi-omniscient narrator. The motif of Mycéa's journey through a dark night, first sounded in *La Lézarde*, is here equated with the suffering of Martinique itself, a country where the majority are unable to come to terms with their own history as a prerequisite for determining their identity and destiny. Marie Celat lives under a double shadow: her tragic sense of the Caribbean past, and her deep disillusionment with Martinican political attitudes. It is a shadow that she tries to escape by adopting the lifestyle of an 'ordinary woman'; but the death of her sons and her own obsession with the meaning of the past provoke an emotional collapse that causes her admission to a psychiatric hospital. Only on escaping into the primeval forest, symbol of maroon freedom in all of Glissant's work, does she achieve a mystical reunion with her ancestors on the Trace of the Time Before – the track of past violence and pain that must be relived in order to be transcended. This initiatory experience is expressed by metaphors that invoke the highest senses: an illusion of music, an almost physical impact of light. They herald Marie Celat's abstract role in Glissant's later novels, *Mahagony* (1987) and *Tout-monde* (1993). Her yearning for authenticity becomes an aspect of her loyalty to the notion of Martinican independence, and her violence of speech and manner is symptomatic of the 'night' that falls within her uninvited and that represents the island's forgotten history.

The restrained, physically imprecise portrayal of Marie Celat is at the opposite extreme to the presentation of other women characters in the late 1980s as incarnations of sensuality. In such novels, the female image is essentially a physical one, conjured up by a male narrator as the focus of sexual desire. Thus the theme of burning passion is whimsically explored in Xavier Orville's *Laissez brûler Laventurcia* (1989) through a figure that is a transmutation of the folktale witch: a pyromaniac spirit who is 'blazingly beautiful', who sets men's hearts and loins on fire and whose eventual death at the stake is described in terms of a slow carnal seduction by caressing flames.[19]

Raphaël Confiant, one of the theoreticians of the 'Creoleness' school, has made sexual references a trademark of his evocations of Martinican folk life. In his childhood memoirs, he recalls the way in which he and

19. Xavier Orville (1989), *Laissez brûler Laventurcia*, Paris: Grasset, pp. 150, 215–16.

his cousin used to spy on the assignations between their grandfather's valet and Léonise, the servant girl with long cinnamon-coloured legs.[20] Something of the same youthful prurience informs his fictional portraits of women. They remain a psychologically unexplored other, generally reinforcing a tourist-board image of the exotic Caribbean female. She-who-has-no-equal, a beautiful, tall, wide-hipped country wench who figures in Confiant's first novel, *Le Nègre et l'amiral* (1988) – 'This firm black body, these ample breasts swelling beneath the fondling of his maddened hands, this hot pussy with its violently pink lips'[21] – prefigures the voluptuous females in his other novels: Antilia of the elastic brown breasts, half-human, half-spirit, whose enthusiastic coupling with a delivery man in a storeroom is viewed by a group of excited schoolboys;[22] Justine, whose curvaceous bronze body holds the white master in thrall;[23] Sylvanise, who flashes her splendid thighs as she dances, and whose dress is so low-cut that it would make a priest stop believing in God.[24] Confiant presents his female characters through an external vision, and often in a picaresque setting. Women do not usually play a principal role in his work. In *Eau de Café* (1991), where there are two female protagonists, neither is truly human: the supernatural waif Antilia is surrounded by the trappings of magical realism, while Eau de Café herself, with her divination, charms and spells, is another manifestation of the witch – not the folktale hag who frightens children, but the seductive monster of patriarchal tradition, the 'dark double' of idealized, passive femininity.[25]

In characters such as the overbearing Eau de Café, one can also discern some of the features of *Man Tigre*, the *femme matador* beloved of the 'Creoleness' school, and earlier evoked by Glissant in his description of the 'indomitable haughtiness' of Mycéa's mother: 'Cinna Chimène was at that time a *matador*. She had her own way of bending her body to tie cane stalks together, one hip thrust out as if to begin a polka . . . She strode forward thrusting her legs, wrapped in rags, straight in front of her, as if to defy a snake that the canecutters might have missed.'[26] This description

20. Raphaël Confiant (1993), *Ravines du devant-jour*, Paris: Gallimard, pp. 13–14.

21. Raphaël Confiant (1988), *Le Nègre et l'amiral*, Paris: Grasset, p. 211. Translation mine.

22. Raphaël Confiant (1991), *Eau de Café*, Paris: Grasset, p. 52.

23. Raphaël Confiant (1994), *Commandeur du sucre*, Paris: Ecriture, p. 209.

24. Raphaël Confiant (1994), *L'Allée des soupirs*, Paris: Grasset, p. 221.

25. See the discussion of angel/monster types in Toril Moi (1985), *Sexual/Textual Politics: Feminist Literary Theory*, London and New York: Routledge, pp. 58–60.

26. Edouard Glissant (1981), *La Case du commandeur*, Paris: Seuil, pp. 20–1. Translation mine.

hints at the underlying masculinity of the *femme matador* tradition, harking back to the merciless era of slavery, when women, deprived of the support of partner or family, needed physical endurance and an unflinching, even aggressive, spirit in order to survive. Patrick Chamoiseau builds his third novel, *Texaco* (1992), around an urban version of the *femme matador*. Marie-Sophie Laborieux is herself the narrator of a tale that is part fictional autobiography, part history of the evolution of former Martinican slaves into an urban proletariat. In her time, she has encountered the familiar setbacks of the woman of humble origins: difficult employers, faithless lovers, confrontations with unfeeling officialdom and constant financial struggle. Having become the founder and dominant personality of a hillside slum on the edge of Fort-de-France, she composes her memoirs from a position of relative security. Although she has the independence of a *matador* and is cynical about men, she does not conform to the conventional image of a feminist: 'I knew moments of abandon, I made men suffer, they made me suffer everything, I often mistook a sudden stirring of the flesh for an emotion. I learnt to write letters, to be sweet to a man who wasn't worth it, to be sweet all the same without really knowing why.'[27] In fact, the plantation subculture whose memory she celebrates is above all the province of men: subversives like the storyteller, the maroon, or her own father Esternome, the house slave who survived through cunning to become the focal point of his daughter's attention and loyalty. Marie-Sophie's significance in the narrative is not primarily as a woman, but as an early representative of a Caribbean working-class type, and as a curator of the folk history to which Chamoiseau grants a privileged place in his approach to cultural identity.

Chamoiseau depicts the contemporary *femme matador* in his second novel, *Solibo Magnifique* (1988), where she takes the form of a middle-aged street pedlar, the memorable Doudou-Ménar. Doudou first appears as a bustling, self-important figure, whose lack of grace is comically emphasized. But Chamoiseau also hints at the hardships behind her lively, inquisitive façade: the money worries, the layabout son, the drunken husband, the unrelenting competition from other street hawkers, the swollen varicose veins. Yet another viewpoint on Doudou is provided by the police sergeant, who unexpectedly recognizes in her the pretty, naïve country girl whom he once met and seduced in a dancehall. Fat Doudou, who is touchingly proud of travelling back in an official car to the scene of the medical crisis she has reported, falls foul of her police escort and permanently disables one of them before she is beaten into a coma. This

---

27. Patrick Chamoiseau (1992), *Texaco*, Paris: Gallimard, pp. 342–3. Translation mine.

defiant proletarian stands in contrast to the timid figure of Sidonise the sherbet vendor, who disputes police authority only when questions touch too disrespectfully upon her private life. Sidonise, the former companion of Solibo the storyteller, has never ceased to love him, although financial hardship caused them to separate. Her recollection of his final visit, and the superb fish stew that he made by way of wooing her, introduces the archetypal *Mari-Baleine* theme of female fidelity. With warmth and humour, Chamoiseau introduces nuances into his depiction of female sensuality by showing the tough *matador* in her early days of luscious, impressionable vulnerability, and working-class women like Sidonise as creatures of both passion and modesty.

Gisèle Pineau, in *La Grande Drive des esprits* (1993), deploys a number of female types in her 'Creoleness'-style evocation of rural Guadeloupe: witch, healer, domineering mother, beautiful peasant girl, *femme matador* and rebellious daughter pining after life in town. Her most sustained portrait of a woman, however, is to be found in *L'Espérance-macadam* (1995), a novel boldly centred not upon youth, but on old age. The protagonist, Eliette, although in her late sixties and living alone in a run-down locality, is not dehumanized in the folktale tradition of the witch, or depicted as unfeminine thanks to poverty and hard labour, as are M'man Tine and other female emblems of slavery. But her existence has been flawed by a distant trauma, deeply repressed, which is gradually revealed to be her own father's savage rape of her in early childhood. The narrative describes the painful return of her lost capacity for feeling, through her reluctant assumption of responsibility for an adolescent neighbour, Angela, who is also a victim of incest and parental assault. Eliette is no *femme matador*, but her determination to surmount the past illustrates the theme of female strength as convincingly as the active struggles that mark the narratives of other female survivors.

The story of Eliette is framed by a multiple unfolding of pain and betrayal within her impoverished rural community. In dramatizing the issue of incest, Pineau throws into prominence a subject generally neglected by francophone Caribbean writers; an exception is Glissant's Nameless Woman, who shields herself from the same unspeakable reality with her ceaseless chatter.[28] Pineau presents the abuse of children as part of a wider pattern of social and emotional disorder – the same pattern, born of slavery with its brutal disregard for individual rights, that forms the background to Télumée's village world in the first half of the century. Presiding over the narrative is the violence of nature itself. Two natural disasters bracket

28. Glissant, *La Case du commandeur*, p. 144.

Eliette's story and are fused with the idea of male aggression: the hurricane during which she was assaulted sixty years before, and the one from which she flees with Angela. The second hurricane coincides with her recovery of the memory of rape and her resolution to offer an emotional commitment, for the first time, to another human being.

Although Caribbean women writers most frequently give women characters the primary role in their work, their preoccupations are not always gender-specific. Pineau's *L'Espérance-macadam*, for instance, presents incest partly as a gender issue involving the abuse of young daughters; but the narrative suggests that the root problem is misdirected violence against a child of either sex. Female and male novelists alike are concerned with aspects of colonial and post-colonial society that have affected both sexes in the West Indies equally, although the resulting problems may manifest themselves differently according to gender. Alienation, racial prejudice, economic deprivation, ambivalence regarding slave ancestry and the pursuit of cultural identity are common themes. These themes are dealt with by authors of both sexes, and in relation to characters of both sexes: Lacrosil chooses a male protagonist to illustrate the theme of racial neurosis in *Demain Jab-Herma* (1967), as does Schwarz-Bart, in *Ti Jean L'horizon* (1979), to illustrate the impossibility of Caribbean reintegration with Africa; both Glissant and Chamoiseau choose female protagonists to embody aspects of the search for cultural identity, alongside women writers like Condé, Warner-Vieyra or Maillet.

Gender-specific issues do arise in connection with female sexuality. For writers like Confiant or Orville, a provocative type of sensuality is a key element in the portrayal of women whose major function is viewed as physical rather than intellectual. Elsewhere, the balance of power between the sexes becomes an important motif. The *Bèbelles* of the autobiographical novels, whether lucid or disturbed, are young women living through a time of emotional and sexual yearning, who fear alienating their lovers through any gesture of protest or independence. Writers like Schwarz-Bart and Pineau present women as the actual or potential victims of male violence, a violence that these authors relate to the psychological destabilization of the male slave, who was denied the right to responsibility in every aspect of his life, including permanent sexual and parental relationships. The traces of slavery in present-day family structures are recorded in the depiction of matrifocal households by Zobel, Schwarz-Bart, Glissant and Chamoiseau.

Caribbean patterns of domestic life have encouraged a vision of woman as autonomous provider and protector. However, in a society where the majority of males were once deprived of authority, levels of male and female dominance are constantly being renegotiated, sometimes through coercion. It is perhaps for this reason that figures of self-contained female power – matriarch, witch, *femme matador* – are so often invoked by Caribbean writers as exemplary survivors, while the dependent *Bèbelles* fail to accede to a sense of personal and cultural identity, and the fidelity of amorous heroines – Télumée, Sidonise, *Mari-Baleine*'s beloved – may end in mourning, owing to the intervention of patriarchal force or external cultural pressures that cannot be resisted.

7

Challenges to Writing Literature in Creole: The Cases of Martinique and Guadeloupe

Jane Brooks

The appearance of a chapter concerned with the process and challenges of writing literature in Creole, in a book devoted to Caribbean francophone literature, may seem paradoxical. However, writing in the Lesser Antilles has been shaped by the coexistence of the Creole and French languages since colonization, as, regardless of the language a writer selects, he or she is inhabited by both Creole and French at the moment of writing. The pressure of the two languages on each other has not always been acknowledged, due to their radically different statuses. To this day, French is perceived as the legitimate language of formal written expression and of high culture, whereas Creole is not generally regarded as a fully-fledged language by the population at large. Its lower status, however, has made it the preferred code of in-group solidarity, appropriate for the expression of an Antillean popular oral culture. As will be seen, at key points in history, the denial of the reciprocal influence of the two languages has been overtly inscribed within each literature, in an attempt to underscore the purity of both French and Creole. Nevertheless, this polarization seems unsustainable in the light of recent developments, particularly the increased use of intermediate varieties of both languages in the form of gallicized Creole and creolized French.

This chapter will begin with a brief historical sketch, which traces the changing status of Creole in relation to that of French in the Lesser Antilles, with particular reference to the rejection of Creole by successive groups of the population and to the circumstances which have led to the emergence of the intermediate forms of both languages. A second section will then examine ways in which the relationship between Creole and French has been conceptualized by various linguists, as these conceptualizations have influenced many creolophone writers. These writers generally move in élite intellectual circles and have been involved in debates concerning the use of Creole as a symbol of cultural and political resistance to French hegemony. The chapter will then turn to more literary concerns, with an analysis of a number of challenges that face the creolophone writer: the elaboration of a written, literary variety of Creole, the choice of orthography and the creation of an autonomous literary tradition. All three challenges illustrate Creole literature's continuing dependence on French-language writing and suggest that, at the present time, the conditions necessary for the further literary development of Creole do not exist.

A Brief History

As a consequence of France's enslavement and forced deportation of Africans (from 1680), two exogenous ethnic groups came into daily contact within the contained space of the smaller plantations typical of Guadeloupe and Martinique. Neither group was linguistically homogeneous. The Africans were captured in many different parts of West Africa and therefore had no common language. Moreover, many plantation owners instituted a policy of separating slaves of the same mother tongue in order to break down family or ethnic solidarity and thus diminish the risk of rebellion. Although the colonizers were preponderantly of French origin, they came from diverse regional and social backgrounds, with the result that mutual intelligibility posed a problem for this group too, since *ancien régime* France was far from being linguistically unified.

In the absence of a common means of communication, a restricted and simplified code, called a 'pidgin', arose, which served to carry out the limited number of transactions necessary to the functioning of the plantation. It is likely that this pidgin had a lexical base drawn mostly from dialects of French origin (the superstrate) and a grammatical structure drawn from West African languages. The pidgin would also have been less complex than any of the languages which had contributed to it, given that it was the mother tongue of none of its speakers. However, children born into this situation on the plantations inevitably acquired the pidgin as a first language, and this shift marked the evolution of the pidgin into a fully-fledged Creole. In becoming the mother tongue of a speech community, any Creole undergoes a process of expansion and development. Since it has to be capable of expressing the full range of its speakers' experiences and communication needs, its vocabulary increases and a more complex syntax develops. As a result of this process, the slaves eventually became monolingual Creole speakers, whereas the majority of whites spoke Creole and French.

In Martinique and Guadeloupe, the evolution of the plantation system and of Creole were interdependent processes. Plantation society constructed and consolidated itself through Creole, while the expansion and elaboration of the language was motivated by developments in plantation society. As a result, Creole was founded upon the violent social relationships of plantation society and upon the ambiguities contained within the colonial project. This has had important ramifications for the status of Creole since its very inception, as the attitude of successive sections of the creolophone population has become marked by hostility towards and an eventual rejection of Creole.

The first rejection of Creole was by the whites around the time of the *Code Noir* (1685), which served to legitimize discrimination against non-whites.[1] After the 1660s, the white population began to be outnumbered by non-whites, with the result that this disparate group of fixed-contract fieldworkers, former prostitutes, ex-buccaneers and younger sons of noble families sought to affirm its power by coalescing into a 'caste', creating a symbolic solidarity through a shared set of values. As part of this effort to preserve white hegemony, this group rejected its role in the creation of Creole, which it redefined as a sign of barbarity and depravity. In so doing, the whites, known as *békés* in Martinique and *blancs créoles* in Guadeloupe, also symbolized the importance of the economic and political link between their 'caste' and France, the mother country. This is not to say that the whites no longer spoke Creole. It remained the language used in the day-to-day running of the plantations and, in the case of the poor whites, was possibly their only language. The middle and upper echelons of the white 'caste', however, chose to identify themselves linguistically with the mother country.

In contrast, successive generations of slaves had no choice but to identify themselves with Creole, as it was their mother tongue and the only language available to them. By extension, Creole came to be associated with the condition of slavery and the denigrated status of the slaves. Thus, the *gens de couleur libres* (free coloureds), who were freed during the period of slavery and eventually formed an intermediate group seeking

---

1. Information on the first two rejections of Creole is summarized from GEREC (1982), *Charte culturelle créole*, Fort-de-France: CUAG, pp. 10–16. The explanation of the origins of Creole put forward here is only one of a number of competing theories. The theory favoured in the *Charte culturelle créole* emphasizes the contribution of the whole population and thus all languages present on the islands in the first half of the seventeenth century. Other theories tend to privilege the contribution of one group over all others, thus suggesting that Guadeloupean and Martinican Creoles have their origins more or less exclusively in the French language, or alternatively in African languages.

power, symbolically distanced themselves from the stigma of a slave past by rejecting Creole. In turn, they espoused French, the language of civilization, power and personal advancement.[2] This rejection became of particular importance among this group with the abolition of slavery (1848), as, in theory, the free coloureds and the freed slaves enjoyed the same status. At this time, education became a key strategy for this intermediate group to maintain their social superiority, as French was the sole medium of education.

The free coloureds' rejection of Creole and idolization of the French language also marked their alliance with the more liberal ideas emerging from mainland France at that time. While these democratic ideals served the interests of this group, they ran counter to those of the *blancs créoles* and *békés*, who had felt themselves increasingly betrayed by their mother country post-1789. Indeed, many of the whites in Guadeloupe had either fled or been put to death when the Revolutionary government had attempted to abolish slavery, in line with, on the one hand, its fundamental principles of liberty, equality and fraternity and, on the other, the need to create an army to defend the colonies from a British invasion. With the abolition of slavery in both Martinique and Guadeloupe, this betrayal was complete in their eyes and the *békés* increasingly re-identified themselves with Creole, distancing themselves from the values of Republican France.

Despite the promise of mandatory primary education offered by the Jules Ferry laws in the early 1880s, implementation was delayed by vested interests in Martinique and Guadeloupe, so the majority of slave descendants (known locally as the *petit peuple*) remained, for the most part, monolingual Creole speakers well into the twentieth century. The vitality of the Creole language among this group is illustrated by the fact that it was rapidly acquired by the East Indian and Chinese indentured plantation labourers who arrived on the islands after the abolition of slavery.

This situation began to alter after changes in the two islands' political status in 1946. Departmentalization enabled the expansion of the French education system and the *petit peuple*'s initiation into the French language, which remained the sole medium of schooling. With rising unemployment, the school qualification became increasingly important to this group and, by association, the value of the French language, especially its written variety. The *petit peuple* had to adopt and identify themselves with French, particularly within the school. Moreover, the use of Creole began to be

---

2. An interesting literary representation of these attitudes is to be found in Léon Gontran Damas's poem 'Hoquets', in Léon Gontran Damas (1972), *Pigments. Névralgies*, Paris: Présence Africaine, pp. 35–8.

seen as a liability when looking for work.[3] As Creole was (and, in most cases, still is) excluded from the classroom after 1946, increasing numbers of the population were able to speak, read and write French, while Creole remained an oral language. To this day, the vast majority of its speakers remain illiterate in Creole.

With the introduction of a state francophone radio service in the 1960s and a state francophone television broadcasting service in the 1970s, the French language now has access to the homes of the poorest in Guadeloupe and Martinique. Since the 1980s, French has been undergoing a process of vernacularization. Monolingual Creole speakers are now in a minority group, usually older people who live in rural areas of the two islands. In both Martinique and Guadeloupe, there is a marked movement towards urbanization. It seems likely that in the future this group of monolingual Creole speakers will disappear, due to the effects of old age and urbanization. Moreover, there is the suggestion that, within the last ten years, French has begun to displace Creole as the 'mother tongue' of an increasing number of the Martinican *petit peuple*.[4] This would point to a possible third rejection of Creole in Martinique.

Concurrently, a fourth rejection of Creole may occur among the women of both islands, as a further recent trend has been the impact of gender on language acquisition and use. A growing body of research suggests that, in many situations, women appear to speak French more easily than Creole, in both Martinique and Guadeloupe.[5] According to the psychologist, Jacques André, this arises from the association of Creole with the 'sexual', resulting in the fact that Creole functions nowadays as a marker of a virile masculinity, whereas French denotes female respectability.[6] This view is supported by the sociolinguistic research of Ellen Schnepel, who notes that, in middle-class francophone households, a little girl is encouraged to speak French to her father and male visitors as a matter of politeness, whereas it is socially acceptable for a little boy to address these same

3. A perusal of the job columns in *France-Antilles*, the only daily local paper in Guadeloupe and Martinique, shows that the ability to speak Creole is never asked for by employers, whereas a French-language requirement often is.

4. Christian March (1989), 'Une approche épilinguistique de la question de la langue maternelle en Martinique: Une enquête chez les mères au centre PMI du Lamentin', Mémoire de DEA en linguistique, Université de Rouen-Haute Normandie.

5. Madeleine Sainte-Pierre (1972), 'Créole ou français? Les cheminements d'un choix linguistique', in Jean Benoit, ed., *L'Archipel inachevé*, Montreal: Montreal UP, pp. 257–8, and Jacques André (1987), *L'Inceste focal dans la famille noire antillaise*, Paris: Presses Universitaires de Paris, pp. 64–5.

6. Jacques André (1985), 'Le coq et la jarre: Le sexuel et le féminin dans les sociétés afro-caribéennes', *L'Homme 96*, 15:4, pp. 51–3.

men in Creole. Moreover, in many such households, girls are far more likely to be addressed in French, with the result that they do not learn Creole.[7] Notably, this situation may well have repercussions for the future success of literature written in Creole, as the local readership is preponderantly female.

Sociolinguistic Models

The relationship between Creole and French has undergone enormous change in this century, leading to a reconceptualization of the sociolinguistic situation by various linguists. Until the 1950s, a 'classic' diglossic situation, as outlined by Charles Fergusson, pertained, with French and Creole held in a stable hierarchical relationship. French, the High variety, was perceived as the official and prestigious code of formal and non-domestic situations, in strong contrast to Creole, the Low variety, which was seen as the language of informal speech, strongly associated with the home and popular culture. As such, each language had its traditional domains of use and Creole and French were seen as distinct entities with separate identities.[8]

From the middle of the twentieth century, this stable situation has given way to one in which both languages compete for hegemony within language domains formerly reserved for the other language. Creole has made an incursion into more formal spheres beyond the domestic setting, whereas French has penetrated the home. A greater proportion of the speech community now has a choice between Creole and French, resulting in more acute linguistic conflict. Although Creole is now spoken by greater numbers of people, due to a growing population, in the absence of an effective collective promotion of the status of Creole, a qualitative decreolization has occurred. This means that the distinction between French and Creole is no longer so clear, and intermediate varieties have come into being. Examples of an intermediate variety of French influenced by Creole may, perhaps, include:

'Il est comparaison.' (instead of 'Il est trop fier.')
'Elle l'a acheté dans la main de Mirta.' (instead of 'Elle l'a acheté de Mirta.')

7. E. Schnepel (1993), 'The Other Tongue, The Other Voice: Language and Gender in the French Caribbean', *Ethnic Groups*, 10, p. 254.
8. See Charles Fergusson (1959), 'Diglossia', *Word*, 15, pp. 325–40, for more information on the diglossic model.

Equally, the influence of French on the Creole spoken by sections of the speech community is also clear. For example, in Guadeloupean and Martinican Creole, to make the plural form of a noun the word 'sé' is traditionally used. However, a growing number of people are beginning to use 'les', the plural marker of the French language, when speaking Creole. The influence of French on the pronunciation of Creole is also clear, with many differences between the two languages disappearing, as in the case of the Creole word for money, 'lahan', which in the Creole speech of many Martinicans and some Guadeloupeans now sounds far closer to the French term for money, 'l'argent'.

Within the twentieth century, the language situations in both islands have shared these same broad currents, although French offers far less of a threat to Creole in Guadeloupe than in Martinique, where the penetration of French into domains formerly reserved by Creole has been far more pronounced.[9] This has led to two different models of the relationship between the two languages in Guadeloupe and Martinique, which can be explained, in part, by the greater importance of a local variety of French in Martinique. Guy Hazaël-Massieux has proposed for Guadeloupe a triglossic model, which distinguishes Standard French, Regional French and Creole. According to his analysis, Guadeloupean Regional French is far closer to Creole than it is to Standard French, in both linguistic and sociolinguistic terms, as the school system tends to reject all that is not Standard French as being Creole. He therefore maintains that the most important distinction is between Standard French and all other varieties spoken locally.[10]

In contrast, the Martinican linguist, Jean Bernabé, has proposed a tetraglossic model of two continua of varieties, one ranging from Standard French to creolized French, the other from the most gallicized variety of Creole to the variety of Creole maximally deviant from French, which he calls basilectal Creole.[11] Moreover, he holds that, in the Standard French–creolized French continuum, the prestige of Standard French is so great that a speaker will try to produce an utterance as close to this variety as his or her competency allows. Indeed, the anxiety caused by the pressure of Standard French is so great that the speaker may produce a hypercorrect form. This occurs when a linguistically insecure speaker hesitates between

9. For further discussion of this point, see Ellen Schnepel (1993), 'The Creole movement in Guadeloupe', *International Journal of Society and Language*, 102, pp. 119–20.

10. Guy Hazaël-Massieux (1978), 'Approche socio-linguistique de la situation de la diglossie français-créole en Guadeloupe', *Langue Française*, 37, pp. 106–18.

11. Jean Bernabé (1983), *Fondal-natal: Grammaire basilectale approchée des créoles guadeloupéen et martiniquais*, 3 vols, Paris: L'Harmattan, vol. 1, pp. 72–4.

Creole and French, with the result that he or she creates a form that belongs to neither language system.[12]

From the mid-1970s to the mid-1980s, Bernabé and the Guadeloupean/Martinican research group Groupe d'Etudes et de Recherches en Espace Créolophone (GEREC), based at the Université Antilles-Guyane, sought to promote basilectal Creole, chosen due to its maximum deviancy from Standard French, as a symbol of an oppressed local identity. An attempt was made to create a standard form of written Creole, based on this basilectal variety. However, this enterprise has had a mixed reception among the local population, for a number of reasons. Most importantly, for many Martinicans, the basilectal variety is stigmatized by its associations with slavery. Secondly, the attempt at standardization does not take into account the other varieties of Creole increasingly used by the speech community, so that it is difficult for the population at large to identify themselves with this initiative.[13]

Ultimately, divided opinion on the efficacy of promoting basilectal Creole caused a division within GEREC. One of its former members, Lambert-Félix Prudent, argues for greater attention to be paid to the intermediate (interlectal) varieties as a more accurate reflection of the actual sociolinguistic situation. Prudent characterizes local daily speech as hybrid ('métissé'), arguing that it is difficult to establish boundaries between different varieties, as speakers often alternate between Creole and French (code switching) or produce hybrid varieties (hypercorrection).[14] Prudent's work thus suggests that French and Creole are no longer discrete languages with easily separable identities for a sizeable section of the Martinican speech community.

Ironically, much energy has been expended by various sociolinguists in the defence of their models, without any serious effort being made to

12. Patrick Chamoiseau frequently portrays *petit peuple* characters whose speech is marked by hypercorrection, particularly with regard to the /R/ phoneme, as its production is subject to different rules in Creole and French. For example, in *Solibo Magnifique* the police inspector, Bouafesse, is often addressed by the witnesses as 'monsieur l'inspectère'. The Creole form of this word in Chamoiseau's orthography would be 'inspectè'. However, in this formal interview situation the witnesses attempt to speak as prestigious a variety of French as possible and thus add an 'r' sound at the end of the word. Through the use of this mark of hypercorrection, Chamoiseau succinctly points to the deep distress and anxiety of these characters, who feel socially and linguistically out of their depth.

13. For a criticism of GEREC's initiatives at this time, see Lambert-Félix Prudent (1993), 'Political illusions of an intervention in the linguistic domain in Martinique', *International Journal of Society and Language*, 102, pp. 140–2.

14. Lambert-Félix Prudent (1981), 'Diglossie et interlecte', *Langages*, 61, pp. 25–31.

carry out research into the actual speech habits of the Guadeloupean and Martinican populations, so these models are heavily reliant on the intuition and ideological persuasion of their proselytizers.[15] However, if these debates have had a lesser impact on the local speech communities, they have had considerable influence on a number of Guadeloupean and Martinican writers, many of whom have been engaged either directly or indirectly in the discussion. The conceptualization of a maximally deviant basilectal Creole as a vector for a nationalist identity can be traced, for example, in the work of such Guadeloupean poets as Djanma[16] and Hector Poullet,[17] and in the poetry and novels of the Martinican writer, Raphaël Confiant,[18] although the interpretation of the basilect varies from writer to writer.[19] In contrast, the divide between French and Creole is far less certain in the francophone works of the Guadeloupean writer Simone Schwarz-Bart[20] and the Martinican novelist Patrick Chamoiseau,[21] in whose writing French is made to resonate with the meanings, world-views and rhythms of Creole to such an extent that the authority of French is

15. Prudent, 'Political illusions', p. 141.

16. Djanma, 'Kòzman lanmè et autres poèmes', in Lambert-Félix Prudent, ed. (1984), *Anthologie de la nouvelle poésie créole*, Paris: Editions Caribbéennes.

17. Hector Poullet (1982), *Pawol an bouch*, Fort-de-France: Editions Désormeaux, and (1990), *Tibouchina*, Paris: Editions Messidor.

18. Raphaël Confiant (1979), *Jik dèyè do Bondyè*, Fort-de-France: Editions Grif an tè; (1980) *Jou baré*, Fort-de-France: Editions Grif an tè; (1985) *Bitako-a*, Fort-de-France: Editions du GEREC; (1986) *Kod yanm*, Fort-de-France: Editions Kréyòl pou divini péyi-a; (1987) *Marisosé*, Fort-de-France: Presses Universitaires Créoles.

19. Both Poullet and Confiant have an ongoing concern with the promotion of basilectal Creole. Poullet was one of the driving forces behind a dictionary of Guadeloupean Creole. Confiant participated in producing a basilectal Creole newspaper, *Grif-an-tè*, which was published between 1977 and 1982, and is also a member of GEREC. Although both writers have a deep commitment to basilectal Creole, their approaches are somewhat different. Poullet finds his poetic language in the day-to-day speech of contemporary Guadeloupean rural dwellers, often constructing a poem from traditional proverbs and sayings. Confiant places the emphasis on creating a literary variety of Creole in preference to 'transcribing' everyday spoken basilectal Creole. As part of this project, he creates neologisms either by unearthing archaic lexis and giving it new meanings or by inventing new words in accordance with the rules of basilectal Creole as he perceives them.

20. Simone Schwarz-Bart (1972), *Pluie et vent sur Télumée miracle*, Paris: Seuil, and (1979), *Ti Jean L'horizon*, Paris: Seuil.

21. Patrick Chamoiseau (1986), *Chronique des sept misères*, Paris: Gallimard; (1988) *Solibo Magnifique*, Paris: Gallimard; (1988) *Au temps de l'antan*, Paris: Hatier; (1990) *Antan d'enfance*, Paris: Hatier; (1992) *Texaco*, Paris: Gallimard, and (1994) *Chemin-d'école* Paris: Hatier.

called into question, although it is doubtful whether either succeeds in subverting the dominant literary language.[22]

Theoretical and Practical Challenges

Constructing a Written Language

Literacy is gained in Martinique and Guadeloupe through the school system, which concerns itself solely with the promotion of Standard French. Creole may be heard in the school yard at break times but is resolutely barred from the classroom, in most cases. Reading and writing remain the almost exclusive domain of French. Few institutions exist which promote literacy in Creole, the exceptions being the Université Antilles-Guyane, a limited number of creolophone publications, which seek to promote an orthography developed by GEREC, and the Paris-based Radio Mango, which has attempted to encourage Creole literacy among the sizeable population of Antilleans living in France, 'la troisième île'. Guadeloupeans and Martinicans therefore learn to read and write French as children and then a tiny proportion of them learn to read and write Creole at a later stage.

With the French language's monopoly of written forms, all creolophone writers face the dilemma of how to write a language that is essentially oral. In the 1970s linguists tended to interpret this question in terms of developing an acceptable orthography, but in the following decade there was a growing awareness that orthography was only part of a much wider issue, as it became clear that the process of transcribing oral Creole could not be equated with the development of a written variety of the language. This is in itself a complex topic and space does not permit a detailed discussion here. However, the following may serve to illustrate some of the ways in which a transcription of Creole may only be a pre-stage to the development of a written code. In speech, intonation plays a crucial role in communicating grammatical meaning. For example, in speech, a statement and a question may have the same grammatical form. It is through differentiated intonation patterns that clarity is achieved. Said with a falling intonation, 'Bili pati' is a statement that 'Billy left', whereas said with a

22. For an analysis of Schwarz-Bart's use of Creole in her later novel, see Bernabé, *Fondal-natal*, vol. 1, pp. 237–73. With regard to Chamoiseau, see Marie-Christine Hazaël-Massieux (1988/1989), 'Chronique des sept misères: une littérature en français régional pour les Antilles', *Antilla Spécial*, 11, pp. 13–21, and (1988/1989), 'Solibo Magnifique, le roman de la parole', *Antilla Spécial*, 11, pp. 32–6.

rising intonation it becomes a question about whether Billy left. The written form thus needs to develop alternative ways to communicate meanings carried by intonation in the spoken variety. In this particular case, the elaboration of a punctuation system allows clarification. However, other resources specific to spoken Creole may pose greater problems for the writer. Recourse to onomatopoeia is common in the oral variety in order to communicate the manner in which an action takes place, hence there are few adverbs in Creole. In the written code, this onomatopoeic function is lost and the writer may need to develop a more or less new grammatical category. How to do this is not preordained and, in the initial stages of elaborating a written code, there may be as many solutions to this problem as there are writers. These choices have implications, as will be seen below.

Given the inevitable differences between speech and writing, the creolophone author does not have a ready-made written code at his or her disposal but is obliged to construct one. This burden lies heavily on those who have taken up the challenge. Raphaël Confiant's comments are instructive in this respect. He states that writing in French is a pleasure, whereas writing in Creole is work. He adds that he can play with the French language when he writes, as it has a pre-established written code, making French, paradoxically, a language of freedom. In contrast, he does not associate the process of writing in Creole with pleasure, because he is labouring to reshape, for literary purposes, a language which habitually designates a less abstract reality and is therefore limited in its ability to communicate concepts.[23]

The process of writing in Creole is also impeded by the prestige of written French. Given the contemporary sociolinguistic situation, there are no monolingual Creole writers in the Antilles; thus the resources of written French present a constant temptation to the Creole writer. The case of adverbs discussed above is interesting in this respect. Confiant has attempted to solve this problem by borrowing the French suffix '-ment' and appending it to Creole words to create adverbs: for example, taking the onomatopoeic Creole 'blip', which denotes a sudden action, to construct the adverb 'blipman' (suddenly). Arguably, this may be viewed as an instance of the decreolization and artificialization of written Creole.[24] This example points not only to the temptation of written French, but also to the challenges and risks involved in constructing a written variety of Creole.

23. Raphaël Confiant (1992), 'La bicyclette créole ou la voiture française', *Le Monde*, 6 November.

24. For a critique of Confiant's creation of adverbs, see Guy Hazaël-Massieux's introduction to Confiant's *Marisosé*, pp. 11–12.

Orthography

The existence of a literary tradition presupposes an interaction between literary works and audience, but this dynamic relationship is crucially absent from the present-day Antillean cultural scene. As the evidence above suggests, the French language's monopoly of the written domain has contributed to this situation, and arising from its hegemony are two practical considerations for the creolophone writer. The first of these is the question of selecting an orthography acceptable to the reading public. The choice of a writing system has an ethnographic aspect, which is of importance in the Lesser Antilles, where negotiations between competing representations of identity, at both personal and national level, are particularly acute. Accordingly, the selection of an orthography is in no way a neutral or unproblematic process.

Until the 1970s, creolophone writers tended to employ an etymologizing orthography – that is to say, an orthography very close to French. This etymologizing orthography was not codified in any way; rather, each writer represented the Creole variety of their choice in a personal and often inconsistent manner. This practice did not necessarily reflect their political persuasions, but rather the unconscious belief that orthography was not a legitimate domain in which to affirm the sense of a distinct Antillean identity. The 1970s were marked by two fundamental changes: first, political militants chose to define their interests through their use of Creole in domains that were previously reserved for French, and, second, language militants employed Creole as a symbol of cultural and political distinctiveness. Among the latter group, the politicization of Creole led to the development of a standardized and codified orthography of Creole, which served to mark its maximum deviance from French. The first instance of this was the pamphlet *Kèk prinsip pou ékri kréyòl* (Some Principles for Writing Creole), which was published in 1975 by the Guadeloupean linguist, Dany Bebel-Gisler. In this creolophone work, which was received with enthusiasm by many of the political militants, she attempted to popularize a phonological orthography. This is an orthography based on the principle that each sound of a language is consistently represented by an individual letter, with no one letter representing more than one sound and with no silent letters. Her proposal was soon followed by another writing system, designed by GEREC in 1976, which followed a similar approach. This latter system enshrined the principle of maximum deviancy, and thus included such letters as 'k' and 'w', which rarely appear in French orthography. The inclusion of these letters was highly symbolic as they functioned to represent the Creole language's autonomy from French.

These attempts to promote a standard Creole orthography have met with little success beyond nationalist circles. Indeed, popular indifference to these orthographies reflects the gap between the aspirations of the political and linguistic militants, on the one hand, and those of the population at large, on the other. Research carried out by Marie-Christine and Guy Hazaël-Massieux in Guadeloupe in the mid-1980s suggests that, in general, Antilleans reject the GEREC orthography, as they find it neither attractive nor easy to read, with the result that it meets neither their aesthetic nor their practical needs.[25] Prudent suggests that there is, however, a growing use of written Creole, but that this flourishes in a limited number of domains, associated with popular culture: advertising, cartoons and *zouk* music. Here the orthography remains for the most part unsystematic, but is immediately accessible to the public.[26] This raises the question of whether the general population's sense of Creole precludes any acceptable formal system of rules governing orthography at the present time, and whether the attempt to do so in creolophone literature will meet with resistance.

Literary Tradition and Genre

Although creolophone literature was represented as a potential medium for the expression of a distinct local identity by certain intellectuals during the 1960s and 1970s, this promise remains largely unfulfilled at the close of the twentieth century. This situation is due to creolophone literature's position between two poles of constant attraction: on the one hand, creolophone oral literature (oraliture) and, on the other hand, French-language literature.

As noted above, the Creole language is associated with a long tradition of popular local culture which was shaped by the violent and unequal relationships of plantation society. This oraliture has its own genres, such as the folktale, the song, the proverb and the riddle, which are seen as being in opposition to the dominant culture. These oral genres promote a specifically Antillean world-view through a distinct performance context. Taking the example of the folktale, this is dominated by three

---

25. For further details of this survey, see Marie-Christine Hazaël-Massieux (1993), *Ecrire en créole: oralité et écriture aux Antilles,* Paris: L'Harmattan, pp. 89–107.

26. Lambert-Félix Prudent (1989), 'Ecrire le créole à la Martinique: Norme et conflit sociolinguistique', in Ralph Ludwig, ed., *Les Créoles français entre l'oral et l'écrit,* Tübingen: Narr, pp. 73–5.

major themes, which reflect plantation society: ruse, hunger and revolt. Traditionally, the tales are told outside at night, in a rural setting, with the audience encircling the storyteller. From the outset, the audience plays an active role, as they are invited to participate through an opening call and response. The tales have a limited number of archetypal characters, whose anarchic and amoral behaviour reflects the nature of plantation society, and the tales are often set in a magical non-time and undescribed place, which creates a sense of detachment, enabling the audience to laugh at the injustices of life.[27] The tales have four functions: to give the community a medium of self-expression, to store memories, to entertain and to voice resistance.[28] In the case of riddles, this genre traditionally has played two important roles. They are often used to preface storytelling, as they help to create a feeling of solidarity among the listeners. They have also been part of a child's education to engender a particular way of relating to and understanding the natural environment, and also to bind different generations of the community together, as the riddles were often posed by respected elders.[29]

These oraliture genres are thus closely associated with a rural way of life, which is rapidly disappearing, due to a high level of urbanization and the diminishing importance of the agricultural sector for the islands' economies. Accordingly, the communities and customs that sustained traditional oraliture are diminishing and, with them, the genres themselves. This has created pressure on written creolophone literature to take up the baton, in order to 'save' a disappearing world. However, if creolophone writers look to oraliture for genres, they may run the risk of increasing their writing's dependence on spoken narrative modes. Creolophone literature may fail to develop an appropriate level of autonomy from oraliture, and transcription rather than literature will be produced. A cursory glance at the folktales collected and transcribed by ethnographers serves to illustrate the deadening effect that transcription can have, as many performative aspects central to storytelling are lost. For example, the storyteller's use of tempo, call and response, gesture and mimicry of

27. Information about the folktale is summarized from Ruth Pevsner (1993), 'People create stories create people: history, language, content and performance in the oral Créole folk tale in Martinique', unpublished PhD thesis, University of Manchester, pp. 102–72.

28. Patrick Chamoiseau and Raphaël Confiant (1991), *Lettres créoles: Tracées antillaises et continentales de la littérature 1635–1975*, Paris: Hatier, pp. 62–3.

29. For a literary representation of this, see the relationship between José and M. Médouze in Joseph Zobel (1950), *La Rue Cases-Nègres*, Paris: Présence Africaine, pp. 52–4.

the characters' ways of moving or speaking tends either to be defused or effaced by the act of transcription.[30]

The second pole of attraction for creolophone literature is French-language literature, which greatly overshadows it in terms of prestige and publishing success. At present, creolophone literature has received little recognition, as it has failed to challenge what Bernabé describes as the 'narrative monopoly' of the French language in the Antilles and is thus condemned to social inexistence. A visit to Martinique's largest bookshop, La Librairie Antillaise, confirms this. The ground floor is dominated by metropolitan literature and foreign literature in translation and in the original, with one small corner devoted to francophone literature, among which a tiny number of creolophone works can occasionally be found. Unsurprisingly, the first floor is almost completely devoted to French-language educational textbooks.

Confiant notes that a literature's autonomy is signalled by the practice of intertextual reference to other works belonging to the same tradition and argues that French literature did not exist until the practice of referring to Graeco-Latin literature ended. He therefore finds it highly significant that creolophone literature flaunts its dependence on metropolitan litera-ture, citing the example of Marbot's *Les Bambous: Fables de La Fontaine travesties en patois créole par un vieux commandeur*,[31] and concludes that at present creolophone literature only exists through reference to a pre-existing French-language literature. Historically, francophone literature of the Antilles has been inspired by European models. The same seems to be true of much creolophone literature, and thus the use of the Creole language has in no way guaranteed the expression of a distinct local identity, as was originally hoped by some. Indeed, the borrowing of metropolitan genres in both literatures has, to a certain extent, called into question the relevance of Antillean literature to the local reality and imagination.[32] A further challenge to the creolophone writer is thus to invent genres that engage with local perceptions.

---

30. For examples of this, see Ina Césaire and Joëlle Laurent (1976), *Contes de mort et de vie aux Antilles*, Paris: Nubia, and Ina Césaire (1989), *Contes de nuits et de jours aux Antilles*, Paris: Edition Caribéennes.

31. François Marbot (1976), *Les Bambous, Fables de La Fontaine travesties en patois martiniquais par un vieux commandeur*, Paris: Casterman. First published in 1846.

32. Raphaël Confiant (1997), 'Kréyòl palé, kréyòl matjé: Analyse des significations littéraires, linguistiques et socio-historiques de l'écrit créolophone de 1750 à 1990 aux Antilles, en Guyane et en Haïti', thèse du doctorat en langues et cultures régionales, Université des Antilles-Guyane, pp. 82–99.

Conclusions

In Guadeloupe and Martinique, the future of creolophone literature may differ from that of spoken Creole. Spoken Creole continues to play a central part in daily life, and has entered new domains. For example, it enjoys great popularity on the radio, and in certain television programmes that reflect popular oral culture. Here, the spoken language flourishes because it draws on its own resources. Radio and television have the advantages of being recordable mass media and thus the process of modernization may help to sustain spoken Creole rather than hasten its demise. At present, creolophone literature remains largely marginal to the preoccupations of Guadeloupeans and Martinicans. They perceive it as difficult to read, since the orthography has an estranging effect for many of them. Also, the written code seems artifical, particularly as writers have sometimes looked to written French when developing a written variety of Creole. There has been recognition of this among some writers who, in the past, were committed, above all, to political independence for the two islands and the promotion of a creolophone literature as symbolic of movement in this direction. This was a goal for Confiant in the 1970s and early 1980s. Since then, he has not published any substantial literary works in Creole, but has enjoyed success as a writer whose continued commitment to Creole culture is expressed through francophone novels. This, in turn, has repercussions for those who read Martinican and Guade-loupean literature, be it creolophone or francophone. As readers, perhaps, we should remember that the literature written in both islands has always been shaped by the relationship between Martinican and Guadeloupean Creoles, on the one hand, and French, on the other. Indeed, this history has contributed to the distinctiveness of Martinican and Guadeloupean literature.

8

Collective Narrative Voice in Three Novels by Edouard Glissant

Celia Britton

In the introduction to *Le Discours antillais*, Glissant describes the Caribbean Overseas Departments as being trapped in a contradictory fantasy of assimilation, which cuts them off from any real knowledge of themselves as a community. On the one hand, the numerous uprisings which occurred from the seventeenth century onwards not only failed in their immediate aims but incurred such brutal repression that 'all that happened was a progressive abdication, more and more marked as time went on, of the collective spirit and the common will that alone enable a people to survive as a people'.[1] On the other hand, the abolition of slavery and then departmentalization offered at least some of the people the 'solution' of an illusory participation in metropolitan French society and culture:

> After the 'liberation' of 1848, the struggle for freedom in the French Caribbean is replaced by an urge to claim French citizenship. The colonizers launch their protégés into political life. The middle class, greedy for honours and respectability, is happy to go along with this game, which brings them jobs and status. Up until the 1946 law making Martinique a 'département', which formed the apotheosis of this whole process, *the French Caribbeans were thus led to deny their collective identity, in order to win an illusory equality as individuals.*[2]

This absence of a collective sense of identity is one of the fundamental social problems of the islands, and is both a cause and an effect of what Glissant sees as their political passivity and stagnation. In this situation, he argues, 'cultural action' assumes a particular importance; writers have a significant role to play in trying to develop a collective consciousness

---

1. Edouard Glissant (1981), *Le Discours antillais*, Paris: Seuil, p. 15. All translations mine.

2. *Le Discours antillais*, p. 17. My italics.

in the people.[3] He takes it for granted throughout his work that Caribbean literature – unlike that of Europe – is inescapably political, and that it is a collective practice: 'the words of the Caribbean artist do not therefore stem from an obsession with expressing his inner being; that being is inseparable from the evolution of the community'.[4] In this he differs from the more individualist stance of many of his predecessors. Michael Dash argues that Glissant's writing represents a turning-point in French Caribbean literature, which previously centred on:

> The great themes of Romanticism – the quest for identity, the idea of originality and the search for origins, the glorification of uniqueness and the creator considered as privileged being, as 'bestower of order'. In rejecting the temptation of this mystification, Glissant's work stands out as a recent and subversive phenomenon in French Caribbean literature.[5]

It is, then, the writer's responsibility to help the Martinican people achieve a sense of themselves as a political and historical subject – a community that can act in its own name. For this to be effective, the collective subject must be constituted in the actual structures of the literary text. That is, rather than merely being represented thematically, it must occupy the position of narrating subject, i.e. a collective narrative voice. However – and this is the whole point – this voice does not (yet) exist in social reality: the fiction has to create it. There is for Glissant an exact parallel between the political and the literary projects, not only because they are working towards the same goal but also because they are both in the situation of trying to bring into existence something as yet unformed:

> A politics and a poetics of liberation can only emerge, they cannot be prompted. The first collective word of this poetics has still to be uttered. And despite so many heroic and obscure battles fought by the Martinican people, the initial and initiating act of this politics has still to be performed.[6]

The problems associated with the construction of such a collective narrative voice involve a number of different areas. It will, for instance, be by definition incompatible with a conventional realist framework, since it cannot be represented as an existing reality: it can have no fictional referent in the usual sense. It will also, as an element in a literary text,

3. Ibid., pp. 208–19.
4. Ibid., p. 439.
5. J. Michael Dash (1990), 'Le Roman de nous', *Carbet*, 10, p. 22.
6. Glissant, *Le Discours antillais*, p. 93.

have to negotiate a relationship with orality. On the one hand, this may mean recovering and re-presenting the unselfconsciously collective oral tradition of folktales, which, however, according to Glissant, survives only in a fragmented, marginalized and trivialized form in contemporary Martinican culture (as folklore for tourists, for example). More generally, the community's speech is seen as the site of its greatest vitality and potential renewal, and thus as the only possible basis to build on; the writer therefore has to find a 'synthesis' of 'the solitary nature of writing and the sharing in the common song'.[7]

Perhaps most important of all, however, is the political and also ethical question of the writer's legitimacy – what gives him or her the right to speak in the community's name? In saying 'we/us' ('nous'), Glissant may appear to be laying claim to a unity that does not exist. It is therefore essential that the collective narrative voice does not impose a false, coercive uniformity; rather, it must be sufficiently fluid and flexible to include all the different voices within the community. And, if it is to do this without merely collapsing into vagueness, it must be able to situate these differences in relation to each other. Here, in other words, the literary problem of narrative voice connects with Glissant's main philosophical concept of 'relation'. Relation is a form of combined solidarity and openness, a promotion of 'the Diverse' and 'the necessity . . . of accepting the Other's difference'.[8] It alters the concept of community from a monolithic entity to a diverse, non-hierarchical collectivity, a constantly changing matrix within which identities, languages and narratives circulate. Thus in *Poétique de la relation* Glissant writes: 'Relation does not relay or connect items that are already in principle assimilable or comparable with each other, because it is constantly differentiating them and deflecting them from any kind of totality – since its work is always to change each of the elements which constitutes it, and thus to change the link which forms between them and which itself changes them again.'[9]

As far as literature is concerned, this means that 'Glissant's project', as Dash puts it in 'Le Roman de nous', 'can be seen as a sustained effort to dismantle the poetics of the singular and to re-establish the circuits that make the "we" possible'.[10] And establishing these 'circuits' implies that literature's task is to elucidate the relations between individual subjects, their community, and what lies outside it. This is what Glissant

7. Ibid., p. 256.
8. Ibid.
9. Edouard Glissant (1990), *Poétique de la relation*, Paris: Seuil, p. 186.
10. Dash, 'Le Roman de nous', p. 30.

calls 'the novel of the implication of I in We, of I in the Other, of We in We', and he goes on to say: 'Relation outlines a frame for this new episode. People tell me that the novel of "We" is impossible, that it will always have to embody the evolution of individuals. It's a risk well worth running.'[11] It is this 'risk' that I now want to trace through three of his novels, *Malemort*,[12] *La Case du commandeur*,[13] and *Mahagony*,[14] for it is in these texts, rather than in his first two novels or the most recent one, that the problematic of the 'we' can be seen to be working itself out most clearly, in a process whereby the theoretical position developed in *Le Discours antillais* and *Poétique de la relation* is gradually realized in the fiction.

Malemort is usually seen as the most uncompromisingly bitter of Glissant's novels in its representation of Martinican society as disunited, alienated and impotent. Glissant himself has described it as recording 'that which there (here) is relentlessly falling apart . . . We are endlessly disappearing, victims of the friction between worlds.'[15] Its structure is remarkably disjointed: the thirteen chapters recount, not in any chronological order, separate episodes taking place between 1788 and 1974 and tenuously linked only by the recurrence of certain characters. They are also extremely heterogeneous as discourses: one chapter is a poem, one is a satirical monologue, one appears to be quasi-autobiographical, one creates a kind of non-realist mythical discourse, one reproduces the 'delirium' of the character Médellus, and so on. Running through them all, however, there is a persistent, if rather desperate, collective narrative voice: a 'we' that seems to be trying to link everything together. Bernadette Cailler analyses the inauguration of this voice at the end of the first chapter and shows how from then on 'the "*nous*" will invade the fabric of the text, not so much alongside a heterodiegetic omniscient narrator or with a voice in the first person as more or less secretly infiltrated, installed within the different discourses'.[16] This is not an impersonal narration: it

11. Glissant, *Le Discours antillais*, p. 153.
12. Edouard Glissant (1975), *Malemort*, Paris: Seuil.
13. Edouard Glissant (1981), *La Case du commandeur*, Paris: Seuil.
14. Edouard Glissant (1987), *Mahagony*, Paris: Seuil.
15. Glissant, *Le Discours antillais*, pp.14–15.
16. Bernadette Cailler (1988), *Les Conquérants de la nuit nue; Edouard Glissant et l'H(h)istoire antillaise*, Tübingen: Gunther Narr, p. 163. Elinor Miller produces a rather different analysis of the collective voice, seeing it as operating in some chapters and some parts of chapters, but not in others (see Elinor Miller (1979), 'Narrative techniques in Edouard Glissant's *Malemort*', *The French Review*, 53:2, pp. 226–7). But to allocate the others to an omniscient narrator, simply on the basis of the non-occurrence of the actual pronoun 'nous', seems to me to miss the point – which is, as I shall argue, that 'nous' is all-inclusive and non-focalized, if not omniscient.

has many features of colloquial speech, so that it sounds like a distinct 'voice', it addresses both other characters and the reader, and it speaks in the first person plural. But it is never clear who 'we' are. At the beginning of the second chapter, the reader is given a list of individual characters included in 'we': 'It seemed to us (Epiphane . . . Colentroc . . . monsieur Lesprit . . . , etc.)'.[17] But not only does this include an indefinite number of 'those unnamed who on that August morning were waiting by the closed sea for a bit of salt and cassava' – and a pig! – but it is also clear that the list is merely a sample, not an exhaustive count; a different incomplete list is given at the beginning of the second paragraph.[18] The actions and thoughts attributed to 'us' are also, here, expressed in metaphorical terms, which do not help in specifying who 'we' are: 'and to see ourselves milling around ourselves like troops on the edge of a battle: fighting only at our margins without guns or bullets, but occasionally collecting our dead under the all too real fire of the other – and to see ourselves happy laughing our tears, our shaven skulls sweating white death'.[19] In fact, the question of the identity of 'we' is posed in the text precisely as an unanswerable question: 'we, enormous question that gives no answer'.[20] In other words, 'we' has no determinate referent; the voice that speaks in the text is plural and inclusive, but also completely undefined and undifferentiated.

All the named characters are referred to both in the third person and in the first person plural, as part of 'we'. Indeed, the three main characters – Dlan, Médellus and Silacier – seem to have been chosen at random to represent everyone: 'and after all why not those three, themselves us, themselves mad'.[21] 'Themselves us', they are both 'them' and 'us', both narrators and narrated. The language they use is equally ambiguous, both separate and communal; Dlan, for instance, is described as: 'already talking to us in his (our) particular language, and so already beginning not to be understood by the two others who nevertheless (Silacier, Médellus) were, are part of us (us, part of them) and who each talks in his (our) particular language'.[22] Thus although the 'we' is beginning to counteract the splintered, dispersed existence of the community, it is still a very inchoate, unformed entity in which the relations between those who make it up have not yet been clarified. The same section of *Malemort* in fact alludes to the historical development of a collective consciousness from the first

17. Glissant, *Malemort*, p. 22.
18. Ibid., p. 23.
19. Ibid.
20. Ibid., p. 34.
21. Ibid., p. 23.
22. Ibid., p. 34.

moment of revolt – the slave escaping into the forest: 'when "we" (undifferentiated, intact, humiliated, thing and soul) escaped into the woods without
perhaps knowing what was driving it on, and yet more alive, more ardently
dead and victorious than it ever would be'[23] – in a way which suggests
that at this stage there is no individual consciousness and no explicit
awareness of why the individual is acting in this way – although the
ambivalence of the attributes ('intact'/'humiliated', 'thing/soul', 'alive/
dead/victorious') prevents us from undervaluing this state. But the text
continues: 'and when 'we' . . . learnt to say I, to think I, to start (continue?)
its infinite aggregation, its miniscule totality' – and so seems to equate
the beginnings of an individual subjectivity with the capacity for forming
together into a collectivity: 'to start . . . its infinite aggregation'.[24] The
narrative voice, however, never reaches this stage of differentiation in
Malemort.[25] The ideal of collective unity in difference is present only as
the utopian dream of the mad Médellus, who imagines 'a single song full
of different voices'.[26]

   La Case du commandeur represents Glissant's second attempt at 'the
novel of We', and it adopts a similar narrative position, except that the
short central section, 'Mitan du temps', has an entirely impersonal narration. In the other two sections, however, the 'we' is even more prominent
than in *Malemort*. *La Case du commandeur* opens and closes with direct
references to the problem of building a collective identity. Firstly, we read:
'We who perhaps, when all is said and done, were never going to make
up that single body by which we might begin to enter into our portion of
land'.[27] And the final sentence of the narrative is: 'We, who so impatiently
gather together these disjointed I's [ces moi disjoints], in the stormy
upheavals in which we flail around, digging up time as well, time that
falls and rises unceasingly; determined to contain the anxiety of each body
within this difficult darkness of us [contenir la part inquiète de chaque
corps dans cette obscurité difficile de nous].'[28]

23. Ibid., p. 23.

24. Ibid,

25. Jean-Yves Debreuille sees the narrative voice, in its unstructured plurality, as staging
the impossibility of order: 'a "we" which far from assigning, ordering or hierarchizing,
fuses together with this lack of differentiation . . . Moreover, its own discourse is by no
means unified, it expands in the process of describing, and takes over other ways of
speaking' (Jean-Yves Debreuille (1992), 'Le langage désancré de *Malemort*'', in Yves-
Alain Favre, ed., *Horizons d'Edouard Glissant*, Biarritz: J & D Editeurs, pp. 324–5).

26. Glissant, Malemort, p. 200.

27. Glissant, *La Case du commandeur*, p. 15.

28. Ibid., p. 239.

La Case du commandeur differs from *Malemort* in that it conveys a stronger sense of historical continuity; instead of the abruptly discontinuous episodes of the latter, we move steadily backwards in time, retracing a family history back through four generations, each one occupying one chapter of the first section. The third section then follows the life of the main character, Marie Celat, straightforwardly from 1945, where it left off in Glissant's first novel *La Lézarde*, to the present time of 1979. Perhaps because of this, the novel conveys a greater sense of hope and possible progress; although collective consciousness is still seen as far from achieved and still the major problem, the struggle towards it is at least more vigorous: for instance, in the phrase which is repeated until it becomes a kind of refrain running through the text: 'disjointed I's each of us struggling towards this we [Moi disjoints qui nous acharnions chacun vers ce nous]'.[29]

In one of the final scenes, Marie Celat, who has been more or less forcibly taken to a mental hospital, escapes, together with Chérubin, another inmate. The journey he takes her on through the forest is also a psychological journey, achieved through language ('They crossed the road and plunged into the thickets: the thickets of Chérubin's suddenly fluent speech just as much as of the maze of leaves and roots'.[30]) The new form of narrative which this produces is also first person plural; rather than 'we', however, Chérubin says 'not-yet-us' ('non-nous-encore'): 'Not-yet-us haven't finished . . . looking at not-yet-us wandering about'.[31] After six occurrences of this, however, it suddenly changes to: 'but look not-yet-us-but-already [non-nous-encore-mais-déjà] . . . it's not-yet-us-but-already rising up from the filthy earth at the entrance to the offices do you understand what Chérubin is saying . . . it's not-yet-us-but-already rising up from the office to kiss the earth'.[32] The 'mad' narrative of Chérubin, in other words, illuminates the status of the collective subject, revealing it as both as yet unconstituted and already existing on the margins of 'normal' consciousness.[33] The lack of definition of 'we' can thus

29. Ibid., p. 42.
30. Ibid., p. 230.
31. Ibid., pp. 230–1.
32. Ibid., pp. 231–2.
33. In answer to a question about the relation of *La Case du commandeur*'s narrative style to 'verbal delirium', Glissant stresses the latter's significance as a mode of understanding and enlightenment: 'Verbal delirium is a desperate gesture towards a syntax, a rational system, a relationship with the world, whose progress one tries, if not to control, at least to experience as a continuum. Is not that – minus the desperation – the position of the writer in our countries?' (*CARE* (1983), 'Entretien du *CARE* avec Edouard Glissant', *CARE,* 10, p. 25).

become a positive force; its extreme elasticity provides a point of view that is not limited to any one character or period of time but moves around from one to another. It constitutes a form of narrative that is different both from impersonal omniscience – because it is often overtly personal and subjective – and from the usual type of focalized narrative, which is limited to a single circumscribed point of view. As Cailler comments, 'If the narrator is omniscient, as he is in *La Case du commandeur*, this omniscience is of a truly communal character, not tied to individualistic categories of the subject.'[34] As such, its use also creates a different representation of intersubjective relations between the individual characters, suggesting that people's most intimate feelings are known to the community. The narrative, in other words, has a kind of communal knowledge of individuals, even if how it is acquired remains obscure – for instance: 'But Augustus had already made his declaration . . . , and (we knew all its details as though from the leaves of the surrounding tamarind trees) this is how'[35] – and this effect is created simply by the use of 'we' as a narrative voice.[36] Knowledge also involves participation and a sense of responsibility: 'we' know, for instance, how Marie Celat is experiencing her nervous breakdown, and link her feelings to 'ourselves':

> Through an obscure need we established, those of us who were hovering on the edge of this misfortune, a common measure between Marie Celat's suffering and the uncertainties that wore us out day after day: each of us saying privately to ourselves that with the ending of her torment there would also come, for us, an end to that unbearable contentment which, we already knew without yet knowing anything, was the only advantage we got from allowing ourselves to be controlled. So we never stopped hoping that she would get over it and climb up out of the dark.[37]

In this sense the strength and flexibility of the collective voice are more clearly present than in *Malemort*. But *La Case du commandeur*, ending with a restatement of 'this difficult darkness of us',[38] has still not really

34. Cailler, *Les Conquérants de la nuit nue*, p. 166.
35. Glissant, *La Case du commandeur*, p. 90.
36. Barbara Webb makes the point that by this kind of presentation Glissant is working against the Western tradition 'that tends to isolate the individual from the community. The source of [Marie Celat's] alienation is not conflict with her community but the lack of community. The "we" narrator stands as a constant reminder of this absence' (Barbara Webb (1992), *Myth and History in Caribbean Fiction*, Amherst: University of Massachusetts Press, p. 123).
37. Glissant, *La Case du commandeur*, p. 225.
38. Ibid., p. 239.

begun to work on the 'implication of I in We' which, as we have seen, is the basis for 'relation'.

This, however, is the principle structural concern of *Mahagony*, which in this respect represents a distinct break with the two previous novels. It is formally more complex, and it abandons the anonymous 'we' in favour of a narrative divided into separate sections, which each have a named individual narrator. The most dominant of these – the narrator of five of the eighteen sections – is Mathieu, who has already featured as a character in all of Glissant's previous novels. But, in now assuming the status of narrator, Mathieu uses his new autonomy to criticize the author who had originally created and used him: in other words, Glissant himself, whom Mathieu calls 'the author', 'the chronicler' or 'my biographer', and whom he accuses of 'endowing me with an exemplary quality, the mechanical simplicity of which was quite alien to me'.[39]

This odd device of a character supposedly escaping from his author's control enables Glissant to present the reader with a critique of his own earlier work.[40] One major aspect of this critique is the collective voice as used in *Malemort* and *La Case du commandeur*. Thus Mathieu complains that 'The author took a lingering pleasure in merging the villagers, their descendants, their faces, into one single indistinct and over-powerful identity.'[41] The author, in other words, is guilty of obliterating the difference whose recognition is the necessary basis of 'relation' (as opposed to what Glissant calls 'the pseudo-collectivisms in which the We has diluted the I'.[42]) The undifferentiated collective voice is now seen as a kind of bad faith, a 'temptation' to 'merge myself into a beneficial us which would equally have allowed me to obliterate myself in it',[43] whereas honesty requires that he retain his separateness and acknowledge that much of his narration is simply of no interest to the community he would be claiming to speak on behalf of – in this case, an 'episode which had apparently made little impression on that We that I sometimes wanted to express or to experience'.[44] No one voice, in other words, can express the totality of

39. Glissant, *Mahagony*, p. 18.

40. In the words of Georges Desportes: 'So this becomes Glissant's confrontation with himself, face to face with his writings and his narratives, through and within recreated characters who assume responsibility for themselves and rehabilitate themselves for us and for history' (Georges Desportes (1988), 'L'illusion vraie de l'art chez Edouard Glissant', *Antilla*, 272, p. 11).

41. Glissant, *Mahagony*, p. 33.

42. Glissant, *Le Discours antillais*, p. 153.

43. Glissant, *Mahagony*, p. 85.

44. Ibid., p. 86.

the community's experience, and to attempt to do so is now seen as a kind of authorial arrogance. Instead, the solution is to have a number of narrators, each making a particular and different contribution to the narrative.

The narrative in question, moreover, is not wholly containable within the boundaries of *Mahagony* alone. Some of the events related here have already figured in Glissant's previous novels; but what *Mahagony* does is to show these earlier representations as incomplete and one-sided because of their unitary narrative point of view.[45] *Mahagony* thus relates intertextually to the rest of Glissant's fiction, retelling the same stories but from a different point of view, enlarging and relativizing their original significance. Mathieu says: 'I went back to the chronicler's text . . . The chronicle had wound the first thread of the story, but still could not account for the whole network: other words would have to join in the work.'[46] The clearest example of this is perhaps the story of Beautemps, who disappeared into the forest and eluded capture for seven years after attacking the white master who had raped his woman, Adoline. This is a central incident in *Malemort*, but the new version of it in *Mahagony* introduces two previously unmentioned characters: Adélaïde, who tells the story, and Artémise. These are both women who were secretly in love with Beautemps; but Adélaïde's portrait of him is distinctly less heroic than that given in *Malemort*. Moreover, her narrative is supplemented in *Mahagony* by that of Papa Longoué (another character who appears in all the novels), who, we now 'discover', was secretly in love with Adoline and therefore has yet another perspective on the story.

If the character Mathieu has now become the 'author' of *Mahagony*, Glissant has conversely become a character/narrator in his own book,[47] and as such has his own section of narrative (entitled 'He who comments'). Marie Celat refers to him as the 'friend' who has previously (i.e. in *La*

---

45. '*Mahagony* is written by Mathieu, Hégésippe, Eudoxie, Longoué, Adélaïde, Odibert, Marie Celat and Ida in succession: characters spaced out along the road of time, who will redefine their living space by making individual corrections to the over-schematically or confusedly typical figures originally created by the writer-poet in the course of the gestation of his various novels' (Desportes, 'L'illusion vraie de l'art chez Edouard Glissant', p. 11).

46. Glissant, *Mahagony*, p. 16.

47. The novel itself thus accomplishes the manoeuvre which Barthes recommends to the critic: 'the critical enterprise will thus consist in turning the documentary figure of the author *inside out*, to become a fictional figure, unidentifiable, irresponsible, caught in the plurality of his own text' (Roland Barthes (1970), *S/Z*, Paris: Seuil, p. 217).

Case du commandeur) written her story,[48] just as she comments on Mathieu's role as author.[49] The various narrators, in other words, are all on the same level of textual reality and are aware of each other's existence. The text as a whole has become a dialogic matrix of voices, in which no single author or narrator has a privileged position.

This, however, is not immediately apparent in the case of Mathieu, who claims some kind of overall control over the other narrators. It is he, he tells us, who has consulted the sources and put together the different partial accounts to arrive at the full picture; the other narratives are, as it were, embedded in and dependent upon his. He stresses his ambition to be detached, objective and scientific; and this initial ambition, while it is humbler than the previous all-encompassing 'we', is nevertheless still an assumption of control and an imposition of order.

But it soon fails. The hierarchy of voices that he had hoped to set up falls apart and he finds himself 'compromised' by the others, rather than being able to reduce them to his own order: 'I ended up compromised by these successive languages that I had sought to clarify. I was one speaker among others, full of a juice whose quality I was incapable of judging.'[50] Thus both Glissant as author and Mathieu as principal narrator are challenged and undermined by the plurality of the narration. Neither can keep their own voices 'pure' and supreme; both have to enter on equal terms into a dialogue of mixed voices; so, Mathieu concludes, 'the search for *order* yielded to *contamination*'.[51]

A key verb that recurs in *Mahagony* – and which Glissant elsewhere links to 'relation' – is 'to relay' ('relayer'). It describes the process of handing on information from one person to another, but also that of handing over control of the narrative, and, as 'se relayer', of working together to produce a collective but non-uniform narrative that will emerge out of the incomplete individual contributions. The narrators take it for granted that their story will be continued by others. Hégésippe, for instance, the slave who secretly learns to write and has to stop when he goes blind, buries his manuscript underground but still assumes that it will be found, read and completed:

What follows is no longer my story, forthwith I will dig the earth and place the summary in its night with my eyes for ever until discovered. My work is

48. Glissant, *Mahagony*, p. 173.
49. Ibid., p. 182.
50. Ibid., p. 31.
51. Ibid., p. 32. My italics.

done, in the name of the Most Holy Virgin of the needy, I send it forth, leaving
it to chance or the opening of time, for the fortunate one who will come across
it. My eyes have finished closing.[52]

This pattern of handing on the story is repeated throughout, most explicitly
in the third part of the novel, where, first of all, Marie Celat explains why
she is unable to continue with the story and must hand over to her daughter
Ida;[53] then Ida hands over to Mathieu ('I feel that what follows can only
be told by my father Mathieu',[54]) who in turn hands over to the 'author':
'What follows can only be my author's commentary. I am letting him
take my place.'[55] The cumulative effect of this process is that the events
and characters of the stories become almost less relevant than the intersubjective structures of narrators that support and relay them; Nathaniel
Wing comments: 'The importance of an original content and of the point
of origin of a narrative is obliterated in these novels in favour of *relation*,
in the double sense of an act of *handing on* ['relayer'] multiple versions
of a narrative and of a *link* established between these diverse versions by
an interpreter, whether reader or character.'[56]

The structure of *Mahagony* is superficially far more familiar and
conventional than the 'we' narrative, in so far as it fits unproblematically
into the category of novels narrated from a number of different individual
points of view, a category that includes such well-known texts as Sartre's
Chemins de la liberté, for instance, or Gide's *Les Faux-monnayeurs*. But
there is an important difference between novels like these and *Mahagony*.
For the European novel, the multiplicity of viewpoints is motivated by
the divergences between them, and the overall effect is one of ironic
disjunction arising from the way in which the different narrators undermine
one another: the main point of Gide's *La Porte étroite*, for instance, is
that Jérôme misunderstands Alissa's feelings for him, and the reader
realizes this through having privileged access to their separate accounts.
But, in *Mahagony*, the plurality of voices is not disjunctive: their differences do not undercut or cancel each other out, nor, as we have seen, are
the voices isolated from each other. The result is a kind of stereoscopic,
multidimensional, open-ended representation of an interwoven fictional

52. Ibid., p. 70.
53. Ibid., p. 187.
54. Ibid., p. 211.
55. Ibid., p. 227.
56. Nathaniel Wing (1992), 'Ecriture et relation dans les romans d'Edouard Glissant',
in Favre, ed., *Horizons d'Edouard Glissant*, p. 297.

reality.[57] Moreover, towards the end of the novel there is the suggestion that, in fact, there is no end; the intertextual network or 'trame' will go on expanding indefinitely, extending beyond the existing corpus of Glissant's own novels to meet up with other stories and form new combinations. Mathieu refers to 'that moment when every story dilates in the air of the world, perhaps to be diluted in it, sometimes to reinforce another network ['trame'] which has appeared far off in the distance'.[58]

Thus *Mahagony*, in basing itself on the notions of the relay and the 'trame', comes closer than the previous novels to the ideal of the dynamic, internally differentiated collective consciousness. The relays have to be clarified before we can effectively know ourselves and act together; Mathieu describes discussions with his friends as being like the different lights coming on and going out in the countryside as secret messages to the fugitive on the run: 'They went out one after another, so that we never saw the whole field of stars spread out over the night. *Our lamps light up in turn, they have yet to burn all together [Nos lumignons se relaient, il leur reste à brûler ensemble]*.'[59] In other words, the collective voice is always a multiplicity of individual voices whose unity can only be based on the relations between them, relations here materialized as narratives. Glissant underlines the connections between 'relation', 'relative', 'relay' – and also 'related' in the sense of 'told': 'Relation . . . is given in a narrative . . . But, since what it relates does not in reality derive from an absolute, it is revealed to be the totality of relatives placed in contact with each other and told.'[60] In the same vein, *Mahagony* gives a final restatement of the relay, as Mathieu writes on the last page:

Thus have I traced the curve of this story of mingled voices . . . If we mean to record our driftings or our futures, we will have to agree to share the task between each of us in turn: for our words are worth something only if they follow on from each other [se relaient]. Writing is strange, when one who was considered or taken as the model, or pretext, then takes it upon himself to do the modelling. This to-and-fro fits with our moods. It points to our place among the future stars, in the infinite relay of singular voices.[61]

57. Or, as Catherine Mayaux puts it: 'Far from enclosing the real in a prism, these multiple points of view seem on the contrary to enlarge the field of vision and to extend further the investigation of others and the world' (Catherine Mayaux (1992), 'La structure romanesque de *Mahagony* d'Edouard Glissant', in Favre, ed., *Horizons d'Edouard Glissant*, p. 359).
   58. Glissant, *Mahagony*, p. 242.
   59. Ibid., p.157. My italics.
   60. Glissant, *Poétique de la relation*, p. 40.
   61. Glissant, *Mahagony*, pp. 251–2.

9

In Praise of Creoleness?

Lise Morel

In their manifesto In Praise of Creoleness, two writers (Patrick Chamoiseau and Raphaël Confiant) and a linguist (Jean Bernabé) laid down the foundations of what they believe could lead peoples of the Caribbean towards a wider sense of identity, unlimited by geographical boundaries: 'neither Europeans, nor Africans, nor Asians, we proclaim ourselves Creoles'.[1] In Praise of Creoleness is clearly to be seen as the manifesto of a new generation of writers, but it is nevertheless inscribed within a continuum of thought, as is suggested by the quotations heading the essay, from the work of Segalen, Césaire, Glissant and Fanon. In Praise of Creoleness is to be read not only as crystallizing but also as surpassing the ideas of these writers, while at the same time continuing to recognize their historical necessity. If they proclaim, for instance, that they are 'forever Césaire's sons',[2] they nevertheless denounce the role of negritude a few pages later, declaring that for them: 'Negritude replaced the illusion of Europe by an African illusion.'[3] In his iconoclastic *Aimé Césaire: Traversée paradoxale d'un siècle,*[4] Raphaël Confiant further challenges the traditional image of Césaire as an innovative political and intellectual leader, exposing the inadequacies of negritude (perceived as a dogmatic ideology), and contrasting its monolithic approach with the power of change which is seen to characterize Creoleness. As for Glissant, although undoubtedly indebted to his theoretical works, they nevertheless consider that the Caribbeanness (*'antillanité'*) that he has described is more of a 'vision' than a real attempt to change things, and they see their own Creoleness as existing within the

1. Jean Bernabé, Patrick Chamoiseau and Raphaël Confiant (1989), *Eloge de la créolité/In Praise of Creoleness* (bilingual edition), trans. M.B. Taleb-Khyar, Paris: Gallimard, p. 75.

2. Ibid., p. 80.

3. Ibid., p. 82.

4. Raphaël Confiant (1993), *Aimé Césaire: Traversée paradoxale d'un siècle*, Paris: Stock.

gaps between negritude and Caribbeanness: 'We cannot reach Caribbeanness without interior vision. And interior vision is nothing without the unconditional acceptance of our Creoleness.'[5]

Creoleness is actually defined as an intellectual and political tool with which the peoples of the Caribbean, as well as those from other former (French) colonies, may confront the shared issue of hybridity, fight oppression and alienation and accept a common consciousness under the aegis of 'joyful diversity'. As an appendix to In Praise of Creoleness, they acknowledge the need for Creoleness not to remain confined within the aesthetic domain, and they assert its political insight, outside all dominant, now obsolete, ideologies: 'Creoleness sketches the hope for the first possible grouping within the Caribbean archipelago . . . a grouping which is only the prelude to a larger union with our anglophone and hispanophone neighbours.'[6]

Creoleness therefore implies several demands, which are developed in In Praise of Creoleness. An essential component of the Creolists' project is to be found in what they call 'fundamental orality' ('l'enracinement dans l'oral'). To them, this orality has been buried under alienation, through French cultural imperialism (particularly in terms of literature). 'We shall create a literature which will obey all the demands of modern writing while taking roots in the traditional configurations of our orality',[7] they declare, and they further assert their debt to the oral Creole tradition in the determination they display in publishing Creole folktales in French.[8] This fundamental interest in traditional Creole folktales can primarily be explained by a will to show that their writing does not blossom out of nothing, but is firmly embedded within a solid Creole tradition of storytelling – a tradition which is not yet extinct. In the foreword to *Les Maîtres de la parole créole*, indeed, Confiant declares that these younger storytellers 'have relieved the old guard although their wording is different . . . They have to adapt their tales to a universe which is now ruled by a new type of orality brought about by television.'[9] As he later points out, they represent 'modern Creoleness'. In any case, the Creolists' motivation lies

---

5. Ibid., p. 87. All translations from French texts are my own.

6. Ibid., p. 116.

7. In 1988, Patrick Chamoiseau edited a collection of Antillean folktales, *Au temps de l'antan*, Paris: Hatier, while Confiant was subsequently responsible for the publishing of two anthologies of Creole folktales: (1995) *Les Maîtres de la parole créole*, Paris: Gallimard, and (1995) *Contes créoles des Amériques*, Paris: Stock. These three books were written in French.

8. Bernabé *et al.*, *In Praise of Creoleness*, pp. 97–8.

9. Confiant, *Les Maîtres de la parole créole*, p. 15.

in a will to restore dignity to the Creole imagination – and to do so in a lively, non-academic way. Chamoiseau takes a clear stand against what he calls 'cultural deportation':[10] 'the tales, he argues, were [previously] translated from Creole into French by people who had, consciously or not, the idea that it was their duty to turn Creole coarseness into French civilized stylishness'.[11] This is what leads Confiant to emphasize the fact that the material presented has not been rearranged, but is rather 'the most accurate reflection possible of a speech ['parole'] or a language ['langue'] which is still alive'.[12] This does not mean that they do not acknowledge the usefulness of some of the previous collections of folktales, but rather that they regret their anthropological outlook and coldness – along with the lack of effort to transpose the tales' idiosyncrasies. This idea is linked to the literary practice advocated in In Praise of Creoleness and to the Creolists' preoccupation with the crossover from the oral to the written form. Confiant explains in *Contes créoles des Amériques* that he wishes to contribute to the establishment of 'an original literary genre which will try to draw from the richness of both orality and writing',[13] ultimately vowing to 'graft – almost in the botanical sense of the word – Creole orality on to French literariness'.[14] This oral heritage is therefore clearly inscribed in the overall project of the Creolists, as they hope to find in it the spirit which will lead them to the completion of their vision of Creoleness.

The second point emphasized in In Praise of Creoleness is the need to re-create a history that corresponds to Antillean reality, as opposed to the Cartesian globalizing vision of history imposed by the metropole: 'our chronicle is behind the dates, behind the known facts'.[15] We have to note here the deliberate use of chronicle, as opposed to H/history, as well as their systematic addition of the words 'our (his)stories' after 'our history': 'Our history (or more precisely our histories) is shipwrecked in colonial history. Collective memory is the first thing on our agenda.'[16] We shall see later the importance of this statement in relation to the interest they display towards individual stories in their novels.

10. Patrick Chamoiseau (1994), 'Que faire de la parole?', in Ralph Ludwig, ed., *Ecrire la parole de nuit*, Paris: Gallimard, p. 152.

11. Chamoiseau, 'Que faire de la parole?', p. 153.

12. Confiant, *Les Maîtres de la parole créole*, p. 14.

13. Chamoiseau, *Contes créoles des Amériques*, p. 12.

14. Ibid.

15. Ibid., p. 99.

16. Bernabé *et al.*, *In Praise of Creoleness*, p. 98.

The idea that memory is to be found in the gaps of official history, rather than in chronological events, is associated with the new sense of vision that they advocate – something more 'interior', 'without the alienating logic of his [the other's] prism'.[17] In this respect, they tend towards a certain Adamic perception of the world,[18] as well as towards a sort of systematic examination of all realities close to popular imagination (beliefs, language, feelings). This double movement towards an inner perception of outside reality also involves a re-evaluation of 'our whole [Antillean] literary production'.[19] And, indeed, in 1991, Chamoiseau and Confiant published an essay, *Lettres créoles: Tracées antillaises et continentales de la littérature 1635–1975,*[20] which discusses the various movements of the literary history of the French Caribbean, ultimately establishing a set of canonical texts. The term 'tracées' suggests the idea that Caribbean literature is not a continuum, but rather a series of brush-like strokes, gaping with silences. Their study covers much ground, starting with the 'martyrs of the decimated original Caribbean people' and their 'silent literature' in the shape of millennial carved stones. It then goes on to explore *béké* literature, the exterior gaze on the Antilles, with its numerous travel chronicles, descriptions of the 'New World' and inscriptions on slave registers. The authors then move on to examine the 'cri de la cale' of the slaves themselves (Walcott's 'packed cries' from the cargo hold[21]) – cries which, as they point out, narrowly coexisted with the silence of resistance, 'le silence du cri' (the silent cry), physically and mentally revealed in the swallowing of the tongue by the slave and in the learning of the strategies of 'détour' (circumlocution) and 'ruse' (trickery). Such strategies, as Glissant similarly points out elsewhere,[22] were of particular importance to the plantation's storytellers, emblematic figures for Chamoiseau and Confiant, whose deliberately ambivalent discourse expressed resistance and revolt, while remaining apparently innocuous in the eyes of the master. Indeed, as we shall see later, such discourse is advocated by Chamoiseau and Confiant as a strategy also for contemporary Caribbean

17. Ibid., p. 102.

18. 'We want, thanks to Creoleness, to name each thing in it [the world], and to declare it beautiful' (ibid., p. 101).

19. 'We can revisit and re-evaluate our whole literary production' (ibid., p. 100).

20. Patrick Chamoiseau and Raphaël Confiant (1991), *Lettres créoles: Tracées antillaises et continentales de la littérature 1635–1975*, Paris: Hatier.

21. Derek Walcott (1992), 'The Sea is History', in *Collected Poems 1948–1984*, London: Faber and Faber, p. 364.

22. See Chamoiseau and Confiant, *Lettres créoles*, p. 37 and Edouard Glissant (1997), *Le Discours antillais*, Paris: Gallimard, pp. 48–51.

writers, like themselves, who may wish to render their texts in some way 'opaque', and thus produce a subversive 'counterpoetics'. Indeed, it is the strategies utilized within the oral tradition which are of primary interest to Chamoiseau and Confiant, for, as they point out, with the collapse of the plantation system, silence reigned once again ('l'oraliturain créole va se taire').[23] And with the development of literacy and the movement towards writing came a number of literary practices (mimetism, Gallicized Creole, exoticism, eroticism and humour), which, implying as they do the subjection of the Antillean intellectual to what they call the 'French cultural superego',[24] Chamoiseau and Confiant largely reject.

It is, however, the acute problem of language which preoccupies the Creolists the most: in In Praise of Creoleness, Chamoiseau, Confiant and Bernabé are all aware of the difficulties of developing, not yet what Brathwaite calls a 'nation-language', but a language at least capable of including all of the various influences that the peoples of the Caribbean bear within themselves. This alone, they feel, will then enable the realization of the full potential of the 'interior vision' which is so important to them. The Creolists aspire to make use of everything that was once imposed on Antilleans, and this applies perhaps especially to language. Thus they recommend that the reverence and respect commonly bestowed upon the French language be abandoned, and they insist instead on the fact that 'we did conquer it, this French language',[25] thus inverting the accepted view that French language 'tamed' the Caribbean people. At the same time, they also insist that Antilleans should keep a certain distance from Creole, because of the affective rapport that they have with it: 'they [the Creole poet and novelist] will mistrust this language, while accepting it completely'.[26] Their main enemy, in any case, is an overinvestment in either language, which can only lead to confusion: 'For a Creole poet or novelist, writing in an idolized French or Creole is like . . . having no language within the language, therefore having no identity.' [27] The double movement, the friction between the two languages, they argue, far from impoverishing their literature, will on the contrary nourish it and, instead of favouring a 'narrow specificity',[28] will lead them on to 'live the world'.[29]

23. Chamoiseau, Confiant, *Lettres créoles*, p. 65.
24. Ibid., p. 68.
25. *In Praise of Creoleness*, p. 106.
26. Ibid.
27. Ibid., p. 108.
28. Ibid., p. 110.
29. Ibid.

In *Aimé Césaire: Traversée paradoxale d'un siècle*, Confiant describes Césaire's suspicions of Creole as a rejection of what is not pure – of the diverse: for Confiant, Césaire is simply reiterating Western concepts of unicity, universality and essentialism.[30] His use of the French language is criticized very strongly by Confiant: Césaire should have 'exultantly chewed the French language',[31] instead of being 'cannibalized'[32] by it. The conclusion of In Praise of Creoleness is a vibrant appeal to diversality (not only, but also, linguistic), a notion which they set against the Western siren of universality: 'Creole literature will have nothing to do with the Universal, or this disguised adherence to western values.'[33] The world is, according to them, 'evolving into a state of Creoleness';[34] therefore Creoleness offers the most adequate means of expressing this modern, diffracted world.

Although Confiant and Chamoiseau have thus published important theoretical works, their prime concern remains with their vocation as writers. Between them, they have published an enormous amount of literary works, ranging from novels to short stories, in French and in Creole. Their novels in French have won them critical acclaim and a wide audience, as they took mainland France by storm in the early 1990s. Chamoiseau obtained the all-important Prix Goncourt for his novel *Texaco*, while Confiant gathered various prizes for *Le Nègre et l'amiral* and *Eau de Café*, to name but two.[35] What is more, their literary strategies are clearly linked to the theoretical views that they explore in In Praise of

30. Ibid., p. 114.
31. Ibid., p. 44.
32. Ibid., p. 45.
33. Ibid., p. 111.
34. Ibid., p. 112.
35. Prizes won by these two writers are as follows:
    Chamoiseau:
    (1986) *Chronique des sept misères*, Paris: Gallimard – Prix Kléber Haedens, Prix de l'Ile Maurice;
    (1988) *Au temps de l'antan*, Paris: Hatier – Grand prix de la littérature de la jeunesse;
    (1991) *Antan d'enfance*, Paris: Gallimard – Grand prix Carbet de la Caraïbe;
    (1992) *Texaco*, Paris: Gallimard – Prix Goncourt 1992.
    Confiant:
    (1988) *Le Nègre et l'amiral*, Paris: Grasset – Prix Antigone;
    (1991) *Eau de Café*, Paris: Grasset – Prix Novembre;
    (1993) *Ravines du devant-jour*, Paris: Gallimard – Prix Casa de Las Americas, Prix Jet Tours;
    (1994) *L'Allée des soupirs*, Paris: Grasset – Grand prix Carbet de la Caraïbe.

Creoleness. In the fictional works of both Chamoiseau and Confiant, the idea of Creoleness as a structure of resistance against French imperialism is demonstrated in various ways. If they claim, in In Praise of Creoleness, that they wish to 'present insignificant heroes, anonymous heroes, those who are forgotten by the colonial chronicle',[36] then their novels introduce a predominantly urban universe populated by those who have been shunned by bourgeois mulatto society or who have voluntarily chosen to 'drop out'.[37] This urban frame, reminiscent of Rabelais's 'place publique', operates like a catalyst towards a common consciousness. Confiant places his characters in areas which belong to the domain of the Parisian Cour des Miracles (an area of Paris famed for its 'disreputable' population): there is the 'Cour Fruit-à-Pain', for example, where the prostitutes in *Le Nègre et l'amiral* work; the 'Cour-aux-trente-deux-couteaux', a place of danger and endless night-time brawls; or Terres-Sainvilles of *Ravines du devant-jour*, where 'the most dangerous rogues' live and work, and where 'you only hear the roughest Creole, made up of words which cannot be pronounced by the mulattos from the centre of town and of the most delightful swear-words which never seem to end.'[38] Thus, a 'Creole space' is set up, filled with all those figures once excluded from Antillean literature – 'djobeurs'[39] with uncertain futures, prostitutes and thieves – while the authorities and the mulatto bourgeoisie are completely ridiculed. Indeed, Césaire himself is no exception, with Confiant cruelly parodying him in *Le Nègre et l'amiral* as the grotesque Amadeus Césare. The characters are often flamboyant and may be seen to belong to the burlesque vein of Creole folktales, as is suggested by their evocative nicknames,[40] and by the comic and often outrageous incidents in which they become involved. In Chamoiseau's *Chroniques des sept misères*, for example, Marguerite Jupiter, *femme formidable*, stands up to the social worker who wants to take her children away into care. After a heroicomic description of the fight that takes place between the two women, the scene is concluded

36. Bernabé *et al.*, *In Praise of Creoleness*, p. 100.

37. In Chamoiseau's 1988 novel *Solibo Magnifique* (Paris: Gallimard), the cast of characters is introduced through a police report about the death of storyteller Solibo and they are obviously marginalized, as each of their professions is followed by the comment: 'Presumably unemployed'.

38. Confiant, *Ravines du devant-jour*, pp. 196–7.

39. The Creole word 'djobeur' refers to those (men) who were forced from the country-side to find work in the markets in towns, earning money by transporting goods on their wheelbarrows and performing other odd jobs for the market traders.

40. Bec-en-Or, for instance, is full of connotations, as it is the name given to a character who speaks very good French.

with the scatological remark of the hero, Pipi, who advises the social worker (by now sitting on the ground) that the garden is not an appropriate place to use as a toilet ('venir faire caca').[41]

On another level, too, the novels and short stories of Chamoiseau and Confiant are deeply rooted in traditional Creole orality, and this anchoring within a tradition of storytelling is of paramount importance to them. In fact, the figure of the storyteller himself takes on an almost mythical dimension, as with Solibo Magnifique in Chamoiseau's novel of the same name. Here, the role of the Caribbean writer is primarily defined in terms of having to relay the spoken word: Chamoiseau, 'present' in the novel under the same name, appears as the 'marqueur de paroles', the scribe of Solibo's words as transmitted by collective memory. Similarly, in Confiant's *Le Nègre et l'amiral*, it is quite interesting to see how one of the main characters, Rigobert, changes status during the course of the novel: at first, he expresses some sort of resistance towards the established order by continually swearing and blaspheming, but at the end of the novel, regenerated by a long stay in the country, he himself becomes a storyteller, relaying the story of the writer Amédée, who dies before finishing his book (*Mémoires de Céans et d'ailleurs*). At a linguistic level, it is similarly interesting to see how the whole body of the written French text becomes 'contaminated' by speech: exclamations and swearing are an inherent part of the narrative process, dialogue and narration are intertwined, narrative voices are multiplied and free indirect speech is a constant recourse. Thus, the course of *Le Nègre et l'amiral* is interrupted three times by extracts from Amédée's novel, while, in the rest of the novel, the reader is often presented with several versions of the same event (such as the meeting of Rigobert and Lapin Echaudé, a professional town crier[42]), all of which suggests that the narrative is actually relayed by rumour. Indeed, neatly summarizing Confiant's own literary practice, Amédée declares: 'Repudiating Cartesianism, I learnt . . . to narrate with the truthfulness of a man denying thirty and twelve thousand versions of the same event at the stake. Once you have embarked upon that kind of spiral, you have only to believe in each one after the other.'[43]

Rumour seems in effect to be the foundation of history, of individual stories and, in a sense, of the story narrated by the writers. This has the double result of suggesting that Martinican people do have a common voice, hence a common consciousness, and also of conveying the impression

---

41. Chamoiseau, *Chronique des sept misères*, p. 206.
42. Confiant, *Le Nègre et l'amiral*, pp. 19–26
43. Ibid., p. 347.

that H/history belongs to the domain of relativity. This, in turn, is confirmed by the way in which the characters themselves view time, for they relate to time not by calendar dates but by using historical events that were important to themselves or were natural disasters: 'I was born just before Admiral Robert,' answers one of the suspects when told: 'the inspector wants to know after which cyclone you were born', while under police examination in *Solibo Magnifique*.[44] The characters' attitude to time corresponds precisely to the diegetic principles used by the novelists: in their novels, their stories – events that would be considered in mainland France as trivia – are equivalent, if not superior, to history, which is stamped with the mark of the colonizer. Along with Bernabé, Confiant and Chamoiseau repeatedly insist in In Praise of Creoleness upon the necessity of considering the history of the Antilles as plural. In the same way, in their novels, they suggest that absolute historical truth is absent, and that common memory is of more relevance, thereby reversing once again concepts that Antilleans have unwillingly received from the West.

In Praise of Creoleness suggests the existence of a link between the Creolists' relationship with H/history and the one that they entertain with language ('Our chronicle is behind the dates, behind the known facts: *we are Words behind writing*'[45]). In fact, and once again taking full advantage of their cultural heritage, they are interested in developing a language distinct from mainland French, one which would fully utilize their Creole/ French diglossia. Creoleness being the 'annihilation of false universality, of monolingualism, and of purity',[46] Confiant and Chamoiseau want to subordinate what they call 'le français de France' and rearticulate it around Creole orality, but they both hold different opinions in terms of practice. Chamoiseau never uses Creole directly, except occasionally in quotations and, although his writing is deeply influenced by Creole, he has created his own style, in which French and regional French are the main linguistic structures and Creole is present as an undercurrent.[47] Confiant, too, has expressed interest in the fact that Creole may subtend his French texts, declaring: 'I am never more touched than when a reader tells me s/he has had the curious impression of reading Creole through my books in French.'[48] However, he has also published three novels in Creole, two of

44. Chamoiseau, *Solibo Magnifique*, p. 133.
45. Bernabé *et al.*, *In Praise of Creoleness*, p. 99.
46. Ibid., p. 90.
47. For a more in-depth study of Chamoiseau's style, see Marie-Christine Hazaël-Massieux (1993), *Ecrire en créole, oralité et écriture aux Antilles*, Paris: L'Harmattan.
48. Raphaël Confiant (1994), 'Questions pratiques d'écriture créole', in Ludwig, ed., *Ecrire la parole de nuit*, pp. 179–80.

which have been translated into French (one, *Mamzelle Libellule,* by Confiant himself), and is in general terms much more intent on working directly with the Creole language than is Chamoiseau. In both writers' works in French, however, Creole words are always occasionally present, with no explanation and no glossary: the non-creolophone reader has only the context to help him or her understand their meaning. It is this textual opacity which may in many ways be compared with the technique of the *détour* used for centuries by the storytellers on the plantation, and outlined in In Praise of Creoleness as an important writing strategy for the new generation of Creole writers, of which they themselves are a part.

In their novels, then, Chamoiseau and Confiant may be seen to put into practice many of the more theoretical ideas which they advance in In Praise of Creoleness. Yet I would like to conclude this chapter with a note on their ambivalence. On the one hand, they are obviously achieving much; yet, on the other, they do not seem to be risking a great deal. Confiant reproaches Césaire for the fact that he has been 'cannibalized' by the French language, but both his and Chamoiseau's novels are published in mainland France, where the authors receive, and gratefully accept, literary prizes. None the less, while it may seem that this behaviour demonstrates a certain complicity with the established (colonial) order, perhaps such an assumption tends towards oversimplification. It is possible, for example, to read this 'complicity' as a double movement of recuperation and mystification, as the French publishing houses and the Creolist writers appear to be exploiting each other: after all, because they are successful, the Creolists can challenge mainland France's perception of Caribbean preoccupations and problems. Indeed, perhaps Creoleness is doing no more than highlighting a scope of possibilities: while it may exercise a critique of Western ideologies, it may not be anything other than a prelude to deeper change. And, since such a question remains unanswerable at this moment, it may perhaps be most useful to follow Guadeloupean writer Ernest Pépin's perceptive comment:

> For me, each era creates its own tool. Creoleness seems well adapted for our times, at the stage we are at as far as our research in literature is concerned. Yet, in my opinion, Creoleness, like others, will be a historical trend in the sense that it will be necessary one day to think about something else . . . Creoleness must not become a dogma![49]

---

49. Ernest Pépin (1992), 'Le débat autour de la créolité', *Antilla Magazine,* 509, p. 29. This interview was first published by the local paper *Lendépendans* (no. 418).

–10–

Breaking the Silence: Cultural Identities and Narrative Configurations in the French Caribbean Novel

Suzanne Crosta

As the globalization of financial markets and information technology weaken national boundaries, questions of migration, citizenship and multi-culturalism have gained strong currency in social and political discourses on identity. Epistemological enquiries and discussions about global relationships have shifted the debate from national origin to subject position, where issues of class, gender, language and race most often take precedence.[1] In the context of the French-speaking Caribbean,[2] literary movements from negritude to Creoleness have forged new discourses on identity and relationships with the other and have become important interventions in French and Caribbean cultural politics. Proponents of these movements (Aimé Césaire, Édouard Glissant, Patrick Chamoiseau . . .) have been concerned with providing a critique of policies and practices that contain cultural diversity rather than establishing and promoting diverse cultural traditions, experiences, achievements and values. Indeed, many Caribbean writers and scholars view French nationalism and global-ization as harmful to the survival and existence of their island communities, since the critical evaluation of Caribbean cultural creativity and activity will predominantly depend on or operate within international markets whose technologies and ideologies may be governed by external agendas and interests.

In light of these ethical and aesthetic concerns, I shall examine French Caribbean writings and their increasing emphasis on being plural or

---

1. For extended treatment of these issues see, Walter D. Mignolo (1994), 'Are subaltern studies postmodern or postcolonial? The politics and sensibilities of geo-cultural locations', *Dispositio*, 19:46, pp. 45–73.

2. This study will focus primarily on the French Overseas Departments of Guadeloupe, Martinique and French Guiana.

cross-cultural and I shall identify some thematic and formal preoccupations which underline subdued silences and voicelessness, as well as speaking of the need to articulate and share past and present experiences of slavery, colonialism and racism in Caribbean history, fiction and daily living. Consequently, this first section will also explore four specific areas of investigation: crossing conceptual and aesthetic boundaries, naming, story-telling and lastly figuring resistance in Caribbean writings. These features share common traits: the need to transform social and economic relations of inequality; the need to establish a new vision and a suitable literary form, one which is both traditional and subversive and yet open to a poetic of cultural crossovers. In the second section, I shall concentrate on Maryse Condé's novels in order to show how her writings are concerned not simply with celebrating cultural diversity but with problematizing it as well. My aim in these two sections is to sketch out some critical paradigms and readings which will allow us to link works by French Caribbean writers to their cultural politics and aesthetic practices. In effect, many of them advocate through their literary endeavour theoretical pluralism, a rehabili-tation of their communities' cultural past and daily living and a vision of human possibility wherein diversity and 'opacity' are given value.

From Subdued Silences to Political and Cultural Assertions

In former slave societies such as Martinique, Guadeloupe and French Guiana, affirmation of one's identity was, and for many still is, a political act. Inevitably, any attempt to assess a Caribbean aesthetic must clearly take into account the influence which the French policy of assimilation has exercised over notions of identity, culture and artistic sensibility. Suppressed or oppressed elements of Caribbean culture re/surface not only in artefacts but also in the 'telling' of stories whether they be riddles, proverbs, folktales or myths. Whether one includes books, paintings, sculptures, textiles, pottery . . . , Caribbean cultural artefacts bear witness to competing sites of power and desire. Even the raw materials (stone, mud, wood, paper, textiles . . .), used by Arawaks, Caribs, peoples of African or European descent, are important elements to consider, for they provide insights into the communal imagination and vision.[3] This is particularly relevant to oral narratives transmitted by African slave

3. For more information see René Louise (1980), *Le Marronnisme moderne*, Paris: Éditions Caribéennes; René Louise (1984), *Sculpture et peinture en Martinique*, Paris: Éditions Caribéennes; Patrick Chamoiseau and Raphaël Confiant (1991), *Lettres créoles. Tracées antillaises et continentales de la littérature 1635–1975*, Paris: Hatier.

workers, storytellers and artists within the plantation system. Their use of oral traditions, in particular their mastery in communicating their stories, confronted assumptions and definitions of race and class that denied them recognition of their fundamental human rights. The slightest infraction of imposed codes of conduct was met with zero tolerance, even when it supported the status quo. The legal case of Adèle, a young Martinican woman condemned to twenty-five lashes in 1831 for singing 'La Parisienne', is a powerful case in point.[4] Her lawyers' plea for a waiver of her sentence due to her delicate health after childbirth is a fierce indictment of the rigorous constraints of the plantation system on individual expression and liberties.

This historical case provides a fitting backdrop, and a reminder of the enormous challenge for slaves, indentured labourers and workers of African or Asian descent to gain any voice at all and of the extreme cost to anyone contesting slavery, colonialism and racism within the plantation system. In his *Poétique de la relation,* Edouard Glissant, influential Caribbean theorist, poet and novelist, describes the creative subterfuges, practice/s of 'diversion' ('détour') and 'reversion' ('retour'),[5] whereby the storyteller would mask or fragment his narrative so that the militant or subversive message could pass while still remaining cryptic to figures of authority, in particular to the *béké* élite. In *La Case du commandeur*, for example, Glissant re-creates the master/slave paradigm and subverts it by undermining the assumption upon which it rests, namely political and cultural authority. The mere idea that his slave Anatolie may be hiding information or knowledge from him drives the master of the plantation close to madness. Anatolie uses his seductive prowess to his political advantage. He confides to his many lovers fragmented pieces of a seemingly subversive text. Entitled to a piece of the oral text, each of the slave women whom he has seduced becomes actively engaged in the turning of the plot. Together they are able to assemble the pieces of the text and participate in the construction of a counter-discourse.[6] In Glissant's view, personal commitment and collective solidarity allow for creative responses to contested spheres of power and discursive practices, both within and outside the confines of the plantation. The portrayal of the slave women's

4. *Demande en grâce pour Adèle, jeune esclave de la Martinique, condamnée à la peine de fouet, pour avoir chanté La Parisienne*, Paris, Auguste Mie, 1831 (signed Bissette and Fabien).

5. See Edouard Glissant (1990), *Poétique de la relation,* Paris, Seuil. These terms have been translated by Michael Dash in Edouard Glissant (1989), *Caribbean Discourse: Selected Essays*, trans. J. Michael Dash, Charlottesville: Virginia UP, pp. 14–26.

6. Edouard Glissant (1981), *La Case du commandeur*, Paris: Seuil, pp. 109–33.

active participation against oppression by the white planter class brings to the forefront the issue of racism and sexism in Caribbean historiography. This presence/absence of a rhetoric of resistance becomes an effective strategy to undermine the plantation system and its discourses of legitimacy.

Glissant's *La Case du commandeur* highlights two important features of Caribbean literature: the desire to decolonize and redefine cultural paradigms (for example, white master/black slave) and the desire to celebrate the communal imagination of a people whose history, geography, identity and voice have been silenced or challenged. Glissant's novel invites, by its very allusive and historically webbed narrative, what Edward Said calls a 'contrapuntal reading' which takes into consideration discourses to which the writer or intellectual is responding. The point that Said judiciously raises is that: 'contrapuntal reading must take account of both processes, that of imperialism and that of resistance to it, which can be done by extending our reading of the texts to include what was once forcibly excluded.'[7] This contrapuntal reading corresponds well to Glissant's literary practices. *La Case du commandeur*, for example, invokes in its configuration the colonialist discourse of the white planter class and the wave of resistance to it.

Similarly, when examining the literary history of Martinique, Guadeloupe and French Guiana, it is possible to trace the varying degrees of acceptance or refusal of French mainstream critical aesthetic and the responses to it. Nineteenth-century and early twentieth-century Caribbean writers sought to produce works that would rival their French counterparts. Although for these writers taking up the pen was a political statement in itself, Caribbean criticism, from political and social theorists (Étienne Léro, René Ménil, Frantz Fanon) to proponents of Creoleness (Jean Bernabé, Patrick Chamoiseau and Raphaël Confiant), would condemn the literary landscape and language of their writings, labelling them Parnassians, romantics, symbolists and so forth.[8] The crux of the argument rests upon the need to break with colonial expectations of literature at the level of both form and content.

---

7. Edward W. Said (1994), *Culture and Imperialism*, New York: A.A. Knopf, pp. 66–7.

8. See Etienne Léro's 'Misère d'une poésie' and René Ménil's 'Généralités sur *l'écrivain* de couleur antillais', which both appeared in the same and only issue of *Légitime Défense*, 1 (1932), pp. 10–12 and pp. 7–9, respectively; Frantz Fanon (1961), *Les Damnés de la terre*, Paris: Maspéro, in particular, Chapter 4, 'Sur la culture nationale'; Jean Bernabé, Patrick Chamoiseau and Raphaël Confiant (1989), *Eloge de la créolité/In Praise of Creoleness* (bilingual edition), trans. M.B. Taleb Khyar, Paris: Gallimard, p. 124.

The call for a new epistemology was to a great extent inspired by the Harlem renaissance and Haitian indigenism, both of which laid the groundwork for negritude writers. Aimé Césaire was among the first to weave the historical absences and silences of Caribbean identity and textuality into his writings. Literary criticism on *Cahier d'un retour au pays natal* [9] has pointed to his new articulation of the Caribbean landscape, identity and community, as well as to his experimentation with aesthetic forms that were drawn from African oral traditions. Césaire's cultural shift towards Africa, its mythologies, histories and stories, was perceived as a first step towards forging an African aesthetic within an anti-colonialist framework.

In response to negritude, Glissant advocated a recentring of Caribbean identity and subsequently coined the term 'Caribbeanness' ('antillanité').[10] According to J. Michael Dash, Glissant's analysis of this new 'vision' of the Caribbean, first articulated in *Soleil de la conscience* (1956) and then in *Le Discours antillais* (1981), developed into theoretical reflections on the Caribbean condition, which culminated in his articulation of a 'cross-cultural poetics' in *Poétique de la relation* (1990) and, more recently, of a 'poetics of diversity' in *Introduction à une poétique du divers* (1995). For Dash, all of these works have the common purpose of ascribing value to the process of creolization and the pluralism of (French) Caribbean culture.[11] In his literary works, the vitality of diverse utterances develops as a narrative strategy or, on a larger scale, as a discourse of resistance against conventional modes of representation associated with colonial domination or colonizing structures. Glissant thus offers the Caribbean as a prodigious site for theoretical reflections on cultural contact in all its various forms and moments (forced migrations, slavery, colonialism . . .).

Glissant's theoretical concepts of Caribbeanness and cross-cultural poetics have influenced the next generation of intellectuals and writers, such as Bernabé, Chamoiseau and Confiant, who have shifted the debate towards a reactivation of the Creole language, culture and imagination.

9. For a fuller discussion of critical approaches to Césaire's *Cahier d'un retour au pays natal*, see Chapter 2 of the present volume, and for extended treatment of Césaire's writings, see, among many others, the collective essays in Jacqueline Leiner, ed. (1984), *Soleil éclaté* Tübingen: Gunter Narr Verlag, and Jacqueline Leiner, ed. (1987), *Aimé Césaire ou l'athanor d'un alchimiste*, Paris: Éditions Caribéennes.

10. Glissant, 'Lieu clos, parole ouverte', in *Poétique de la relation,* pp. 82–9.

11. For a more detailed study of Glissant's theoretical 'development', see Richard Burton (1984), 'Comment peut-on être Martiniquais? The recent work of Edouard Glissant', *The Modern Language Review*, 79:2, pp. 301–12; and J. Michael Dash (1995) *Edouard Glissant*, Cambridge: Cambridge UP.

Their literary manifesto challenges past and present discourses on Caribbean identity and calls for new paradigms to reflect inclusivity and accept diversity. Although politics and art remain linked through their projection of a Caribbean federation or confederation, their focus is clear: 'for the moment, *full knowledge of Creoleness will be reserved for Art,* for Art absolutely'.[12] This declaration is qualified extensively in the authors' explanatory note:

> The valorization of our Creole daily experience should not be done through slogans but rather through an effort of poetization, for reality is in itself revolutionary when reviewed through the prism of a writing concerned with revealing its bases. That is why we believe that the best way of taking part in the old struggle our peoples are leading against the colonial or imperial constraints, is to consolidate in our writings this Creole culture that our oppressors have always tried to belittle.[13]

Since Creole culture is embedded in the orality of the Creole language, literature and world-view, Bernabé, Chamoiseau and Confiant give renewed importance to the literary language and expressions of Caribbean writings.

Transgressing Boundaries

The search for an artistic form or an aesthetic has led many Caribbean writers to question the notion of boundaries and reclaim alternative cultural traditions. In his full-length study of Glissant's theoretical and literary work, Dash opens his chapter on the early writings of Glissant with the following remarks:

> Glissant began his career as a poet and continues to produce books of poetry in conjunction with his fictional narratives and theoretical discourses. This sustained refusal on his part to abandon poetry, or even to recognise the conceptual boundary that traditionally exists between poetry and prose, creative and critical writing, is central to the understanding of Glissant's entire literary enterprise.[14]

Glissant's formal interrogations and innovations correspond to his reflections on notions of reference and identity in the Caribbean. In effect, his literary essays and works insist upon cultural crossovers and exchanges

---

12. Bernabé *et al.*, *In Praise of Creoleness*, p. 90.
13. Ibid., p. 124.
14. Dash, *Edouard Glissant*, p. 26.

in the realm of ideas and creativity. On a larger scale, writers from the French Caribbean such as Patrick Chamoiseau, Maryse Condé, Daniel Maximin, Gisèle Pineau, Simone Schwarz-Bart have all, in their own way, focused their attention on establishing new dialogues which may help to bridge the gaps between races, languages and cultures, and this with the intention of entering in relation with what Glissant has called 'the Whole-World' (*Le Tout-Monde).*[15]

In his novel, *La Case du commandeur*, Glissant explores the multi-layered components of Caribbean identity, oscillating between the singular 'I' and the collective 'we'. In doing so, he creates a spiral configuration of time that structures the story-line and gives substance and form to the quest for meaning. Hence, Glissant is not interested in attempting to represent reality transparently but is interested instead in liberating it from inherited essentialist categories. Character selection and representation are not developed in order to give the reader a unifying subject but precisely the opposite, to show the range of divergent voices which constitute communities. The reader, like the characters of his novel, never fully understand or grasps the identity of the other (for example, Odono, Béhanzin, Pythagore, Mycéa . . .). In Glissant's view, transparency is an illusion, a reflecting mirror that does not allow one to recognize and appreciate the 'opacity', or 'unknowability', of the other.

This engagement with the other has led many Caribbean writers like Condé, Glissant and Schwarz-Bart to embed blueprints of their own signifying practices within their narratives. Such a move enables readers to derive their own understanding of a given writer's artistry from her or his theoretical posturing and material selection, and to gain an insight into what Michel-Rolph Trouillot calls the 'moment of retrospective significance'.[16] *La Case du commandeur* becomes itself a theoretical reflection on the development of different reading strategies, since the narrator guides the readers through the symbolic maze that hampers the characters' speech, memory and search for freedom and fulfilment. According to Glissant, this form of theorizing through fiction critiques traditional ways in which we categorize literature while broadening our concept of literary studies. In his *Introduction à une poétique du divers,* Glissant contends that the many challenges of cultural pluralism and exchange have not been met, and that this has generated ethnic violence around the globe. This state of affairs, in his view, begs for a much needed

---

15. Edouard Glissant (1993), *Tout-monde*, Paris: Gallimard.

16. For extended treatment of this concept, see Michel-Rolph Trouillot (1995), *Silencing the Past*, Boston: Beacon Press, pp. 136–54.

dialogue and theorization of a new cross-cultural approach, for which he lays the groundwork. His own theoretical description of the process of creolization, an open-ended model, is a step towards what he hopes might become a spiritual renewal of humanity.[17]

Naming

This spiritual renewal of humanity engages individuals and communities to recognize and accept each other. This world-view is also a response to the effects of French colonial rule in the Caribbean, where naming was never a personal issue but a political and cultural one, given its impact on race and power relations on the plantation. In raising the issue of naming and its historical, political and social significance, Caribbean writers speak of their struggle (and by extension their communities' struggle) to name themselves and express from multiple perspectives and positions their personal and collective experiences.

Both Glissant's *Le Quatrième Siècle* and Condé's *Traversée de la mangrove* are poised between the weight of history on the present and the tensions and conflicts that arise from their characters' quest for identity and meaning. Cast in the role of the 'other', the struggle to name oneself, one's child and one's community, as well as to find one's place in the world, becomes a political and personal imperative. In *Le Quatrième Siècle*, the assuming and relinquishing of imposed names and the election of new names not only reveal power relations between races and cultures but also the knowledge to be recovered in the daily encounters and experiences of people's lives. In *Traversée de la mangrove*, the narrator frames a seemingly ordinary event in Mira's life (the discovery of the full name of the mysterious man with whom she is smitten) within the historical experience of slavery and colonialism. Mira's observation ends with an ironic twist staged by the implied author: 'it [the letter] bore a rare and unusual name, Francisco Alvarez-Sanchez, so different from those in Rivière au Sel who were called Apollon, Saturne, Mercure, Boisfer, and Boisgris. The masters really had fun baptizing their slaves!'[18] Mira's fascination with the stranger is set against the whole community of Rivière-au-Sel, whose history and identity have been conditioned by colonial rule. Her desire to escape that reality leads her ironically to perpetuate the power

17. Edouard Glissant (1995), *Introduction à une poétique du divers*, Montreal: PUM, pp. 14–15.
18. Maryse Condé (1989), *Traversée de la mangrove*, Paris: Mercure de France. The quotation here is taken from the English edition: Maryse Condé (1995), *Crossing the Mangrove*, trans. Richard Philcox, New York: Anchor Books, p. 41 (translation modified).

structure in place, since Francis Sancher's genealogy is tied to the *béké* élite. Here Condé brings home the issue of naming and its effects on young women like Mira, whose liaison with Sanchez is very much dictated by her need for self-validation. Elsewhere, as Schwarz-Bart's *Pluie et vent sur Télumée miracle* clearly indicates, external definitions can pull the individual in so many different directions that it becomes next to imposs-ible to grasp a theoretical certainty or premise from which to challenge meanings or propose a counter-history that opens up a space for individual presence and autonomy. To combat these constraints, Schwarz-Bart develops images of resistance such as alternative ways of naming, saying and invoking ancestral traditions, among the most powerful of which is the drum with its symbolic resonances. It is Man Cia, Télumée's age-old mentor, who recommends that she be 'a fine little Negress, a real drum with two sides. Let life bang and thump but keep the underside always intact.'[19] Schwarz-Bart calls for a new language that will allow the individ-ual to resist social constraints and self-loathing.

Storytelling

An effective strategy to combat negative perceptions of self is to propose alternative world-views through the telling and sharing of stories. Many Caribbean writers today have chosen to ground their works in oral forms, drawing liberally upon the oral traditions of Caribbean cultures. The rich repertoire of oral narratives (myths, proverbs, songs . . .) provides insight into the histories, aesthetic practices and cultural values of Creole culture. In his successive novels, Chamoiseau has beyond a doubt greatly refined the art of reconciling and negotiating cultural differences in epistemology. In most of his works, Chamoiseau has established a series of conventions to facilitate this attempt to merge oral and written discourses. In both *Chronique des sept misères* and *Solibo Magnifique*, the narrator re-creates a storytelling context, in which he addresses his public overtly and builds upon episodic sequences, where the use of Creole, popular idioms and proverbs reflects the subjectivity and personality of his cast of characters. These strategies invite the reader into the perceptual position of listener involved in a storytelling event. The narrator, through various disguises (storyteller, marker of speech, writer, historian, photographer), embodies multivocality through the diversity of voices and perspectives he occupies.

19. Simone Schwarz-Bart (1972), *Pluie et vent sur Télumée miracle*, Paris: Seuil. The quotation here is taken from the English edition: Simone Schwarz-Bart (1982), *The Bridge of Beyond*, trans. Barbara Bray, London: Heinemann, p. 39.

The composite and diverse nature of Caribbean identity becomes an important feature of the Creoleness movement. Indeed, Bernabé, Chamoiseau and Confiant perceive and use vernacular cultural forms, specifically orality, within a world-view marked by resistance to French cultural policies:

> Orality is our intelligence; it is our reading of this world, the experimentation, still blind, of our complexity. Creole orality, even repressed in its aesthetic expression, contains a whole system of countervalues, a counterculture; it witnesses ordinary genius applied to resistance, devoted to survival.[20]

These authors' multiorientated search for a new discourse on the Caribbean implies an uncovering of myths, tales, stories and interpretations that are deemed vital to the survival and empowerment of Caribbean peoples in their daily living. For these reasons, the relationship between ideology, culture and aesthetics is inextricably woven into the fabric of Caribbean societies.

Figures of Resistance

In revisiting oral traditions, one interesting area of investigation involves the rich cast of characters embodying or symbolizing resistance to slavery, colonialism and racism. For example, the historical figures of the maroons, of the rebel, of the negator (s/he who says 'no' to colonial oppression) take on mythical proportions in the works of Glissant and Schwarz-Bart. Other interesting figures include the *quimboiseur* (traditional healer), the *houngan* (voodoo priest) and the *mambo* (voodoo priestess), all of whom offer insights into the sacred, the rituals which still permeate people's lives. The forgotten figures of the *djobeurs*[21] or the *tanbouyès* (traditional drummer) bear witness to the 'irruption' of modernity, which strips individuals of their social function and livelihood. The magical figures of the Caribbean imagination, such as the *jan gajé* (also *gens gagés, engagés*, night spirit), *bête à sept têtes* (seven-headed monster), *soukouyan*,[22] *zombi*

---

20. Bernabé *et al.*, *In Praise of Creoleness*, p. 95.

21. The term *djobeur* refers to individuals who were forced from the countryside to perform odd jobs in town. Chamoiseau calls them the 'nègres-marrons de l'en-ville', evoking the historical figure of the maroon, the fugitive, in an urban context. See Patrick Chamoiseau (1992), 'Les nègres-marrons de l'en-ville', *Antilla*, 473, pp. 29–33.

22. I refer readers to the 'Glossary' of the English edition of Maryse Condé's *Moi, Tituba, sorcière . . . noire de Salem*, in which Richard Philcox gives the following definition of *soukouyan*: 'literally, "bloodsucker"; word derived from the African language of the

(the living-dead), reveal the composite dimensions of a Caribbean world-view.

The representation and valorization of these mythical figures can be seen as attempts to conceptualize distinctions and contradictions between appearance and reality, political and cultural assertions against different forms of oppression. Chamoiseau's *Chronique des sept misères*, Condé's, *Moi, Tituba, sorcière . . . noire de Salem*, Ernest Pépin's *Tambour-Babel*, Gisèle Pineau's *La Grande Drive des esprits* and Schwarz-Bart's *Ti Jean L'horizon* are but a few examples of the rich body of literature which explores the popular beliefs and rituals of their Creole culture and sensibility. In these texts, the mythical figures of the Caribbean imagination evoke ways to mediate between the natural and supernatural worlds, between fact and fantasy. As figures of cultural resistance, they allow readers to identify and derive theories that pertain to the historical and cultural contexts of Caribbean writings. In doing so, these authors give weight to those of Glissant's theoretical and literary works which pronounce themselves in opposition to a 'forced poetics' that seeks to restrain all forms of vitality, including artistic creativity.[23]

Cultural and Aesthetic Interrogations in Caribbean Fiction

In his introduction to *The Ethnic Canon: Histories, Institutions and Interventions*, David Palumbo-Liu advocates a more critical approach to the study of multiculturalism in order to facilitate a discussion of the less positive aspects of the cross-cultural process. As he points out:

> A critical multiculturalism explores the fissures, tensions, and sometimes contradictory demands of multiples cultures, rather than (only) celebrating the plurality of cultures by passing through them appreciatively. It instead maps out the terrain of common interest while being attentive to the different angles of entry into this terrain.[24]

Tukulœr people, where it designates a spirit that attacks humans and drinks their blood like a vampire' (Maryse Condé (1992), *I, Tituba, Black Witch of Salem*, trans. Richard Philcox, Charlottesville: Virginia UP, p. 186). Other translators have opted for the English term 'hobgoblin', to describe this figure.

23. Edouard Glissant (1981), *Le Discours antillais*, Paris: Seuil. The quotation here is from J. Michael Dash's translation, *Caribbean Discourse: Selected Essays*, pp. 120–34.

24. David Palumbo-Liu, ed. (1995), *The Ethnic Canon: Histories, Institutions and Interventions*, Minneapolis, Minnesota UP, p. 5.

In the context of French Caribbean literature, this critical multiculturalism has been difficult to achieve. It is not the production of literary writings that is wanting but their status and consumption within their communities. Glissant has admitted outright that his targeted audience is not to be found in the present but in the future.[25] Furthermore, proponents of Creoleness have reiterated this fact in talking about their writings as a form of preliterature:

> Caribbean literature does not yet exist. We are still in a state of preliterature: that of a written production without a home audience, ignorant of the authors/ readers interaction which is the primary condition of the development of a literature. This situation is not imputable to the mere political domination, it can also be explained by the fact that our truth found itself behind bars, in the deep bottom of ourselves, unknown to our consciousness and to the artistically free reading of the world in which we live. We are fundamentally stricken with exteriority. This from a long time ago to the present day.[26]

Without a home audience, Caribbean writers (Chamoiseau, Condé, Con-fiant . . .) have voiced their concerns that critical reception of their works is too often subject to internal partisan politics or external definitions by the critical establishments abroad.

Subversive Readings in Maryse Condé's Writings

In light of these factors, Maryse Condé's writings, often marked by dis-placement and interrogation, address issues of gender, race, sex, religion across a variety of contexts so as to engage a wide-ranging readership. Having received mixed reviews and harsh criticism, she has herself confessed that 'writing is a very perilous exercise. If you write what you believe to be true, you displease'.[27] Literary critics have stressed on more than one occasion the subversive quality of her writings or her 'politically incorrect' stance. In order to illustrate my point, I have selected for attention three interesting features of her writings which question French and Caribbean expectations of literature and political activism.

---

25. See notably, Priska Degras and Bernard Magnier (1984), 'Édouard Glissant, préfacier d'une littérature future: entretien avec Édouard Glissant', *Notre Librairie*, 74, pp. 14–20; Ernest Pépin (1991), 'J'écris pour un lecteur à venir', *Sept Magazine*, 602, p. 8.

26. Bernabé *et al*., *In Praise of Creoleness*, p. 76.

27. Maryse Condé (1993), 'The Role of the Writer', *World Literature Today*, 67:4, p. 698.

Decentring Narrative Location: Fictive Wanderings and Peregrinations

One distinctive feature that literary critics have underscored in Condé's writings is her refusal to limit her literary landscape to the Caribbean. In her essay on French Caribbean literature, she argues that, conventionally, Caribbean writers confine the story of their narratives to their native islands.[28] In her own writings, Condé has strived to expand the spatial configurations of the settings of her novels, and *La Vie scélérate* provides us with an excellent example. In it, she links Guadeloupe with Panama, San Francisco, New York, France, England, Haiti and Jamaica via the personal stories of Albert Louis and his descendants. The narrative seeks to interconnect these places for a series of cross-cultural journeys into the heart, mind and imagination of her characters. Condé sees herself as breaking with literary tradition in order to expand her narratives to the diverse lifelong experiences of Caribbean peoples.[29] The geographical wanderings permeating Condé's novel give rise to a sense of exile that her characters feel in relation to their families, their race, their gender roles and themselves. This is given ample treatment in *La Vie scélérate*. On the one hand, there is Thécla, who 'took refuge on the far side of the world' because she was not at peace with herself, her race, or her family'.[30] On the other, there is the narrator, for whom this wandering allows her to accumulate, reclaim and reactivate (via her own writings) what was lost or forgotten cultural information. At the end of the novel, Claude (Coco) decides to leave Guadeloupe. Armed with the knowledge of her past, she can now extend her wings and build on her experiences. This coincides well with Condé's position that 'a writer must explore more than his/her island world'.[31]

Relinquishing Grandiose Myths and Exclusive Ideologies

In *Heremakhonon*, *Ségou*, *Une saison à Rihata* and *Les Derniers Rois Mages*, Condé problematizes an uncritical perception of Africa as mother-

28. Ibid.
29. Ibid.
30. Maryse Condé (1987), *La Vie scélérate*, Paris: Seghers. The quotation here, and each subsequent quotation from this text, is taken from the English edition: Maryse Condé (1992), *Tree of Life*, trans. Richard Philcox, New York: Balantine, p. 368.
31. Maryse Condé, quoted in Thomas Spear (1993), 'Individual quests and collective history', *World Literature Today* 67:4, p. 723.

land or paradise lost and takes issue with Caribbean writers who idealize and symbolize Africa as the matrix of Caribbean identity without due consideration of the problems of the continent. In her view, conventional images of Africa in Caribbean literature tend to pass over domestic slavery, tribal warfare and the subjugation of women.[32] Condé feels it is important for writers to come to terms with the idealized image of Africa, especially when they are revisited in the light of personal and cultural definitions. Hence, in *La Vie scélérate*, references to Africa are minimal compared with her previous sagas. In *La Vie scélérate*, the narrator's genealogical search commences with Albert Louis in Guadeloupe and includes places in Europe, the Caribbean and the USA. Although the narrator makes a grand sweep of the history of black activism, Africa does not become the focus of her attention, as in Condé's previous works. She does invoke the conventional image of Africa through the only African character in the novel, Denis Latran. However, his portrayal undergoes a complete transformation in the course of the narrative through the eyes of Thécla. Her idealized image of Denis clashes with the reality of his inability to assume his obligations as father and provider. She becomes bitter with time and finally exclaims that: 'even the lowliest cane cutter has more honesty in him than he did'.[33] Thécla's realization that Denis's human frailties have failed her and their child leads her back to her own roots and experiences. Thus the demystification of the images of Africa serves as a learning experience for Thécla and enables her to re-view her perceptions of her native island.

The implication of this shift is significant. The Caribbean is no longer relegated to the margins but is at the centre of Claude's interrogation of her personal and collective history. This new inward gaze is not only honest but promising for other forms of enquiry into the past, the present and the future of Caribbean realities. This approach might guard against the illusion of reconstructing a paradisaical past. In *La Vie scélérate* and also in *Les Derniers Rois Mages*, Condé comments not only on the impossibility of re-creating objective truth from historical documents but on the effects of this idealized vision of the past. This inward gaze requires personal commitment and a critical stance against discriminatory cultural conventions. At the end of *La Vie scélérate*, Gestner, the musician and folk voice of Guadeloupe, begins to tell a folktale. The woman's role in the story is relegated to that of a subservient object of desire. The story

---

32. Maryse Condé (1993), 'Order, disorder, freedom and the West Indian writer', *Yale French Studies*, 83:2, p. 124.

33. Condé, *Tree of Life*, p. 301.

makes Claude uneasy and Gestner relinquishes his telling of the tale. Condé calls here for a lucid and critical review of old myths and stories which perpetuate sexism. Hence Gestner hands this task over to the new generation, to Claude, whom he calls 'the child of our tomorrows'.[34] On a somewhat different note, in *Les Derniers Rois Mages*, the focus is not on the writer but on the painter, whose ambivalent gaze towards history, life and art is symptomatic of the layers of silence and voicelessness with which Spéro, the protagonist/artist, has to wrestle and give expression. There is here no resolution between the political and the personal but a deep awareness of the tensions and dynamics of their interplay.

Negotiating or Subverting Social Constructions of Identity

In most of Condé's novels, character representation, thematic and symbolic configurations reveal sites of tensions and clashing ideologies, warring emotional needs between couples, families and friends. This is especially true in her most recent novels: *La Vie scélérate*, *Traversée de la mangrove*, *Les Derniers Rois Mages* and *La Colonie du nouveau monde*. These narratives weave complex human relationships, where issues of race, language, sex, age, political and cultural affiliations are raised and given extended treatment. Reflecting upon women's writings in the Caribbean context, Condé makes reference to sexism, in particular, to the stereotypical portrayals of women and states that:

> Whenever women speak out, they displease, shock or disturb. Their writings imply that before thinking of a political revolution, West Indian society needs a psychological one. What they hope for and desire conflicts with men's ambitions and dreams. Why, they ask, fight against discrimination in the world when it exists at home, among ourselves?[35]

She, like many other Caribbean women writers, such as Ina Césaire, Gisèle Pineau, Simone Schwarz-Bart, attacks the ideology that fails to consider personal interrelationships and the limited social role to which women and children are relegated within Caribbean societies.

In *La Vie scélérate*, the Louis family has a long legacy of men (Albert, Jacob, Dieudonné) whose lofty political ideas conflict with the way in which they practise their beliefs. Subscribing to a dichotomy between the political and the personal, Albert, Jacob and Dieudonné all place their

---

34. Ibid., p. 367.
35. Condé, 'Order, disorder, freedom and the West Indian writer', pp. 131–2.

politics before their personal lives. When Claude suggests that Dieudonné's neglect may be justified due to the importance of the 'cares of the nation,' Monique clearly opposes this idea. In defiance, she cries:

> What are you talking about Coco? Isn't it we women who make and unmake the nation? As long as they keep us in the background, they'll never accomplish a thing! And Guadeloupe will remain the last colony for a long, long time![36]

Monique's personal admonition undermines the dichotomy between private and public discourses. Her strong personal stance becomes political as she becomes acutely aware of the marginalization and oppression of women who can bypass neither patriarchy nor unequal power relations. This issue is given extended treatment in *Les Derniers Rois Mages*. In this novel, Condé reverses the gender roles in order to show that women are no less vulnerable to ideological and/or militant social discourses and that they, too, may succumb to the very fate of their male counterparts in *La Vie scélérate*. Similarly, Monique in *La Vie scélérate* and Spéro in *Les Derniers Rois Mages* both suffer from emotional neglect, while their spouses are attending to the political needs of their communities. Although the marginalized characters in *La Vie scélérate* and *Les Derniers Rois Mages* remain to some extent trapped within the boundaries that are imposed upon them, the continued projection of their hopes and dreams represents a way in which they may find meaning and direction in their lives.

In *La Vie scélérate*, the uncovering of the past, its silences, its exclusion, its muffled or suppressed voices, requires personal and communal commitment. This is evident in Claude's desire to salvage the remnants of her family's history. She believes, in much the same way as Bébert does, that 'one cannot live without knowing where one comes from'.[37] In learning about her family history, she learns that she is not alone, that her feelings of marginalization and isolation were also felt by other family members. As she herself states: 'and so I join with Bert and Bébert, and belong as do they to the lineage of those who are never mentioned. From that no doubt comes my instinctive solidarity with them.'[38] It is therefore fitting that Bert, Bébert and Aurélia, formerly marginalized and excluded from the rest of the Louis family, are, at the end of the novel, reintegrated into the familial past. Their names are included on the family crypt alongside

36. Condé, *Tree of Life*, p. 352.
37. Ibid., p. 216.
38. Ibid., p. 186.

the rest of the deceased members of the Louis clan. The inclusion of forgotten or marginalized members into the family tree, the reintegration of excluded elements give weight to the Caribbean notion of *métissage* (hybridity) and Creoleness wherein all elements of Caribbean identity are to be recuperated, evaluated and connected to the present.[39] It is noteworthy that in *La Vie scélérate*, as in many of Condé's novels, building solidarity among family members is a source of strength and healing and the approach may vary according to the circumstances. Since the Louis family members in *La Vie scélérate* are dispersed around the world, correspondence is the favoured mode of establishing and maintaining contact. In their respective letters lie their hopes and expectations, their wishes to reconcile and reunify the family's history. However, when Aurélia finally renews contact with the rest of her family through Claude, she can now establish a new form of dialogue – one that will serve as a basis for future generations, given that their personal reunion highlights interdependence, mutual caring and understanding.

Grounding Art in Daily Life

It is interesting to realize that the ending of *La Vie scélérate* deals with the significance of biographies or life stories to a wider audience. Claude's thoughts converge with the implied author's motivations for writing this novel:

> Would I perhaps have to recount this story? At the risk of displeasing and shocking would I in my turn, perhaps, have to pay my debt? It would be a story of very ordinary people who in their very ordinary way have nonetheless made blood flow . . . I would have to tell and it would be a memorial monument of my own. A book quite different from those ambitious ones my mother had dreamed of writing, *Revolutionary moments of the Black World* and all the rest. A book with neither great torturers nor lavish martyrdoms. But one that would still be heavy with its weight of flesh and blood. The story of my people.[40]

Claude's decision to write something shocking and disturbing, a story about ordinary human beings with all their faults and inconsistencies, is meant to break with literary conventions and expectations for Caribbean

---

39. Françoise Lionnet (1995), *Postcolonial Representations: Women, Literature, Identity*, Ithaca: Cornell UP, pp. 1–29.

40. Condé, *Tree of Life*, p. 357.

fiction.[41] And yet Condé's literary project also negotiates a space in which she engages with the aesthetic principles articulated by the proponents of Creoleness when they define the role of the writer:

> The writer is a detector of existence. More than anyone else, the writer's vocation is to identify what, in our daily lives, determines the patterns and structure of the imaginary. To perceive our existence is to perceive us in the context of our history, of our daily lives, of our reality. It is also to perceive our virtualities.[42]

Like Chamoiseau, Confiant, Glissant, Schwarz-Bart, among others, Condé celebrates the personal lives of ordinary people, recounts stories about hardships and transformation on a personal and collective scale. In doing so, she, like her compatriots, hopes to articulate a vision that will rekindle individual and communal solidarities, value cultural diversity and invite different approaches to Caribbean realities.

As I have suggested in the title of this study, cultural definitions of identity apparent in the poetics of negritude, Caribbeanness and Creoleness have sought to articulate silences and promote cultural assertions by recognizing diverse world-views, the multicultural heritages (African, Asian, European . . .) and multiracial constituencies of Caribbean communities. Conscious of the colonial language and its ideological terrain, French Caribbean writings often delve into the poetics of location: the positionality of characters and narrators; the legitimacy of social discourses; symbolic landscapes and peregrinations; Creole traditions and resonances. It is significant to note that, while Caribbean writers underline tensions and conflicts among members of different cultural groups, they also project in the same breath a vision of mutual understanding and healing through reconciliation with one's cultural past. Lastly, if one considers the social and political imperatives from which French Caribbean literature emerged, the creative struggles and experimentation that it embodies, its openness to connections and interaction between peoples and communities within and outside the Caribbean, there is much to be said about the role of the communal imagination and its need to flourish in order to explore new cartographies and new ways of nurturing the human spirit.

41. Lionnet, *Postcolonial Representations*, p. 133.
42. Bernabé *et al.*, *In Praise of Creoleness*, pp. 99–100.

–11–

Daughters of Mayotte, Sons of Frantz: The Unrequited Self in Caribbean Literature

Clarisse Zimra

Who or what is a Caribbean writer? Every attempt at autonomous self-definition has provoked equally compelling counter-definitions of cultural dependency. Can the master's language, which Frantz Fanon once tagged as the instrument of colonial brainwashing, create a common identity not encaged within the master's *episteme*? Can there be a Caribbean literature identified by a Euro-Caribbean language or need only Creole texts apply? If so, what do we do with those writers who, like Haiti's Frankétienne, Guadeloupe's Sonny Rupaire or Martinique's Raphaël Confiant, write both? Does pride of place override everything else? This might eliminate those who triangulate their literary quest among several spiritual homes, equally at ease in the continent to the north, Europe, and/or Africa. Naipaul, Walcott, Brathwaite, Wynter, Condé, Harris come to mind among our contemporaries, as might have Carpentier or Guillen earlier.

Indeed, this proliferation of mutually exclusive definitions nevertheless remains predicated on the belief – once carried by the Cuban Carifesta movement of 1979 and, for the anglophones, hopes of a lasting West Indian Federation – that the formerly colonized must constitute a cultural unit by virtue of a common past. In this idealized historical perspective, the traumatic middle passage foreshadows the islands' resistance to their continued 'neocolonial' status with respect to the juggernaut of superpowers, whether to the north or across the Atlantic Ocean. This oppositional stance unites any and all cultural production, a conviction that still subtends Paul Gilroy's 1992 text, *Black Atlantic*, for instance, even as he short-changes the francophone contribution. Such was the contention firmly expressed, twenty years ago, by Guadeloupe's Maryse Condé in her 1979 *La Parole des femmes*:

We want to believe that the 'Carib world' is one and, therefore, we refuse any ranking that would selectively discriminate among islands. We start with the preliminary conviction that, within this universe whose fundamental unity we defend, there may occur quite a few differences resulting from distinct economic, social or psychological conditions – conditions probably dictated by their lesser or greater dependency on one or other centre of world domination.[1]

Here, linguistic differences and the different formal results they may dictate become less crucial than overdetermined sociohistorical convergences in deciding who and what makes a Caribbean.

This Universe Whose Fundamental Unity We Defend

This contention has logistical merit. It is the starting-point for self-examination for literary figures as diverse as Martinique's Edouard Glissant, who, with his 'poétique de la relation', discovers the Caribbean self primarily as a subject in an existential relation to other subjects;[2] Trinidad's C.L.R. James, who insists that the conquered recapture their agency by writing their history;[3] or Guiana's Wilson Harris, who demands their full engagement in a multilayered consciousness that leaps over national and ethnic boundaries.[4] And the issue of self-definition becomes ever more complex when one interjects in the process the gender variable so crucial to our modern understanding of human discourse.

The oppositional question was squarely genderized in the text that would forever transform our understanding of the racialized process of

1. Maryse Condé (1979), *La Parole des femmes: essai sur des romancières des Antilles de langue française,* Paris: L'Harmattan, p. 6. Translation mine.

2. Edouard Glissant (1981), *Le Discours antillais*, Paris: Seuil, is the first formulation of the concept, further refined in (1990), *Poétique de la relation*, Paris: Seuil. *Le Discours antillais* was aptly translated in 1989 by Michael Dash as *Caribbean Discourse*, Charlottesville: CARAF Series, University of Virginia Press, but the English version is a selection of relevant passages, hence shorter than the original. For instance, the famous reference to slave women as captive but defiant, who, by practising abortions, knew 'how to refuse carrying within their loins the master's property' ('refuser de porter dans ses flancs le profit du maître', p. 97), is missing in the translation; an omission that erases, for English-only readers, the Fanon–Lacrosil connection that I shall examine here.

3. C.L.R. James (1980), *The Black Jacobins: Toussaint Louverture and the San Domingo Revolution*, London: Allison and Busby. James's preface to the first edition (1938), London: Vintage, set forth these goals admirably: 'I made up my mind that I would write a book in which Africans or people of African descent, instead of being the object of other people's exploitation and ferocity, would themselves be taking action on a grand scale and shaping others to their needs' (p. viii).

4. Wilson Harris (1983), *The Womb of Space*, Wesport and London: Greenwood Press.

self-definition in the Caribbean. Frantz Fanon's 1952 *Peau noire, masques blancs* singled out Mayotte Capécia as its paradigmatic woman writer, transforming an otherwise minor talent into an instant celebrity. These were not laurels she would wear lightly. For, as I have argued in prior essays,[5] much of Capécia's importance depended on her usefulness as a foil to Fanon's primary concern: that of establishing the African Caribbean male's right to full humanity. In so doing, Fanon took it for granted that liberation by reason of race must tactically subsume liberation by reason of sex. A psychiatrist's study *Peau noire, masques blancs* may have been, but it remained blithely unaware of its own hegemonic gendered assumptions.

By the late 1990s, however, the progressive 'genderizing' of literary criticism on the Caribbean seems a *fait accompli*. One can now locate the contested space carved out by women writers, who, as Sylvia Wynter has insisted, all along refused to let the other speak for them. From her incisive 1968 intervention, 'We must learn to sit down and discuss a little culture', to her trenchant 1990 call to battle, 'Beyond Miranda's meanings',[6] the Cuban-born poet-dramatist-critic-teacher from Jamaica has refused the separatist androcentric Caribbean canon, where women were not allowed to position themselves. As epistemological fields are being stubbornly renegotiated in the West, at least with regard to the relationships between the West and its others, they demonstrate that the early unified idealized vision of the Caribbean, once so necessary to force the West out of its hegemonic position, is no longer tenable. It might be useful to remind ourselves how we got here in the first place. Hence, conceding the usefulness of unifying parameters, this essay seeks to excavate two intertwined areas: one, the francophone subset, however contentious the phrase; and, two, the female subset, perhaps the less fractious of the two because easier to isolate.

Although arguing for the specificity of female writing has been a key contribution of feminist theory, I will here limit my own definition of the

---

5. Clarisse Zimra (1977), 'Patterns of liberation in contemporary women writers', *L'Esprit créateur*, 17:2, pp. 103–14. Indeed, it is with the implied primal miscegenation that Fanon is concerned, since, for him, the black Caribbean woman has always already internalized the lactification ideal and thus, either physically or at least symbolically, has 'gone over' to the enemy.

6. Sylvia Wynter (1968), 'We must learn to sit down and discuss a little culture: reflections on West Indian writing and criticism', *Jamaica Journal*, 2:4, pp. 23–32; and (1990), 'Beyond's Miranda's meanings: un/silencing the "demonic ground" of Caliban's woman', in Carole Boyce Davies and Elaine Savory Fido, eds, *Out of the Kumbla: Caribbean Women and Literature*, Trenton, New Jersey: Africa World Press, pp. 355–71.

female subset as the writing of a female subject denied, because biologized and genderized. This move has been suspected of essentialism,[7] but, when applied to colonial societies, the phrase becomes historicized, for these societies did assign colonized women a place and role different from that of men by reason of their reproductive biology. The biological semantics that has dominated the literary discourse on and by women has never lost track of this historical foundation.

The term 'francophone' proves a bit more slippery: first, on linguistic grounds, because it fails to distinguish among writers for whom French is either the mother tongue or the only available written medium (because, in some cases, they were not taught to write their native tongue); second, on ideological grounds, because of the concerted efforts of the French government to maintain a sort of 'mission civilisatrice' – this will to civilize the uncivilized – through language; to wit, the last 'Francophone Summit' in Hanoi, reported with amused wryness in *The Economist* of 22 November 1997. In the French islands, this has brought continued dependence on a 'mother country', which gives the lie to the notion of post-coloniality, mired as the francophone Caribbeans are in a crisis of identity politics that masquerade as identity poetics.

This essay seeks to examine how the androcentric model has functioned within the yoked subsets of francophone/women writers. To focus matters in what is, obviously, a vast panorama, I have selected three writers with common linguistic as well as sociohistorical backgrounds. That they should come from the same island, Guadeloupe, and should write in response to a common intertextual grid (Fanon on Capécia) will permit a finer contextualization of the gender variable.

Michèle Lacrosil (*Sapotille*, 1960; *Cajou*, 1961), Jacqueline Manicom (*Mon examen de blanc*, 1972) and Daniel Maximin (*L'Isolé Soleil*, 1981)[8] share a basic plot, the doomed affair between partners of different racial and class origins. Not surprisingly, they also share an unreliable first-person narrator, instrument of self-fragmentation *par excellence*. If, following Fanon's pronouncements, the Caribbean female is obsessed by what

7. See, for example, some of the arguments surrounding the work of Luce Irigaray: Monique Plaza (1978), '"Phallomorphic power" and the psychology of "woman"', *Ideology and Consciousness* 4 , pp. 4–36; Janet Sayers (1982), *Biological Politics: Feminist and Anti-feminist Perspectives*, London: Tavistock; Mary Jacobus (1986), *Reading Woman: Essays in Feminist Criticism,* London: Methuen.

8. Michèle Lacrosil (1960), *Sapotille, ou le serin d'argile*, Paris: Gallimard; and (1961), *Cajou*, Paris: Gallimard; Jacqueline Manicom (1972), *Mon examen de blanc*, Paris: Presses de la Cité; Daniel Maximin (1981), *L'Isolé Soleil*, Paris: Seuil, translated in 1991 as *Lone Sun*, Charlottesville: CARAF Series, University of Virginia Press.

he scathingly called 'the lactification complex', the desire for children who are ever lighter-skinned, what more apt expression of self-hatred than abortion, the one act that nullifies all reproduction, all self-validation, whether physical or symbolic? Ever present in Capécia, the Fanonian paradigm is doubled up in an act of abortion–suicide with Lacrosil and reversed in Manicom, where abortion becomes a liberating self-birthing. In Maximin, the act leads to an identity poetics that breaches generic as well as gender boundaries.

If I choose thus to circumscribe the issue, it is because a formidable revision of Fanon's contribution to Third World liberation theory and literary history has been under way for the past ten years. This enthronization of Fanon's position, in and on the Caribbean, has been accelerated by Homi Bhabha's vibrant homage, his 1986 preface to *Black Skins, White Masks* found the psychiatrist from Martinique 'either revered as the prophetic spirit of Third World Liberation or reviled as exterminating angel'.[9] In a more measured essay of 1992, 'Critical Fanonism', Henry Louis Gates warned against hypostasizing Fanon's exemplary position to such an extent that we end up totemizing him, 'emptied of his own specificity'.[10] In so doing, we neglect the specificity of the culture and the cultural productions *Peau noire, masques blancs* intended to depict and denounce. It is to these specificities that we now turn.

What They Must Have is Whiteness at any Price

Fanon's first book was crucial in setting up the psychosocial parameters of his native land, by proffering a racialized paradigm for its cultural productions. Yet he remained impervious to its genderized components, something which, unfortunately, his intellectual progeny continues to do.[11] His own take on Caribbean women racializes gender (women reproduce

9. Homi Bhabha (1986), 'Foreword: remembering Fanon', in Frantz Fanon, *Black Skins, White Masks*, trans. Charles Lam Markmann, London: Pluto, p. viii.

10. Henry Louis Gates Jr (1991), 'Critical Fanonism', *Critical Inquiry*, 17, p. 459. Likewise, Edward Said (1989), 'Representing the colonized: anthropology's interlocutors', *Critical Inquiry*, 15, pp. 205–20, has cautioned us against over-generalizing the dyadic relationship in defining 'a great many different, but inferior, things in many different places, at many different times' (p. 207).

11. Particularly virulent is Fritz Gracchus (1979), *Les Lieux de la mère dans les littératures afro-américaines*, Paris: Editions Caribéennes. For a sound corrective, see Julie Lirius (1979), *Identité antillaise*, Paris: Editions Caribéennes; and Gwen Bergner (1995), 'Who is that masked woman, or the role of gender in *Black Skins, White Masks*', *PMLA*, 110:1, pp. 75–88.

the race) as it genderizes race (to be a black woman is, in essence, different from being a black man). The dyad reinstates familiar binaries in the very process of questioning their legitimacy: as white to black, so self to other, so Caribbean man to woman. That his instinct tended to the teleological explains in no small part Fanon's polarized vision, a move as simplifying as it was crucial to his purpose.

The polarization was also carried out by his unswerving use of the 'generic' masculine, 'le Noir', wherein 'the Black man' is made to constitute the normative. This, and the recurrent use of the pronoun 'he', accentuates the fact that the full ontological subject from whom he expects acknowledgement is neither the black woman, nor the white woman, but the white man. Well might one retort that French has always demanded this 'gender-neutral' enfolding of woman into man to designate the species. But that Fanon, so sensitive to linguistic entrapment in the master's language, should use it so unselfquestioningly is worth pondering – as is worth pondering his not so casual dismissal of female sexuality qua female, in the chapter entitled 'The negro and psychopathology': 'Those who grant our views on the psycho-sexuality of the white woman may ask what we have to say about the woman of color. I know nothing about her.'[12] A series of qualifying conditionals traces his discomfort more obviously in the original French: 'on pourrait nous demander' ('some might ask/query', instead of 'may ask'); 'ce que nous proposerions' ('what we might propose/ offer' on the woman of colour, instead of 'what we have to say'[13]). With his unquestioning use of the (now debunked) Freudian positions of Marie Bonaparte on vaginal versus clitoridic women, the Martinican accepts the white androcentric model as primary, to theorize vaguely on the existence of 'juxta-Blanches' ('juxta-Whites', i.e. women next to, almost, white), to whom he devotes exactly three lines. These are Caribbean women who yearn for rape by a coal-black man, 'of the Senegalese type'.[14] Not only is the racist fear of Africa speaking here, but also a particularly French colonial anxiety, since Senegalese were drafted routinely to occupy or pacify other colonials (in Algeria or Vietnam, for example, they had a ferocious reputation).

Before dismissing Fanon's position as altogether 'politically incorrect', we need to remember that he was attacking Ottavio Mannoni's study of neurotic dependency in Madagascar, which asserted that Malagasy were

12. Frantz Fanon (1986), *Black Skins, White Masks*, trans. Charles Lam Markmann, London: Pluto, pp. 179–80.

13. Frantz Fanon (1952), *Peau noire, masques blancs*, Paris: Seuil, p. 145.

14. Fanon, *Black Skin, White Masks*, p. 180.

'pathologically' (i.e. biologically) so predisposed by their submissive culture. Fanon countered that such dysfunctional behaviour was caused by the very abuses perpetrated by the 'great white father'. Whatever his blind spots, Fanon's contribution was to demonstrate that the colonial patients were sick, but that it was colonialism that had made them so. His sharp insight was to politicize the experience in displacing basic Freudian psychology from the individual to the collective. Yet, to maintain his highly politicized binary reading, he ignored the much more supple awareness of skin tones still in place on the French islands into the twentieth century, with the lighter-skinned at the top of the heap, generally. This differential treatment was all that remained of the Sun King's 1685 *Code Noir*, a set of sixty articles with corresponding pigment taxonomies, that had been intended to limit black/white contacts; accordingly, each nuance carried a precise set of discriminatory practices. Instead, Fanon posited a black or white, 'them or us' view of the colonial world, branding all women traitors to the race: 'All these frantic women of color in quest of white men are waiting . . . what they must have is whiteness at any price.'[15] This dissection of female behaviour (chapter 2 of *Peau noire, masques blancs*, on Capécia) comes before that of male behaviour (chapter 3, on Maran), as though the former defined and overdetermined the latter. Viewed as victims, men were treated with compassion, their predicament, in René Maran's 1947 *Un homme pareil aux autres*, deemed a 'tragedy' ('drame'): 'What are the terms of this problem? Jean Veneuse is a Negro. Born in the Antilles, he has lived in Bordeaux for years; so he is a European. But he is black. So he is a Negro. There is the conflict [tragedy].'[16]

It is tempting to speculate on Fanon's own discovery of the master's double standard, since he seems so blind to his own. The confrontation between the republican ideals imbibed in his colonial schooldays and the reality of his first visit to French soil forced him to reconceptualize an identity whose ontological transparency he had not hitherto examined.

---

15. Ibid., p. 49. The slippages between the French and the English versions are telling. The waiting women are not 'frantic' in the original; they are 'échevelées', which is to say, dishevelled, their loose hair simultaneously an image of loose morals and unkempt poverty. Overall, Charles Lam Markmann's translation operates a flattening effect on the differences between male and female conditions. The consequence is to mute the impact of Fanon's Sartrean demand that each object be recognized as subject, and vice versa, in a mutually empowering move.

16. Ibid., p. 64. Here, slippages between the French and the English versions mean that Veneuse's problem is not deemed a 'conflict', but a 'drame'. The original is much stronger ('Voilà le drame'/'There's the tragedy'), a phrase that covers the distance between drama and tragedy.

This was a Sartrean moment: the Caribbean subject rendered specular object by the ready-made identity assigned him, 'Martinican, native-born in one of *our* oldest colonies'.[17] Note that the sarcastic emphasis signalling ownership, '*our* colonies', is Fanon's own. This denied him the self the young medical student had brought from his 'native' land to his metro-politan 'mother' land, that of a French citizen, heir to the Enlightenment and equal to any French person anywhere.[18]

Capécia wrote in the late 1940s. Consider the ambivalence of her first title, *Je suis Martiniquaise*, since by 1946, the island had been granted departmental status and the formerly colonized full citizens' rights. With exquisite irony, the phrase was also the one young Fanon had heard thrown back at him upon his arrival in Paris. Upon his first public foray, young Fanon discovered his place in the mouth of child, fully if unselfconsciously acculturated to the values of the dominant group. The first indeterminate remark, 'Look, mommy, *a* Negro!' mutated to specifics when Fanon smiled back: 'Mommy, look at *the* Negro, I'm scared' (emphasis, mine). To which the upper-class white mother, unable to silence her child ('Shush! The man's going to get angry!'), made the requisite hegemonic apology: 'Take no notice, sir, he does not know that you are as civilized as we . . .'[19] This experience, so common in the francophone corpus (one thinks of Césaire's 'Negro, comical and ugly' in *Cahier d'un retour au pays natal*), marks the moment of truth when the Martinican, until then so proud of

17. Ibid., p. 113.

18. For the circumstances and the contradictions of identity politics surrounding the passage from colonial territory to department, see Richard D.E. Burton and Fred Reno (1994), *French and West Indian: Martinique, Guadeloupe and French Guiana Today*, Charlottesville: New World Series, University of Virginia Press. The status of 'departments' meant, for all practical purposes, that they were the administrative as well as political equals of any department on French soil (actually, they were now French soil). Burton (1993) has commented on this orgy of 'hyper-assimilation', in 'Maman-France-Doudou: family images in French West Indian discourse', *Diacritics*, 23:3, pp. 69–90. As the novelists under scrutiny in the present essay make clear, the change neither ensured an end to prejudice nor created full civil rights. The last salvo to date may well be the defiant 1989 collective manifesto penned by Jean Bernabé, Patrick Chamoiseau and Raphaël Confiant, *Eloge de la créolité/In Praise of Creoleness* (bilingual edition), trans. M.B. Taleb-Khyar, Paris: Gallimard, which declares, 'Neither Europeans, nor Africans, nor Asians, we proclaim ourselves Creoles', p. 75.

19. Fanon, *Black Skin, White Masks*, p. 113. This time, the English translation arbitrarily lowers the register. The white mother does not say, as Markmann has it, 'Hell, he's getting mad' (p. 113); but rather, 'Chut! il va se fâcher' ('Hush/shush, he's going to get angry/upset'). Certainly, a proper bourgeois lady would watch her linguistic register, particularly with regard to teaching this inferior black man, as well as her child, that she is 'as civilized' as he.

maintaining the difference between civilized Caribbeans and primitive Africans, is brought sharply up by another unbreachable series of hierarchized distinctions.[20] French or Martinican? Caribbean or African? Black, coloured or honorary white? Whatever, whoever he is, his identity is chosen for him; he can never be subject to himself.

Thus, we find a Fanon who should know better maintaining another hierarchized distinction still, that between male and female colonized. His acerbic review of Capécia's two novels, the 1948 *Je suis Martiniquaise* and the 1950 *La Négresse blanche*, was followed by a much kinder appraisal of Maran's, whose character's colour obsession is explained away as an 'abandonment neurosis' that goes back to early childhood and cannot be undone. Veneuse will forever fall in love with worthy white women and refuse to marry them because he believes himself unworthy (Lacrosil's *Cajou* will replay this scenario). And yet the quotes Fanon uses from Capécia show, just as equally, that her character's own neurosis goes back to a racially traumatized early childhood. By the age of five, in kindergarten, Mayotte would habitually pour the black ink from her inkwell on her white deskmates before repeated punishments succeeded in taming her. Whereas Fanon works hard to establish that Maran's clinical condition is more important than its racialized manifestation, no such allowance is made for Capécia's. That both mother and older friend should have taught Mayotte to respect white power is not seen as a survival tactic, but as the proof of a female conspiracy.

The psychiatrist is nevertheless correct when he accuses her characters of racist self-hatred. In *La Négresse blanche*, Isaure explains her society to the white, French-born Pétainist officer in blunt terms: 'Believe me, when these dirty niggers are excited, there's no holding them back. They can't control themselves. They are savages. You do not know the black blood, Sir.'[21] Indeed, when Mayotte is abandoned penniless in *Je suis Martiniquaise*, she takes defiant comfort in her child to the end: 'I thought . . . how right I was to have had a son, and how proud I was, *all the same*, that he should be white.'[22]

---

20. The humiliating distinction carefully nurtured between Caribbeans and Africans within the French empire served to divide and conquer. For an unflinching corroboration, see Claude McKay (1957), *Banjo*, New York: Harcourt, Brace. First published in 1928, it is merciless in its depiction of hostility between Africans and other subjects of the French Empire among the dock-workers of Marseilles harbour.

21. Mayotte Capécia (1950), *La Négresse blanche*, Paris: Correa; pp. 11–12. Translation mine.

22. Ibid., p. 201 (of 202 pages). Emphasis mine.

Impervious as Fanon was to issues of gender, he shows himself equally blind to issues of class. Maran's Veneuse is a university-trained professional who tangles easily with upper-class women of his calibre. Capécia's Mayotte is a shack-born brat, who leaves the back country to make her living in the capital by taking in the dirty laundry of whites. While the irony does not escape him, good Marxist Fanon overlooks the abject poverty that eventually teaches this woman that she must work the system or starve; instead, he comments on the phenomenological angle: 'So, since she could no longer try to blacken, to negrify the world, she was going to bleach it. To start, she would become a laundress.'[23]

If Mayotte, to survive on an island blockaded by the Second World War, preferred the blue-eyed sailors of the occupying navy to her swarthier Gaullist compatriots in the first novel, Isaure, in the second one, was on the right side of history. She marries a *béké* in the resistance, who gives her a prophetic lesson in race politics:

> My sisters do not wish to understand that the Allies' victory, the success of communism, is going to abolish once and for all this senseless racism . . . the future belongs to blacks and, five or six years from now, regardless of whether I am in love with you or not, I may be all too glad to have been one of the first to marry a woman of colour.[24]

Her husband is soon murdered in the hunger-triggered riots of black cane-cutters, for whom there can be no 'good' whites. In this, Capécia was not only prescient (a political reading of her works, clearly grounded in contemporary insular history, has yet to be performed), but she gave us a plot Michèle Lacrosil will develop. It is a plot with a long history, born of the nineteenth-century Romantic abolitionist tale with its female-designed variation, the tragic mulatto, whose love is unrequited, whose soul is self-sacrificial to the end.

The connection between Lacrosil and Capécia is more than accidental. By Lacrosil's own admission during a series of conversations with me in summer 1976, her publisher, the powerful Gallimard, whom she had approached on a friend's dare, requested a sequel to Capécia's novels. Lacrosil had not cared for the comparison but produced instead what she called, 'a mock Capécia' ('une fausse Capécia'). Indeed, if her heroines suffer from the famous lactification complex and find their own dark features unbecoming, they nevertheless twist the tragic mulatto plot into

---

23. Fanon, *Black Skin, White Masks*, p. 45.
24. Capécia, *La Négresse blanche*, p. 132. Translation mine.

a very different conclusion, one that exposes racism's power to inflict worse evil by turning the hatred inward.

Lacrosil was convinced that Capécia's novels were written 'on orders' ('sur mesure'). This casual remark expresses how gingerly one must tread with any Capécia material – particularly, beliefs that her novels are 'autobiographical,' a claim made by Fanon himself and one that the latest Fanon scholar accepts uncritically.[25] It was commonly said, at least among the older generation of writers in Paris to whom I also spoke in 1976 (to wit, Léonard Sainville, Gilbert Gratiant, Marie-Magdeleine Carbet and Guy de Chambertrand), that Capécia wrote 'under the aegis, if not the whip' ('sous l'aile et la férule') of a white admirer and probable lover, which they took to be the proof that her stories were not worth reading. This essay, however, prefers to treat Fanon's equations of Maran-Veneuse and Capécia-Mayotte as rich sources for interpretive paradigms, without shipwrecking itself further on the autobiographical issue. Modern criticism has blurred the conventional distinction between autobiography and fiction within the discursive continuum of self-actualizing narratives. The figurative system of representation we call literature stands at the intersection of the individual and the collective 'imaginary', the common storehouse of ideas and images we inhabit and to which we respond, by virtue of our private lives (the autobiographical) as well as our collective lives (the imaginary socius).

Lacrosil ended up deconstructing the formulaic mulatto. Instead of Capécia's triumphant passage away from island to 'motherland', a passage history – and Fanon – tells us was fraught with obstacles, she strikes a sarcastic note with the ending of *Sapotille*: 'The French do not know the compartmentalization prevalent in Caribbean society, the taboos from one class to another. I've always loved their country; *I have yet to know it,* but I do know that it is my homeland.'[26] This narrator yearns for the land she's never seen as for a beloved (one hears echoes of Fanon's 'waiting women'), in the crippling fantasy of the colonized's compensatory mechanisms. With a light-skinned lover who refuses to be seen with her, and a black husband who beats her up so savagely that she loses her child, the novel revisits the female yearning for full presence by means of her procreative function in a much more sinister way. The character welcomes the miscarriage, driving home the twinned reproduction of racism, political as well as biological: 'I did not want a little girl who'd learn, in her history book, "Our ancestors the Gauls carried spears and wore breeches" . . .

25. See Bergner, 'Who is that masked woman'.
26. Lacrosil, *Cajou*, pp. 239–40. Emphasis added, translation mine.

Nor did I want a little boy, sweet and mischievous, at first, then soured; one who would become an embittered man because each insult would have left behind this urge to torment another.'[27]

Cajou, in Lacrosil's next novel, goes to the logical extreme by choosing suicide as a way to end both the pregnancy and the self. One could argue that this educated, middle-class, biracial woman, a successful research scientist soon to be married to an equally successful white colleague, is neurotic, whereas Sapotille is simply maladjusted. Yet there is an uncanny repetition here. In Capécia's second novel, Isaure's white mother-in-law offers to receive the woman she would not see when her son was alive, because she believes her to be pregnant. Likewise, it is only after Germain has told Cajou that, knowing her reluctance to marry him, he has made her pregnant to force her hand that he triumphantly announces that he, too, has won his parents over: '"They told me I should have brought you to meet them long ago." I look at him in disbelief. "They know you are carrying my child. They accept." I see. Germain looks away. I should have known.'[28] This is the very moment when she decides upon suicide. Lacanians would find this character obssessed by mirrors that never reflect back an acceptable, fully integrated self, an exemplary case, down to the last and most unforgiving mirror of all, the river. Leaning over the Seine, she realizes in her final moment that this child will never be hers: 'I would like to shatter the mirror, hurl my body as if it were a cannonball in order to destroy…Who? Germain's child?'[29] Albeit presented as a plunge into insanity, the suicide becomes a vindication of the humanity too long denied her – tentative, still, since the book ends on a question.

I am less inclined than some to limit Lacrosil's novel to a descent into madness,[30] because the author does provide a clue to inflect our reading; this is the mysterious word that haunts Cajou with such force that she often blanks out under its unspoken power: ' I felt empty. I had not really fainted, but objects no longer registered on my consciousness. They had escaped me … At one point, the window disappeared.'[31] Forced by her fiancé to say it, yet physically unable to, she ends up vomiting up the disconnected syllables that sound off her own fragmented self:

27. Ibid., p. 236.

28. Ibid., p. 223.

29. Ibid., p. 232.

30. For example, Robert P. Smith (1974), 'Michèle Lacrosil, novelist with a color complex', *The French Review*, 47, pp. 783–90; and, Elizabeth Wilson (1990), 'Le voyage et l'espace clos', in Boyce-Davies and Fido, eds, *Out of the Kumbla*, pp. 45–58.

31. Lacrosil, *Cajou*, p. 207.

'dia-spo-ra! dia-spo-ra!'[32] The term is so valorized these days that one can speak positively of a black diasporic identity and, perhaps, forget its uglier subtext. This mutilated and mutilating word enacts her psychic dismemberment. 'Diaspora, dispersion, dissolution, destruction,'[33] she answers to his proposal of marriage – a response he pronounces 'not important' and diagnoses – scientist that he is – as the case of nerves of a pregnant woman.

This diasporic connection is fully present in Jacqueline Manicom's *Mon examen de blanc*, the phrase – my white exam, my exam in white/ about whites – itself a Guadeloupean idiom that refers to passing as white. Reminiscing on her arrival in Paris, the narrator wryly evokes the Fanon–Capécia–Lacrosil legacy:

> This particular summer, she still believed in what she had been taught in her Caribbean school: the Gauls were her ancestors, but of course! She was thus doubly French: first, because she had been born in a French colony; second, because she had been so assured during the departmentalization of 1945; she was but a little girl, but she did understand. She had been told that the African negroes were savages, whereas Caribbeans were practically whites. How then could there be any insurmountable obstacle between Xavier and herself?[34]

The author's own experience in France as a medical student presents more than an accidental convergence with Fanon's, and we shall find Maximin making hay of both the Fanon and the Manicom personae in his own later novel.

Dia-spo-ra, Dia-spo-ra

Manicom's narrator toys – like Cajou – with suicide. What saves her is her political awakening. Like Isaure and Cajou before her, Madévie falls in love with an activist killed trying to organize the cane-cutters; but, this time, he is black. The novel eviscerates the tragic mulatto plot whose predictable ending operated to contain its subversive message, and does so by politicizing it brazenly. Playing on racial ambivalence, this protagonist of East Indian parentage is called 'mulâtresse', to align her with any and all people of mixed descent, although the term had hitherto designated someone with clearly African features. Appropriating it, Manicom indicates that, to the still racist 'new' whites, all others are 'mulattos', whatever

32. Ibid., p. 208.
33. Ibid., p. 209.
34. Ibid, p. 43. Translation mine.

their ancestry. They must join together or hang separately. Things have changed since the joyous entry into the French family. These are the 1960s, and the novel maps harsh socio-economic conditions and race riots, bloodily put down by imported French paramilitary riot troups (over 50,000 strong in 1967). Born like the author in an East Indian cane-cutting family, the character displays her awareness of class and a bitter-clear perception of the human cost of 'departmentalization', the massive exodus of unemployed islanders to factories and hospital bedpan detail in France: 'Today, Boeings have replaced the slave ships of the middle passage, give or take a few nuances.'[35] New invaders, French-born civil servants who neither know nor care about the islands, pour in to run the place like so many conquerors.

The requisite Parisian affair is presented by a dry-eyed narrator with a sarcastic bluntness that cancels out the reported idealism of young love:

> How could she not love him, since he had just made a 'woman' out of her, 'his woman/wife' ['femme'], as it were. She had given him the unspent capital of her virginity. In return, he had to marry her . . . Why shouldn't he marry her? She was ready to make herself white to please him; to give him, later, little white children, to forget the sun pouring on Moule harbour, the tiny 'pipirit' bird that salutes the fragrant dawns suffused with the smell of coffee sweetly spiced with 'sépiante'.[36]

More painstakingly – because she is that much more aware in retrospect – an older woman charts for us the slow relinquishing of self-respect that the affair demanded of her youthful self, by reason of class as well as by reason of race. These very upper-crust Christians offer marriage if she will sign a divorce agreement effective on the day she delivers her child. To deflower a coloured virgin and give her a bastard is a sin, but to acknowledge her is a social liability, a serious issue. Far better for the child to be surrendered, since the product of the female's reproductive function remains the property of the patriarchy. The medical student ends up performing her own abortion in a sordid Parisian room. Literally as well as symbolically killing the child within becomes the only way to exorcize the unrequited self. However, determined by and for a man and his beliefs (black Gilbert instead of white Xavier), her identity still defines the (once) colonized in relation to the (once) colonizer. This merely shifts the Fanonian paradigm from the urge to become white to the need to become non-white, operating a doubling of 'same' as 'other' invested in

35. Ibid., p. 167.
36. Ibid., p. 41.

violence; all three novels end with the murder of one of the partners.[37] Oppositional strategies, carried out mimetically as in Capécia and Lacrosil, or up-ended as in Manicom, merely reinstate the legitimacy of a hierarchy that demands cultural, social and psychological self-immolation. Yet Manicom's narrative strategy inflects her unrequited tale to a different end. Whereas Cajou and Mayotte tell their youthful story in the moment of living it, doctor Madévie Ramimoutou is retelling hers long after. The difference is one between passive victimization and active narrative agency, and it is conveyed powerfully. The affair is set off not only in italicized fragments scattered throughout, but also in the third person. The narrative shuttles between time and place and among several narrative selves: not only the young gullible student she was, but the way she read herself then; not only the embittered doctor she has become, but the way she reads herself and the young student now. All comment upon themselves and each other, involving us, the 'real' readers, in elaborating the final version of the narrative truth. This pattern is one that Maximin will borrow, challenging our reading by destabilizing both the position of the reader/s and that of the writer/s.

In Maximin's 1981 *L'Isolé Soleil,* this challenge is carried by the novel's 'epistolary' format, a montage of apostrophes hurled at putative readers or putative characters by still other characters, who trade pieces of letters; exchange snatches of diaries sent, stolen, borrowed or found; reconstitute fragments of private papers once lost and then recovered; edit official documents; pass on oral folktales, retold and transformed. All these criss-cross a dizzying narrative space, the better to underline the collaborative, dialogical and tentative nature of all writing. The result is a post-modern crazy quilt, thoroughly historicized by the restless repositioning of multiple past and present self-representations that give the lie to 'official' white history. The master-text – if one can use this term without ideological blasphemy when it comes to this resolutely dehierarchized narrative – is the wonderfully dissident journal of negritude, *Tropiques,* itself a collaborative montage, as Maximin explains in the 1988 interview that precedes the American edition:

> I discovered Suzanne Césaire in *Tropiques,* particularly the last essay of the last issue – an essay written entirely by herself – which I consider a capital document for the Caribbean. She had titled it 'Le grand camouflage' (one might say, 'the great smokescreen'). I had learned it by heart, I liked it so.

---

37. I am using the psychocultural paradigm found in René Girard (1977), *Violence and the Sacred,* Baltimore: Johns Hopkins Press.

Lone Sun is the dialogue I wanted to have with her, with all of the 'women of four races and dozens of bloodlines,' to borrow Suzanne's unusual phrase.[38]

One must heed this definition of Caribbean identity as a reasoned tactical response to specific conditions. This 'grand camouflage' – so admired by Maximin that he reiterated the homage at the 1997 Würzburg 'Symposium on Post-colonial Autobiographies' – has become an apt definition of the hybrid identity that moves from an oppositonal Fanonian grid to a polyphonic, almost Levi-Straussian 'bricolage' (block building) that heals the 'dia-spo-ra'.[39]

The 'camouflage', smokescreen as well as disguise or mask, structures a meaning constantly shuffling and reshuffling itself, dynamic, interactive, truly collaborative. Not only does this procedure invalidate the simplistic contention that a post-modern narrative always evades history, but it demonstrates that, in a colonial situation broadly construed (here, the unfolding swath from empire to illusionary decolonization), the only available self is contingent. The ancestral heroes of slavery and past history are revisited with a view to ambivalence, plural indeterminacy of meaning and the keen awareness that history, too, demands a subjective reinterpretation of the past and of the self. Maximin's characters share a determined refusal to be penned within strict definitional boundaries of any sort, an insistence that the self is always situational, provisional and relational. They refuse the chronological linearity of ready-made narratives handed down by the ancestors and with them, as I have argued, the heroic ancestral saga.[40] Still, their denial does not refuse history; rather, it reinscribes an autonomous self into a history of its own agency.

What is of interest, here, is that this self claims the mother lineage as primary and foundational, so that, when the young student is made to abort a male foetus, she christens it 'daughter': 'I felt my child pass with the noise of a sickle . . . I lost almost everything, tonight; my mother, love for [my] man, their poetry, my child. No! I keep my son and declare him my daughter.'[41] It is this putative daughter, eventually reborn of a militant

---

38. Clarisse Zimra, 'The present always invents a past out of its own desire', in Daniel Maximin, *Lone Sun*, p. xxv.

39. A fine application of the 'camouflage' structuring paradigm is found in Ronnie Scharfmann (1992), 'Rewriting the Césaires', in Maryse Condé, ed., *L'Héritage de Caliban*, Paris: Jasor, pp. 233–46.

40. Clarisse Zimra (1987), 'Tracées césairiennes dans *L'Isolé Soleil*', in Jacqueline Leiner, ed., *Aimé Césaire ou L'Athanor des cultures*, Paris: Présence du Livre caribéen, pp. 347–67.

41. Maximin, *Lone Sun*, p. 118.

black father as Marie-Gabriel, who rewrites and reinvents parts of her mother's life within the collective narrative we are reading; and, in so doing, gives birth to herself as the new Caribbean. *L'Isolé Soleil* delights in multiple Caribbean intertextualities, openly as well as obliquely. Some of the more blatant borrowings use the prophets of negritude and the whole team of *Tropiques* as putative characters for a polyphonic dialogue: Aimé Césaire, Suzanne Césaire, Damas, Senghor, Ménil, even Charley Hannah, 'the Negro, comical and ugly'. Maximin's *alter egos*, these literary ancestors help him rewrite the literary as well as political history of their common culture. More oblique borrowings provide, for instance, a psychiatrist by the name of Dr Frantz, who works near-miraculous cures on traumatized young patients in a clinic for disturbed children, whose conditions come from such early and brutal encounters with colonial racism as witnessing the violent death of a parent, or the bloody repressions of 1945 and 1967. The Manicom connection is present in this restaging of the riots, to whose memory she had dedicated her own *Examen de blanc,* and in the obstetrician, 'Dr Manykom, a young mulatto intern',[42] who presides over the birth of Marie-Gabriel and the death of her mother in an unstoppable haemorrhage provoked by the sequels of the botched abortion from long ago. For Siméa's long-lost aborted child was torn from her against her wishes, at the behest of her own, too bourgeois black mother, and the complacent indifference of a blue-eyed white lover, an architecture student.[43]

It is by recovering the true meaning of her mother's multiple betrayals, by reason of race as well as by reason of class, that Marie-Gabriel is finally able to birth herself, textually as well as biologically. She writes the story of her own bloody beginnings, the life (her own) and the death (her mother's) that replaced and atoned for the murdered, diasporic male child who preceded her. In Maximin's case, the oppositional stance that pitted male against female, white against black, is but a pre-text that engenders the real text, the subject's move into the transgressive plural self of a new, adiasporic Caribbean that no longer recognizes binaries or needs hierarchies. Hence, to re/claim the fe/male child is also to reclaim the once fetishized mother, de-fetishize her as life-giving, and to dismantle

---

42. Ibid., p. 245.
43. The clear reference is also to the recurring figure of technological evil in Aimé Césaire's work, the famous 'architecte aux yeux bleus' (blue-eyed architect) of (1946), *Et les chiens se taisaient,* Paris: Gallimard; translated in 1990 by Clayton Eshleman and Annette Smith, as *And the Dogs Were Silent,* Charlottesville: CARAF Series, University of Virginia Press.

the male-orientated heroics the better to inscribe in our collective imagination an island beyond all male–female polarity.

The old Fanonian paradigm that reproduced the fragmentation of the 'dia-spo-ra' has been transformed by each succeeding generation of writers: first, by women, who accepted its racialized premises even as they sought to defuse (Lacrosil) or refuse them (Manicom); next, by a man (Maximin), who guts the androcentric model to demonstrate the imbricated nature of any subjugation – the fact that oppression by gender serves to reinforce oppression by race and vice versa, and that, perhaps, the best way to refuse either is to scramble all binaries and all hierarchies. *L'Isolé Soleil* operates a metaleptic 'prophetic re/reading of the past'[44] by staging the self-birthing moment of a non-teleological narrative. In the francophone Caribbean, this is a moment that moves us that much closer towards C.L.R. James's regained agency, the true interrelational, transnational, adiasporic poetics that Glissant and Harris had so confidently called forth.

---

44. I borrow here Edouard Glissant's phrase ('une vision prophétique du passé'), in the preface to (1961) *Monsieur Toussaint*, Paris: Seuil, p. 7.

–12–

The Caribbean: A Multirelational Literary Domain[1]

Régis Antoine

(translated by Roger Baines)

The recent media coverage of Antillean writers and their work has enabled the French, and indeed European, reading public to discover the 'periodization' of the literary history particular to these overseas departments: from the negritude introduced in 1939 by Aimé Césaire (the greatest literary author, as far as we are concerned – or, at the very least, the greatest living French writer); to Caribbeanness twenty years later and creolization – the *Poétique de la relation* of Prix Renaudot winner Edouard Glissant; and, finally, to Creoleness, with Patrick Chamoiseau being awarded the Prix Goncourt for *Texaco* in 1992. And as for Haitian literature, thus far neglected by the mainstream reading public, the number of writers published and read in Paris is similarly significant, as Haitian literature has proved to be highly important and of an excellent standard. What, however, is the position of francophone literature within the Caribbean itself and, more widely, within the American world? What about its Creoleness in relation to the comparable '*Creolidad*'? Excluding Quebec, the Caribbean certainly does not benefit from a close linguistic hinterland in the way that the hispanophone Caribbean has Central and South America, or the anglophone islands have the African-American world, because Louisiana and French Guiana are incapable of sustaining the notion of a continuum of French language.

There is no francophone university which has managed to provide a flexible federal structure, as has the anglophone University of the West Indies. Despite the quality periodical *Chemins critiques*, published in

1. A version of this chapter has already been published in French: Régis Antoine (1995), 'La Caraïbe, aire littéraire de multirelations', *Imaginaires Francophones* (Publications de la Faculté des Lettres, Arts et Sciences humaines de Nice, Centre de Recherches Littéraires Pluridisciplinaires), 22, pp. 285–95.

Montreal, there is no cultural review for the whole of the French Caribbean islands which is as rich and full as *Caribbean Quarterly, Caribbean Review* or, in the past, the Cuban *Anales del Caribe*, published by 'Casa de las Americas'. For a long time, French colonial power has dictated that France should be the exclusive publisher, just as French has been the only language and culture in the Antilles. For example, it took decades for the great Cuban poet Nicolás Guillén, who is particularly representative of the archipelago, to be recognized in Martinique and for his negritude to be compared to that of Césaire. As for Haiti, independent since 1804, it continued to take its inspiration from French literary models up until the 1930s and did not forge any links with its island neighbours except via the political activism of poets such as René Depestre in Havana and Jacques Viaud in Santo Domingo.

The Three-souled Caribbean

Currently, West Indian francophone writers have every reason to turn, as they do, towards the different territories of the 'three-souled Caribbean':[2] Amerindian, European and African. Beyond the differing political statuses of these territories, they share the same history, a history which may be seen to be composed of colonialism, neocolonialism, imperialism, under-development and racism. Indeed, the Martinican Edouard Glissant has been forthright about a common 'popular culture which dates from the time of the plantation system and which is the foundation of our current strength'.[3]

On the positive side, it must be added that there is a relatively uniform anthropology, especially in the case of religious syncretisms, which have similar components: Haitian voodoo, Afro-Cuban 'santeria' and Jamaican 'pocomania'. Also on the positive side, there is the fact that West Indians are characterized more by their ethos than by what they possess. The categories which they use to name class differences are as diverse as those to do with pigmentation but, despite a long tradition of the racialization of social problems, they do not correspond exactly with them. This is true for the following list of people in whom francophone literature has its sources: '*nègres-feuilles*' (farm workers); '*bitaco*' (blacks working on

2. The idea of the 'three-souled Caribbean', or 'le Caraïbe aux trois âmes', was originally expressed in Aimé Césaire's *Cahier d'un retour au pays natal*, where it was used to refer to the indigenous Carib inhabitant of the Antilles ('le Caraïbe') as opposed to the Caribbean region ('la Caraïbe'). Its present use here may be seen to refer to both the Carib and the Caribbean.

3. Edouard Glissant (1981), *Le Discours antillais*, Paris: Seuil, p. 180.

a '(ha)bita(tion)', or plantation); '*grands dons*' (those who benefited, in Haiti, from government 'gifts' of property); *békés*; poor whites who are sometimes called negroes; blacks who only speak French and are referred to as mulattos.[4]

On the negative side, there is no clear notion of an inherited identity and there is the absolute necessity to react to the Eurocentric gaze and its fictionalizing exoticism. Also on the negative side, there is a lack of mastery of time and space: 'there is neither possession of the land, complicity with the land, nor hope in the land'.[5] However, some are of the opinion that those new cultures which are founded in the dispossession of history constitute a golden opportunity. In contrast to the numerous scornful declarations on the cultural possibilities of the archipelago made by V.S. Naipaul, the famous Indian writer from Trinidad, Derek Walcott, the Nobel prize-winning Saint Lucian, displays an optimism associated with beginnings, as he describes the 'innocence' of a 'New World . . . wide enough for a new Eden of various Adams'.[6]

Other common characteristics are the problems involved in the construction of sister nations as far as political and economic dependence are concerned. Lastly, there are the literatures which, in the vast majority, demonstrate a concern with social reality, and which dare to deal with the mathematics of labour, whether this comes from the populism of the Puerto Rican Luis Pales Matos, for example, of the Guadeloupean Simone Schwarz-Bart or of the dub poetry of the poor areas of Kingston, Jamaica; from the magical realism of, for example, the Haitian Jacques-Stephen Alexis, from the anti-dictatorial spiralism of another Haitian, Frankétienne; or from the Marxism which has been present on most of the islands.

I have examined the notion of the 'French tropism' elsewhere, in relation to a period prior to 1932[7] and to a more complex reality which I have called Franco-Antillean literature.[8] There are indeed various levels of interpenetration between the literary realities of metropolitan France and of the islands. The original metropolitan tropism was, of course,

4. As for the estimated 128 names defining mixed race which were to be found in Antillean literature: 'rouge'; 'chabin'; 'capre'; 'zambo'; 'quarteron'; 'octavon'; 'négritte' etc., these were established as early as the eighteenth century by a colonizing magistrate, Moreau de Saint-Méry.

5. Glissant, *Le Discours antillais*, p. 88.

6. Derek Walcott (1990), *Omeros*, London: Faber and Faber, p.181.

7. See Régis Antoine (1978), *Les Ecrivains français et les Antilles,* Paris: Maisonneuve et Larose.

8. See Régis Antoine (1992), *La Littérature franco-antillaise: Haïti, Guadeloupe et Martinique*, Paris: Karthala.

the result of the cultural pressure exerted by the dominant culture. In this way, a writer of the standing of Aimé Césaire, having reached an exceptional stage of maturity, was able to create a topically inspired balance between the demands of negritude, of third-worldism and of 'working-class France' – although he always expressed himself in French. On the other hand, the authors of *In Praise of Creoleness*,[9] who criticize him fairly harshly for this, use Western rhetoric in their own essay, as has been noted before. In Césaire's time, there was a quite justifiable reaction to the following French declaration of 1935 (pronounced on the occasion of the 'Tricentennial Cruise' to mark the settlement of the Caribbean), that 'Haiti is the most far-flung beacon of Latinity in America'. The literary prizes which were hoped for and/or received by Glissant, Chamoiseau, Confiant, Depestre and so on in metropolitan France have attracted scorn, but we should reflect on the French origins of Creole waltzes, *biguines* and Antillean *quadrilles*; we should measure which of the surrealist transplantations to be found in Césaire's *Les Armes miraculeuses* (1946) or Daniel Maximin's *L'Isolé Soleil* (1981) may be seen both as artificial and obscene within a Caribbean framework and yet, at the same time, as very fertile in literary terms.

Glissant notes that:

> When a specifically composite culture, such as that of Martinique, is then touched by another culture which 'gets inside' its composition and continues to determine that composition, not radically, but with an assimilating erosion, the violence of the reaction is sporadic and uncertain. The reaction has no antecedents, as far as Martinicans are concerned, in what is sacred in terms of land and its filiation.[10]

The question is: what, in these conditions, becomes of the cultural hybridity that shapes this literature, what happens to creolization (given that we shall not be carrying out a stylistic study of writers who consider themselves to be 'créolistes')?

Hybridities

The literary promotion of biological hybridities has given rise, in Martinique, not to the equivalent of the famous 'Ballada de los dos Abuelos' by

---

9. Jean Bernabé, Patrick Chamoiseau and Raphaël Confiant (1989), *Eloge de la créolité/In Praise of Creoleness* (bilingual edition), Paris: Gallimard.

10. Edouard Glissant (1990), *Poétique de la relation*, Paris: Gallimard, p. 158.

Guillén[11] or to the poetry of the Jamaican Louise Bennett on the multiple origins of people from the Caribbean ('Gramma Africain', 'Grampa Englishman', 'Jew fada side', 'Frenchie'),[12] but to a long poem by Gilbert Gratiant, 'Le Credo des sangs-mêlés',[13] which is itself based on his own prior reflections on the '"lucky dip" nature of the Martinican family'.[14] The Martinican Chamoiseau, reacting against French, racist hostility towards mixed unions and against the hierarchization produced by the multiple terms used to define mixed race, presents a thrilling Creole 'diversality' in *Texaco*, describing Rosa Labautière, for example, as 'a spindly *câpresse*. She had nine children from different fathers, but all with clear skin, which meant that her litter was shabine-mulatto, banana-yellow, lemon-yellow and passion fruit-yellow'.[15]

Going beyond the linguistic heterogeneity of the archipelago (four European languages have the status of acrolects), Depestre makes multi-culturalism a law of intellectual life', a concrete absolute which is different from the abstract absolute inherited from the French Revolution. The Trinidadian Marion Patrick Hones (whose text *Jour ouvert Morning* itself has a hybrid title) insists upon the vitality of heterofertilization, of 'inter-fertilization', among the countries of the Caribbean.

However, in a desire to avoid the trap of black/white dualist thinking, and of negritude's polarized aesthetic, which does not correspond to the intercultural realities of the Caribbean, George Lamming, a Barbadian who is well known in the francophone Antilles, argues for a functional hybridity which 'disessentializes',[16] while his compatriot Edward Kamau Brathwaite describes creolization as 'a way of seeing Jamaica and, by extension, Caribbean society, not in terms of white and black, masters and slaves, in separate units, but as contributory parts of a whole'.[17]

11. Nicolás Guillén (1934), 'Ballada de los dos Abuelos', in *West Indies, Ltd.*, Havana: García y Cía.

12. See Louise Bennett (1966), *Jamaica Labrish*, Kingston: Jamaica Book Stores, and Mervyn Morris, ed. (1982), *Selected Poems: Louise Bennett*, Kingston: Jamaica Book Stores.

13. Gilbert Gratiant, 'Le Credo des sangs-mêlés', in Isabelle Gratiant, Renaud Gratiant and Jean-Louis Joubert, eds (1996), *Fables créoles et autres écrits*, Paris: Stock, pp. 618–36. The poem was originally published in Gilbert Gratiant (1950), *Fab' Compè Zicaque*, Fort-de-France: Imprimerie du Courrier des Antilles.

14. See Gilbert Gratiant (1935), 'Mulâtres, pour le bien et le mal', *L'Etudiant noir*, 1.

15. Patrick Chamoiseau (1992), *Texaco*, Paris: Gallimard, p. 332.

16. See George Lamming (1992), *The Pleasures of Exile*, Michigan: University of Michigan Press.

17. Edward Kamau Brathwaite (1971), *The Development of Creole Society in Jamaica 1770–1820*, Oxford: Oxford University Press, p. 307.

The Islands as Crossroads

All the islands serve as crossroads.

- There is the cultural exchange of music and of dance, e.g. the salsa (sauce); the circulation, between the islands, of steel bands and of the Trinidadian limbo, of the Haitian dance 'compas direct' and of the multiple rhythms which come out of Cuba.
- There is cross-culturalization, through the presence, for example, of the same Shango cult in Jamaica and Haiti in the north and its cross-culturalization to Trinidad in the south.
- There is the exile of Cuban and Haitian writers; the cosmopolitanism of writers such as Anthony Phelps, who calls himself 'an American negro', or René Depestre, who, on the one hand, favours the quasi-status of stateless individual (*heimatlos*) over the return, like Garvey, to Mother Africa and, on the other hand, demonstrates an island nostalgia which today appears to be at least as literary an experience as it is a lived one.
- The literary domain of the francophone Caribbean, corresponding to the diaspora of the francophone Caribbean community and to the paths taken by its writers, is also the place where characters arrive, pass through or disperse: the return from Cuba to Haiti in the magnificent works of Jacques Roumain (*Gouverneurs de la rosée*, 1944) and Jacques-Stephen Alexis (*L'Espace d'un cillement*, 1959); the presence of a central character who comes from elsewhere in Maryse Condé's *Traversée de la mangrove* (1989); the departure for Panama, on the other hand, in the same author's *La Vie scélérate* (1987).
- Concepts also travel between islands. The French translation of *Capitalism and Slavery* (1994) by Eric Williams, the former progressive Trinidadian Prime Minister, has been very successful in Martinique and Guadeloupe. The Cuban Alejo Carpentier, who has disseminated a considerable mass of historical and theoretical reflections which can be applied to the whole archipelago, provided his Haitian friend and neighbour Jacques-Stephen Alexis with the concept of 'magical realism'; in turn, Alexis provided the word 'malemort', which Glissant went on to use as the title for one of his novels; while the Guadeloupean Daniel Maximin may have borrowed the title *L'Isolé Soleil* from the Cuban painter Wifredo Lam, himself of classic African-Asian mixed race. In addition, there are links, too numerous to be examined in any detail here, between Derek Walcott and Edouard Glissant; between Maryse Condé and the Nobel prize-winning African-American Toni Morrison; between René Depestre and Nicolás Guillén.

It is the sea, however, which forms the archipelago and which links its islands: the 'fraudulent' sea of the Guadeloupean Alexis Leger/Saint-John Perse,[18] or the *Wide Sargasso Sea* of Jean Rhys's 1966 novel set in Jamaica and Dominica. Even given the potential that air travel offers, Caribbean men and women are always placed in a world that is surrounded by sea, sea which can become a bond of solidarity or the opposite, an existential barrier. In the first case, it is the author as hero: Shabine-Ulysses-Derek Walcott himself, whose coastal navigation enables us to read the history of the peoples of these West Indies as closely as possible;[19] and the Guadeloupean Sonny Rupaire, who never sailed:

> I come from overseas
> from the sea of despair
> where, from Caracas to Guantánamo
> the green hands of shipwrecked humanity
> flutter tirelessly on the waves
> I come from overseas
> from Santo Domingo to Trinidad
> a green parenthesis of American islands.
> [Je suis d'outre-mer
> de la mer de désespérance
> où de Caracas à Guantanamo s'agitent
> sur les flots inlassablement
> les mains vertes d'une humanité naufragée
> Je suis d'outre-mer
> de Saint-Domingue à Trinidad
> parenthèse verte d'îles américaines.][20]

However, if, for example, the Morne des Sauteurs, in Grenada (the cliff over which the last remaining Caribs were chased to their deaths), has, for a very long time, represented the pathos of protest, now the cold imagination of the ocean's depths appears to prevail. This replaces, most notably, the ardour of Césaire's subterranean revolutionary symbolism, since the non-eruption of Guadeloupe's volcano – the subject of Daniel

18. See Saint-John Perse (1972), 'Eloges III', in *Oeuvres complètes*, Paris: Gallimard (Pléiade), p. 35.

19. See Derek Walcott's poem 'The Schooner Flight', the hero of whom is called Shabine, in Derek Walcott (1979), *The Star-Apple Kingdom*, London: Cape, as well as his 1993 play *The Odyssey*, London: Faber and Faber.

20. Sonny Rupaire,'Ultra-marine', in Sonny Rupaire (1971), *Cette Igname Brisée qu'est ma terre natale*, Paris: Parabole.

Maximin's novel *Soufrières* (1987) – favoured not revolution but, on the contrary, neocolonial projects of disintegration and reconstitution.

If all registers are taken into consideration, the general situation described by the Cuban Antonio Benitez Rojo[21] follows on from what Glissant writes in *Poétique de la relation*: a creolization conceived as 'hybridization without limits, whose elements are infinitely multiplied with unpredictable results',[22] with the Antilles as 'an almost organic case' of the relationship of identity which 'exults in the notion of both wandering and totality'.[23]

Literary Riches and 'Rhizomes'

If we take stock, once the literary production of this Caribbean configuration has been identified, and put it into a theoretical framework, it is a good illustration of the title of *The Empire Writes Back*,[24] which rehabilitates the 'peripheries' of the former colonial empires.

Some works (Guillén's *West Indies Ltd.*, 1934; Glissant's *Les Indes*, 1955; Césaire's *Une tempête*, 1969) and some figures (the historical figure of Toussaint-Louverture, for example, or the historico-legendary figures of the maroons from Jamaica's Blue Mountains or the mythical figure of Caliban, who can be found in Césaire, Lamming, Brathwaite, Depestre and Retamar) appear immediately to have a globalizing as well as a founding role: they are magnetic and transnational. And there are other processes in operation:

- The projection of one territory on to another, of Haiti on to Martinique in Césaire's *La Tragédie du roi Christophe* (1963), of Haiti on to Guadeloupe in Simone Schwarz-Bart's *Ton beau capitaine* (1987), of Cuba on to Guadeloupe in Alejo Carpentier's *El Siglo de las luces* (1962).
- Texts which have circumstantial anti-imperial solidarity, provoked by Cuba but also, in times of crisis, by the Dominican Republic and by Haiti.
- Intense intertextual activity, which we cannot address here.

21. See Antonio Benitez Rojo (1992), *The Repeating Island: the Caribbean and the Postmodern Perspective*, Durham: Duke University Press.

22. Glissant, *Poétique de la relation*, p. 46.

23. Ibid, p. 158.

24. Bill Ashcroft, Gareth Griffiths and Helen Tiffin (1989), *The Empire Writes Back: Theory and Practice in Post-colonial Literatures*, New York: Routledge.

- The work of those who confine their voyage to 'their own' archipelago: Saint-John Perse's *Amers* (1957) and Derek Walcott's *Fortunate Traveller* (1981).

- Writings that are situated at various distances from the roots of writing and the roots of orality; the hybridized writings of so many writers, including Alexis, situated between French, English, Spanish, Haitian Creole, and that of Derek Walcott, which, quite naturally, is grounded in English and the French-based Creole of his island.

- The way in which oral creolization comes together, as I witnessed at a meal where we heard, as a unified chorus, as if fused together: Cuban and Dominican songs; the general thoughts of a Puerto Rican novelist; Guadeloupean proverbs; the unifying beating of the tam-tam; and where the Caribbean punch, whichever island it came from, contributed to the atmosphere of conviviality.

Specificities

The demonstration of the richness of this interculturalism between Caribbean islands does not mean erasing the very national specifities which sustain this richness. Being Haitian or Puerto Rican is not the same as being Cuban . . . The folklore of each island and the language spoken on each island (whether Creole or not, bilingual or diglot) provide their own measure of singularity. In some places, social convention has a diverse influence on the phenomena of literary reception: the same Guadeloupean play, *Ton beau capitaine*, has been staged differently and received differently in Guadeloupe, Jamaica and Cuba, i.e. in territories where the problem of relations between the sexes is posed differently.

Each country ('pays') – a word that is fetishized in the French Antilles – is first of all a 'cadastre'[25] and a landscape, to represent, to dream of, to prefigure. These cadastres refer to each other via the force of an insistent shared morphology: sea, volcanoes, the obsessive sway of the cane fields, which can overdetermine the authenticity of a poem or a novel. However, each landscape that is written about reveals its individual physical, anthropological and social features: the characters in Glissant's novels penetrate the highly ideologized opacity of the Martinican uplands ('hauts'); the village of 'Fonds-Rouge' – the Haitian microcosm of *Gouverneurs de la rosée* – has a particular physical and moral colouring; fluids and forces play a remarkable role which will not be found in 'Fond-Zombi', the most important hamlet in Simone Schwarz-Bart's *Pluie et vent sur Télumée*

---

25. See Césaire's 1961 collection of poetry, *Cadastre*, Paris: Seuil.

miracle. Each author has an individual way of taking root in, of conquering places; each one has an individual 'tracée'.[26] In 1992, the urban setting of *Texaco* skilfully expressed to what extent core resistance to changes in identity could be preserved both literally and materially and could be reconstituted in the pride of the Creole heart. In this way, the Antilles are not a cultural area with a strictly ethnic base, like those which made up former European ethnology; on the contrary, they are best described by words such as 'furnace'.[27]

A challenge has been made, and it is one which particularly concerns Depestre: the possibility for the Caribbean person to gain a new sense of identity, a challenge which more than one Antillean writer has already taken up. The challenge is not only to renounce what *In Praise of Creole-ness* terms the two exteriorities, French and African, but also to renounce certain simple polarities that are more or less narcissistic, such as 'American magical realism'.[28] The challenge is to go beyond an idealism that has paralysed notions of identity and its overly normative expressions, such as 'inherent' ('*fondamental*'), 'native-indigenous' ('*natif-natal*') – a word used, remarkably, in Roumain's *Gouverneurs de la rosée*; to go beyond the literature 'of exile' stage, which includes, in Haiti, Jean Metellus's *Louis Vortex*, Frankétienne's play *Pélin têt*, and a great many novels written in Canada;[29] and which also includes the great anglophone texts, Lamming's *Of Age and Innocence* (1991) and Sam Selvon's *Moses Ascending* (1975), but which, in others' work, is merely reduced to being the negative print of an essentialist ideology.

It must be added that, in order to balance the advances made in studying in terms of 'rhizomes', it is desirable to maintain a radicality which goes deep, which is flexible and which is not diminished by the surface standardization that is now prevalent all over the world. And it is equally desirable that the following remain: the dream and the joy of being oneself

26. As Patrick Chamoiseau has pointed out, the word 'tracée', meaning 'track', evokes both the 'path of the runaway slave and the Creole act of crossing' (Patrick Chamoiseau (1991), 'Reflections on Maryse Condé's *Traversée de la mangrove*', *Callaloo*, 14:2, pp. 389–95). See also the stimulating essay by René Ménil (1981), *Tracées*, Paris: Laffont.

27. See, for example, René Depestre's poem 'Me voici Caliban, homme-four de la Caraïbe', in René Depestre (1980), *En état de poésie*, Paris: Editeurs Français Réunis, p. 34, and Jacqueline Leiner, ed. (1987), *Césaire ou l'athanor d'un alchimiste*, Paris: Editions Caribéennes. (Translator's note: both 'four' and 'athanor' can be translated as 'furnace'.)

28. See Alejo Carpentier (1948), 'Lo real maravilloso de América', first published in *El Nacional*, 8 april 1948, and then as the preface to Carpentier's 1949 novel *El Reino de este Mundo*, Mexico: Ediapsa.

29. For a fuller examination of such writers, see Jan Carew (1979), 'The Caribbean writer and exile', *Caribbean Studies*, 19:1–2, pp. 111–32.

without having to make a detour via interdependence; and stories of Creole childhood, of which several have been published recently – an expression of desire, delicious fables of the regrets of an individual whose authenticity is threatened.

The following authors all express better than anyone the interrelation between the here and the elsewhere, which is one of the characteristics of modernity: Patrick Chamoiseau in Martinique, whose fictional masterpiece *Texaco* argues for a culture and an aesthetic of fragments, for what is composite (including what is non-indigenous); Frankétienne, who managed to move from *Dezafi*, a book about tragic national cohesion, to *L'Oiseau schizophrène*, a textual spectography of the dislocated Haitian conscience; and Maryse Condé, especially in *Les Derniers Rois Mages* which depicts the contemporary reverberations of the Antillean psyche between Guadeloupe and the USA. But, above all, the question of 'multirelationality' in the Caribbean has been illustrated and theorized in two works by Edouard Glissant: *Tout-monde* (1993) and *Traité du tout-monde* (1997). *Tout-monde* in particular, following as it does the journey of an Antillean to Italy, describes the endless movements, back and forth, of 'those who, navigating between two impossibilities, are the very salt of the world's diversity'.[30] Not only this, but it contains a splendid 'hymn' to the young women who work as hawkers, or itinerent market traders: 'They go from island to island . . . they weave the Caribbean, the Americas . . . they are the Relation [la Relation].'[31] Here, the word modernity needs to be used in preference to the cumbersome, critical and, as far as we are concerned interchangeable, if amusingly antithetical, terms 'avant'-garde and 'post'-modern. This is because, if one wanted to study the influence of post-modernism in conjunction with the writings of the avant-garde in Caribbean francophone literature, it would be necessary to envisage another literary framework and another theoretical network: the links between Faulkner and Maryse Condé; Rabelais and Raphaël Confiant; Kundera and Patrick Chamoiseau; Deleuze and Edouard Glissant; Marquez and René Menil. However, that would distance us from the geographically situated literary configuration which we have tried to describe here.

---

30. Edouard Glissant (1993), *Tout-monde*, Paris: Gallimard, p. 324.
31. Ibid., p. 545.

Bibliography

Abenon, Lucien-René (1992), *Petite histoire de la Guadeloupe*, Paris: L'Harmattan.

Adélaïde-Merlande, Jacques (1994), *Histoire générale des Antilles et des Guyanes: Des Précolombiens à nos jours*, Paris: Editions Caribéennes.

Alpha, José (1983), *1902. La Catastrophe de Saint-Pierre*, Fort-de-France: Hatier-Martinique.

André, Jacques (1985), 'Le coq et la jarre: Le sexuel et le féminin dans les sociétés afro-caribéennes', *L'Homme 96*, 15:4, pp. 49–75.

—— (1987), *L'Inceste focal dans la famille noire antillaise*, Paris: Presses Universitaires de Paris.

Antoine, Régis (1978), *Les Ecrivains français et les Antilles*, Paris: Maisonneuve et Larose.

—— (1984), *La Tragédie du roi Christophe d'Aimé Césaire*, Paris: Bordas 'Lectoguide'.

—— (1992), *La Littérature franco-antillaise: Haïti, Guadeloupe et Martinique*, Paris: Karthala.

Arnold, A. James (1981), *Modernism and Negritude: The Poetry and Poetics of Aimé Césaire*, Cambridge, Massachusetts: Harvard University Press.

—— ed. (1995), *A History of Literature in the Caribbean: Hispanic and Francophone Regions*, Amsterdam and Philadelphia: John Benjamins.

Ashcroft, Bill, Griffiths, Gareth and Tiffin, Helen (1989), *The Empire Writes Back: Theory and Practice in Post-colonial Literatures*, New York: Routledge.

—— eds (1995), *The Post-colonial Studies Reader*, London: Routledge.

Bajeux, Jean-Claude (1983), *Antilia retrouvée: Claude McKay, Luis Palés Matos, Aimé Césaire, poètes antillais*, Paris: Editions Caribéennes.

Barthes, Roland (1970), *S/Z*, Paris: Seuil.

Benitez Rojo, Antonio (1992), *The Repeating Island: the Caribbean and the Postmodern Perspective*, Durham: Duke University Press.

Bennett, Louise (1966), *Jamaica Labrish*, Kingston: Jamaica Book Stores.

Bergner, Gwen (1995), 'Who is that masked woman, or the role of gender in *Black Skins, White Masks*', *PMLA*, 110:1, pp. 75–88.

Bibliography

Bernabé, Jean (1983), *Fondal-natal: Grammaire basilectale approchée des créoles guadeloupéen et martiniquais*, 3 vols, Paris: L'Harmattan.

―― Chamoiseau, Patrick and Confiant, Raphaël (1989), *Eloge de la créolité/In Praise of Creoleness* (bilingual edition), trans. M.B. Taleb-Khyar, Paris: Gallimard.

Berrou, Raphaël and Pompilus, Pradel, eds (1975), *Histoire de la littérature haïtienne*, 3 vols, Port-au-Prince: Editions Caraïbes.

Bhabha, Homi (1986), 'Foreword: remembering Fanon', in Frantz Fanon, *Black Skins, White Masks*, trans. Charles Lam Markmann, London: Pluto, pp. vii–xxvi.

―― (1994) *The Location of Culture*, London: Routledge.

Blaise, Jean, Farrugia, Laurent, Trébos, Claude and Zobda-Quitman, Sonia, eds (1981), *Culture et politique en Guadeloupe et Martinique*, Paris: Alizés-Karthala.

Boukman, Daniel (1978), *Les Négriers*, Paris: L'Harmattan.

―― (1996), *Delivrans*, Paris: L'Harmattan.

Boyce Davies, Carol and Savory Fido, Elaine, eds (1990), *Out of the Kumbla: Caribbean Women and Literature*, Trenton, New Jersey: Africa World Press.

Brathwaite, Edward Kamau (1971), *The Development of Creole Society in Jamaica 1770–1820*, Oxford: Oxford University Press.

Brichaux-Houyoux, Suzanne (1993), *Quand Césaire écrit, Lumumba parle: Edition commentée de 'Une saison au Congo'*, Paris: L'Harmattan.

Burton, Richard D.E. (1984), 'Comment peut-on être Martiniquais? The recent work of Edouard Glissant', *The Modern Language Review*, 79:2, pp. 301–12.

―― (1993), 'Maman-France-Doudou: family images in French West Indian colonial discourse', *Diacritics: A Review of Contemporary Criticism*, 23:3, pp. 69–90.

―― (1997), *Le Roman marron: Etudes sur la littérature martiniquaise contemporaine*, Paris: L'Harmattan.

―― and Reno, Fred (1994), *French and West Indian: Martinique, Guadeloupe and French Guiana Today*, London: Macmillan.

Cailler, Bernadette (1988), *Les Conquérants de la nuit nue; Edouard Glissant et l'H(h)istoire antillaise*, Tübingen: Gunther Narr.

Capécia, Mayotte (1948), *Je suis Martinquaise,* Paris: Correa.

―― (1950), *La Négresse blanche,* Paris: Correa.

CARE (1983), 'Entretien du *CARE* avec Edouard Glissant', *CARE,* 10, pp. 17–25.

Carew, Jan (1979), 'The Caribbean writer and exile', *Caribbean Studies*, 19:1–2, pp. 111–32.

Bibliography

Carpentier, Alejo(1990), *Obras completas de Alejo Carpentier*, Volumen 13, Ensayos, Mexico: Siglo XXI.

Césaire, Aimé (1946), *Et les chiens se taisaient*, Paris: Gallimard.

—— (1956), *Lettre à Maurice Thorez*, Paris: Présence Africaine.

—— (1959), 'L'homme de culture et ses responsabilités', *Présence Africaine*, XXIV– XXV, pp. 116–122.

—— (1961), *Cadastre*, Paris: Seuil.

—— (1963), *La Tragédie du roi Christophe*, Paris: Présence Africaine.

—— (1990), *And the Dogs Were Silent*, trans, Clayton Eshleman and Annette Smith, Charlottesville: CARAF Series, University of Virginia Press.

—— (1995), *Cahier d'un retour au pays natal/Notebook of a Return to My Native Land* (bilingual edition), trans. Mireille Rosello with Anne Pritchard, Newcastle Upon Tyne: Bloodaxe Books.

Césaire, Ina (1985), *Mémoires d'isles. Maman N. et Maman F.*, Paris: Editions Caribéennes.

—— (1987), *L'Enfant des passages, ou la geste de Ti-Jean*, Paris: Editions Caribéennes.

—— (1989), *Contes de nuits et de jours aux Antilles*, Paris: Editions Caribéennes.

—— and Laurent, Joëlle (1976), *Contes de mort et de vie aux Antilles*, Paris: Nubia.

Chambers, Angela (1997), 'Univeral and culturally specific imagery in the poetry of Aimé Césaire', in Pat Little and Roger Little, eds, *Black Accents: Writing in French from Africa, Mauritius and the Caribbean*, London: Grant and Cutler, pp. 31–45.

Chamoiseau, Patrick (1986), *Chronique des sept misères*, Paris: Gallimard.

—— (1988), *Au temps de l'antan*, Paris: Hatier.

—— (1988), *Solibo Magnifique*, Paris: Gallimard.

—— (1990), *Antan d'enfance*, Paris: Hatier..

—— (1991), 'Reflections on Maryse Condé's *Traversée de la mangrove*', *Callaloo*, 14:2, pp. 389–95.

—— (1992), *Texaco*, Paris: Gallimard.

—— (1994), *Chemin-d'école*, Paris: Hatier.

—— (1994), 'Que faire de la parole ?', in Ralph Ludwig, ed., *Ecrire la parole de nuit*, Paris: Gallimard, pp. 151–58.

—— and Confiant, Raphaël (1991), *Lettres créoles: Tracées antillaises et continentales de la littérature 1635–1975*, Paris: Hatier.

Chauvet, Marie Vieux (1950), *La Légende des fleurs*, Port-au-Prince: Deschamps.

—— (1954), *Fille d'Haïti*, Paris: Fasquelle.

Bibliography

—— (1957), *La Danse sur le volcan,* Paris: Librairie Plon.

—— (1960), *Fonds des nègres,* Port-au-Prince: Editions Deschamps.

—— (1968), *Amour, Colère et Folie,* Paris: Gallimard.

—— (1986), *Les Rapaces,* Port-au-Prince: Editions Deschamps.

Childs, Peter and Williams, Patrick (1997), *An Introduction to Post-Colonial Theory,* Hemel Hempstead: Prentice Hall/Harvester Wheatsheaf.

Clark, Vèvè (1992), 'When womb waters break: the emergence of Haitian new theater (1953–1987)', *Callaloo,* 15, pp. 778–86.

Clarke, Edith (1966), *My Mother who Fathered Me,* 2nd edn, London: Allen & Unwin.

Condé, Maryse (1974), 'Négritude césairienne, Négritude senghorienne', *Revue de la Littérature Comparée,* 3, pp. 409–19.

—— (1976), *Heremakhonon,* Paris: Union Générale.

—— (1979), *La Parole des femmes: essai sur des romancières des Antilles de langue française,* Paris: L'Harmattan.

—— (1981), *Une Saison à Rihata,* Paris: Robert Laffont.

—— (1982), *Heremakhonon,* trans. Richard Philcox, Washington: Three Continents Press.

—— (1986), *Moi, Tituba, sorcière . . . Noire de Salem,* Paris: Mercure de France.

—— (1987), *La Vie scélérate,* Paris: Seghers.

—— (1987), *Segu,* trans. Barbara Bray, New York: Viking.

—— (1988), *A Season in Rihata,* trans. Richard Philcox, London: Heinemann.

—— (1989), *Traversée de la mangrove,* Paris: Mercure de France.

—— (1991), *An tan revolisyon ou Elle court, elle court la liberté,* Basse-Terre: Conseil régional.

—— (1992), *Les Derniers Rois Mages,* Paris: Mercure de France.

—— (1989), *The Children of Segu,* trans. L. Cloverdale, New York: Viking.

—— (1992), *I, Tituba, Black Witch of Salem,* trans. Richard Philcox, Charlottesville; London: Virginia UP.

—— (1992), *Tree of Life,* trans. Richard Philcox, New York: Balantine.

—— (1993), *La Colonie du nouveau monde,* Paris: Robert Laffont.

—— (1993), 'Order, disorder, freedom and the West Indian writer', *Yale French Studies,* 83:2, pp. 121–35.

—— (1993), 'The Role of the Writer', *World Literature Today,* 67:4, pp. 697–9.

—— (1995), *Crossing the Mangrove,* trans. Richard Philcox, New York: Anchor Books.

—— (1995), 'Eloge de Saint-John Perse', *Europe,* 799–800, p. 22.

Bibliography

—— (1996), *La Migration des coeurs*, Paris: Robert Laffont.

—— (1997), *Desirada*, Paris: Robert Laffont.

—— (1998), *The Last of the African Kings*, trans. Richard Philcox, Nebraska UP.

Confiant, Raphaël (1979), *Jik dèyè do Bondyè*, Fort-de-France: Editions Grif an tè.

—— (1980), *Jou baré*, Fort-de-France: Editions Grif an tè.

—— (1985), *Bitako-a*, Fort-de-France: Editions du GEREC.

—— (1986), *Kod yanm*, Fort-de-France: Editions Kréyòl pou divini péyi-a.

—— (1987), *Marisosé*, Fort-de-France: Presses Universitaires Créoles.

—— (1988), *Le Nègre et l'amiral*, Paris: Grasset.

—— (1991), *Eau de Café*, Paris, Grasset.

—— (1993), *Aimé Césaire: Traversée paradoxale d'un siècle*, Paris: Stock.

—— (1993), *Ravines du devant-jour*, Paris: Gallimard.

—— (1994), *Commandeur du sucre*, Paris: Ecriture.

—— (1994), *L'Allée des soupirs*, Paris: Grasset,

—— (1994) *Bassin de l'ouragan*, Paris: Mille et une nuits.

—— (1994), 'Questions pratiques d'écriture créole', in Ralph Ludwig, ed., *Ecrire la Parole de Nuit*, Paris: Gallimard, pp. 171–80.

—— (1995), *Les Maîtres de la parole créole,* Paris: Gallimard.

—— (1995), *Contes créoles des Amériques,* Paris: Stock.

Cornevin, Robert (1973), *Le Théâtre haïtien,* Ottawa: Leméac.

Corzani, Jack (1978), *La Littérature des Antilles-Guyane françaises*, 6 vols, Fort-de-France: Désormeaux.

—— (1992), *Dictionnaire encylopédique Désormeaux*, Fort-de-France: Désormeaux.

Damas, Léon Gontran (1972), *Pigments. Névralgies*, Paris: Présence Africaine.

Dash, J. Michael (1981), *Literature and Ideology in Haiti 1915–61*, London: Macmillan.

—— (1990), 'Le Roman de nous', *Carbet*, 10, pp. 21–31.

—— (1995), *Edouard Glissant*, Cambridge: Cambridge UP.

Dayan, Joan (1991), 'Reading women in the Caribbean: Marie Chauvet's *Amour, Colère et Folie*', in Nancy Miller and Joan DeJean, eds, *Displacements: Women, Tradition, Literatures in French*, Baltimore: Johns Hopkins, pp. 228–53.

—— (1995), *Haiti, History, and the Gods,* Berkeley and London: University of California Press.

Debreuille, Jean-Yves (1992), 'Le langage désancré de *Malemort*', in

Bibliography

Yves-Alain Favre, ed., *Horizons d'Edouard Glissant*, Biarritz: J & D Editeurs, pp. 319–28.

De Chambertrand, Gilbert (1976), *Théâtre d'expression créole*, Basse-Terre: Editions Jeunes Antilles.

Degras, Priska and Magnier, Bernard (1984), 'Édouard Glissant, préfacier d'une littérature future: entretien avec Édouard Glissant', *Notre Librairie*, 74, pp. 14–20.

Depestre, René (1980), *Bonjour et adieu à la négritude*, Paris: Robert Laffont.

Desportes, Georges (1988), 'L'illusion vraie de l'art chez Edouard Glissant', *Antilla*, 272, pp. 10–12.

Dracius-Pinalie, Suzanne (1989), *L'Autre qui danse*, Paris: Seghers.

Dumas, Pierre-Raymond (1985), 'Chauvet: "Amour, Colère et Folie"', *Conjonction*, 167, pp. 17–19.

Fanon, Frantz (1952), *Peau noire, masques blancs*, Paris, Seuil.

—— (1959), *L'An cinq de la révolution Algérienne*, Paris: Maspéro.

—— (1961), *Les Damnés de la terre*, Paris: Maspéro.

—— (1964), *Pour la révolution Africaine*, Paris: Maspéro.

—— (1967), *The Wretched of the Earth*, trans. Constance Farrington, Harmondsworth: Penguin.

—— (1970), *Toward the African Revolution*, trans. Haakon Chevalier, Harmondsworth: Penguin.

—— (1986), *Black Skin, White Masks*, trans. Charles Lam Markmann, London: Pluto.

—— (1989), *Studies in a Dying Colonialism*, trans. Haakon Chevalier, London: Earthscan.

Favre, Yves-Alain, ed. (1992), *Horizons d'Edouard Glissant*, Biarritz: J & D Editeurs.

Fergusson, Charles (1959), 'Diglossia', *Word*, 15, pp. 325–40.

Fick, Carolyn E. (1990), *The Making of Haiti: The Saint-Domingue Revolution from Below*, Knoxville: University of Tennessee Press.

France, Peter, ed. (1995), *The New Oxford Companion to Literature in French*, Oxford: Oxford University Press.

Frobenius, Leo (1952), *Histoire de la civilisation africaine*, trans. D. Back and D. Ermant, Paris: Gallimard.

Gardiner, Madeleine (1981), *Visages de femmes: Portraits d'écrivains*, Port-au-Prince: Editions Deschamps.

Gates, Henry Louis, Jr (1991), 'Critical Fanonism', *Critical Inquiry*, 17, pp. 457–70.

GEREC (1982), *Charte culturelle créole*, Fort-de-France: CUAG.

Gilroy, Paul (1992), *The Black Atlantic*, London: Verso.

Bibliography

Girard, René (1977), *Violence and the Sacred*, Baltimore: Johns Hopkins.

Glissant, Edouard (1958), *La Lézarde*, Paris: Seuil.

—— (1961), *Monsieur Toussaint*, Paris: Seuil.

—— (1964), *Le Quatrième Siècle*, Paris: Seuil.

—— (1969), *L'Intention poétique*, Paris: Seuil.

—— (1975), *Malemort*, Paris: Seuil.

—— (1981), *La Case du commandeur*, Paris: Seuil.

—— (1981), *Le Discours antillais*, Paris: Seuil.

—— (1985), *The Ripening,* trans. Michael Dash, London: Heinemann.

—— (1987), *Mahagony,* Paris: Seuil.

—— (1989), *Caribbean Discourse: Selected Essays*, trans. Michael Dash, Charlottesville: Virginia UP.

—— (1990), *Poétique de la relation*, Paris: Seuil.

—— (1993), *Tout-monde*, Paris: Gallimard.

—— (1995), *Faulkner Mississippi*, Paris: Stock.

—— (1995), *Introduction à une poétique du divers*, Montreal: PUM.

—— (1997), *Traité du tout-monde*, Paris: Gallimard.

—— (1997), *Le Discours antillais* (new edition), Paris: Gallimard.

Gosselin, Jean (1984), 'Paris – Antilles – Guyane', *Bulletin d'information du CENADDOM*, 73, pp. 25–33.

Gracchus, Fritz (1979), *Les Lieux de la mère dans les littératures afro-américaines*, Paris: Editions Caribéennes.

Gratiant, Gilbert (1935), 'Mulâtres, pour le bien et le mal', *L'Etudiant noir*, 1.

—— (1958), *Fab' Compè Zicaque,* Fort-de-France: Imprimerie du Courrier des Antilles.

Gratiant, Isabelle, Gratiant, Renaud and Joubert, Jean-Louis, eds (1996), *Fables créoles et autres écrits,* Paris: Stock.

Guillén, Nicolás (1934), *West Indies, Ltd.*, Havana: García y Cía.

Harris, Wilson (1983), *The Womb of Space*, Wesport, Connecticut and London: Greenwood Press.

Hazaël-Massieux, Guy (1978), 'Approche socio-linguistique de la situation de la diglossie français–créole en Guadeloupe', *Langue Française*, 37, pp.106–18.

Hazaël-Massieux, Marie-Christine (1993), *Ecrire en créole: oralité et écriture aux Antilles*, Paris: L'Harmattan.

Hennessy, Alistair, ed. (1992), *Intellectuals in the Twentieth-century Caribbean*, London: Macmillan.

Henry-Valmore, Simonne (1988), *Dieux en exil*, Paris: Gallimard.

Herskovits, Melville (1972), *Life in a Haitian Valley*, New York: Doubleday.

Bibliography

Irele, Abiola, ed. (1994), *Aimé Césaire: Cahier d'un retour au pays natal*, Ibadan: New Horn Press.

Jahn, Janheinz (1966), *Geschichte der neoafrikanischen Literatur*, Düsseldorf, Cologne: Eugen Diederichs Verlag.

James, C.L.R. (1980), *The Black Jacobins: Toussaint Louverture and the San Domingo Revolution*, London: Allison and Busby.

Jeanne, Max (1980), 'Sociologie du théâtre antillais', *CARE*, 6, pp. 7–43.

Jones, Bridget and Dickson Littlewood, Sita (1997), *Paradoxes of French Caribbean Theatre. An Annotated Checklist of Dramatic Works (Guadeloupe, Guyane, Martinique) from 1900*, London: Roehampton Insititute.

Kesteloot, Lilyan (1967), *Anthologie négro-africaine: panorama critique des prosateurs, poètes et dramaturges noirs du vingtième siècle*, Verviers: Marabout Université.

―― and Kotchy, Barthelemy (1973), *Aimé Césaire: l'homme et l'oeuvre*, Paris: Présence Africaine.

Knodel, Arthur, ed. and trans. (1979), *Saint-John Perse, Letters*, New York: Pantheon Books.

Lacrosil, Michèle (1960), *Sapotille et le serin d'argile*, Paris: Gallimard.

―― (1961), *Cajou*, Paris: Gallimard.

―― (1967), *Demain Jab-Herma*, Paris: Gallimard.

Laferrière, Dany (1983), 'Marie Chauvet: *Amour, Colère, Folie*', in Jean Jonassaint, ed. *Littérature haïtienne*, special issue of *Mot pour Mot*, 11, pp. 7–10.

Laleau, Léon (1931), *Musique nègre*, Port-au-Prince: Collection Indigène.

Lambotte, Robert (1979), 'Les DOM: le sous-développement français', *Options*, 77, pp. 38–42.

Lamming, George (1992), *The Pleasures of Exile*, Michigan: University of Michigan Press.

Laraque, Franck (1975), 'Violence et sexualité dans *Amour, Colère et Folie*', *Présence Haïtienne*, 2, pp. 53–6.

Leiner, Jacqueline, ed. (1984), *Soleil éclaté*, Tübingen: Gunter Narr Verlag.

―― ed. (1987), *Césaire ou l'athanor d'un alchimiste*, Paris: Editions Caribéennes.

Léro, Etienne (1932), 'Misère d'une poésie', *Légitime Défense*, 1, pp. 10–12.

Levillain, Henriette (1988), 'La version de la Guadeloupe: L'Amérique', in Henriette Levillain and Mireille Sacotte, eds, *Saint-John Perse: Antillanité et universalité*, Paris: Editions Caribéennes, pp.159–72.

―― (1992), 'Saint-John Perse et l'Atlantique', *Souffle de Perse*, 2, pp. 33–8.

—— (1994), 'L'enfance de Saint-John Perse', in Henriette Levillain, *Guadeloupe 1875–1914*, Paris: Autrement, pp. 190–9.

Lionnet, Françoise. 1995, *Postcolonial Representations: Women, Literature, Identity*, Ithaca: Cornell UP.

Lirus, Julie (1979), *Identité antillaise*, Paris: Editions Caribéennes.

Louise, René. 1980, *Le Marronnisme moderne*, Paris: Éditions Caribéennes.

—— 1984, *Sculpture et peinture en Martinique*, Paris: Éditions Caribéennes.

Ludwig, Ralph, ed. (1994), *Ecrire la parole de nuit*, Paris: Gallimard.

—— Montbrand, Danièle, Poullet, Henri and Telchid, Sylviane (1990), *Dictionnaire Créole–Français*, Paris: Servedit/Editions Jasor.

McFadyen, Deirdre and LaRamée, Pierre, eds (1995), *Haiti: Dangerous Crossroads*, Boston: Southend Press.

McKay, Claude (1957), *Banjo*, New York: Harcourt, Brace.

Macouba, Auguste (1968), *Eïa! Man-maille là!* Honfleur: P.J. Oswald.

Madiou, Thomas (1989), *Histoire d'Haïti (1492–1846)*, 8 vols, Port-au-Prince: Editions Henri Deschamps.

Manicom, Jacqueline (1972), *Mon examen de blanc*, Paris: Presses de la Cité.

Marbot, François (1976), *Les Bambous, Fables de La Fontaine travesties en patois martiniquais par un vieux commandeur*, Paris: Casterman.

March, Christian (1989), 'Une approche épilinguistique de la question de la langue maternelle en Martinique: Une enquête chez les mères au centre PMI du Lamentin', Mémoire de DEA en linguistique, Université de Rouen-Haute Normandie.

—— (1996), *Le Discours des mères martiniquaises. Diglossie et créolité: un point de vue sociolinguistique*, Paris: L'Harmattan.

Mathieu, Jean-Luc (1988), *Les DOM-TOM*, Paris: Presses Universitaires de France.

Mauvois, Georges (1988), *Agénor Cacoul* (with *Misyé Molina*), 2nd edn, Schoelcher/Paris: Presses Universitaires Créoles/GEREC/L'Harmattan.

Maximin, Daniel (1981), *L'Isolé Soleil*, Paris: Seuil.

—— (1995), *L'Ile et une nuit*, Paris: Seuil.

Mayaux, Catherine (1992), 'La structure romanesque de *Mahagony* d'Edouard Glissant', in Yves-Alain Favre, ed., *Horizons d'Edouard Glissant*, Biarritz: J & D Editeurs, pp. 349–63.

—— (1994), *Les Lettres d'Asie de Saint-John Perse,* Paris: Gallimard.

Ménil, René (1932), 'Généralités sur *l'écrivain* de couleur antillais', *Légitime Défense*, 1, pp. 7–9.

—— (1944), 'Situation de la poésie aux Antilles', *Tropiques,* 11, pp. 127–33.

Bibliography

—— (1981), *Tracées*, Paris: Laffont.

Mignolo, Walter D. (1994), 'Are subaltern studies postmodern or post-colonial? The politics and sensibilities of geo-cultural locations', *Dispositio*, 19:46, pp. 45–73.

Miller, Christopher (1990), *Theories of Africans*, Chicago: University of Chicago Press.

Miller, Elinor (1979), 'Narrative techniques in Edouard Glissant's *Malemort*', *The French Review*, 53:2, pp. 224–32.

Moi, Toril (1985), *Sexual/Textual Politics: Feminist Literary Theory*, London and New York: Routledge.

Morris, Mervyn, ed. (1982), *Selected Poems: Louise Bennett*, Kingston: Jamaica Book Stores.

Ngal, M. a M. (1975), *Aimé Césaire: un homme à la recherche d'une patrie*, Dakar: Nouvelles Editions Africaines.

—— and Steins, Martin, eds (1984), *Césaire 70*, Paris: Editions Silex.

Nisbet, Anne-Marie and Ormerod, Beverley (1982), *Négritude et Antillanité: Etude d'Une tempête d'Aimé Césaire*, Kensington: New South Wales University Press.

Ormerod, Beverley (1985), *An Introduction to the French Caribbean Novel*, London: Heinemann.

Orville, Xavier (1989), *Laissez brûler Laventurcia*, Paris: Grasset.

Palumbo-Liu, David, ed. (1995), *The Ethnic Canon: Histories, Institutions and Interventions*, Minneapolis: Minnesota UP.

Parry, Benita (1987), 'Problems in current theories of colonial discourse', *Oxford Literary Review*, 9:1–2, pp. 27–58.

Pépin, Ernest (1991), 'J'écris pour un lecteur à venir', *Sept Magazine*, 602, p. 8.

—— (1992), 'Le débat autour de la créolité', *Antilla Magazine*, 509, p. 29.

—— (1996), *Tambour-Babel*, Paris: Gallimard.

Pevsner, Ruth (1993), 'People create stories create people: History, language, content and performance in the oral Créole folk tale in Martinique', unpublished PhD thesis, University of Manchester.

Pineau, Gisèle (1993), *La Grande Drive des esprits*, Paris: Le Serpent à plumes.

Placoly, Vincent (1983), *Dessalines ou la Passion de l'indépendance*, Havana: Casa de las Américas.

Poullet, Hector (1982), *Pawol an bouch*, Fort-de-France: Editions Désormeaux.

—— (1990), *Tibouchina*, Paris: Editions Messidor.

Price-Mars, Jean (1928), *Ainsi parla l'oncle*, Compiègne: Bibliothèque haïtienne.

Bibliography

Prudent, Lambert-Félix (1981), 'Diglossie et interlecte', *Langages*, 61, pp. 13–38.

—— ed. (1984), *Anthologie de la nouvelle poésie créole*, Paris: Editions Caribéennes.

—— (1989), 'Ecrire le creole à la Martinique: Norme et conflit sociolinguistique', in Ralph Ludwig, ed., *Les Créoles français entre l'oral et l'écrit*, Tübingen: Narr, pp. 65–80.

—— (1993), 'Political illusions of an intervention in the linguistic domain in Martinique', *International Journal of Society and Language*, 102, pp. 135–48.

Radford, Daniel (1993), *Le Maître-Pièce*, Monaco: Editions du Rocher.

Rinne, Suzanne and Vitiello, Joëlle, eds (1997), *Elles écrivent des Antilles (Haïti, Guadeloupe, Martinique)*, Paris: L'Harmattan.

Rosello, Mireille (1992), *Littérature et identité créole aux Antilles*, Paris: Karthala.

Roumain, Jacques (1944), *Gouverneurs de la rosée,* Fort-de-France: Désormeaux.

—— (1978), *Masters of the Dew,* trans. Langston Hughes and Mercer Cook, Oxford: Heinemann.

Rowell, Charles H. (1989), 'C'est par le poème que nous affrontons la solitude: une interview avec Aimé Césaire', *Callaloo*, 12:1, pp. 48–67.

Rupaire, Sonny (1971), *Cette Igname Brisée qui est ma terre natale*, Paris: Parabole.

Ruprecht, Alvina (1995), 'Performance transculturelle: Une poétique de l'interthéâtralité chez Simone Schwarz-Bart', in Pierre Laurette and Hans-George Ruprecht, eds, *Poétiques et imaginaires: Francopolyphonie littéraire des Amériques*, Paris: L'Harmattan, pp. 313–23.

Said, Edward (1989), 'Representing the colonized: anthropology's interlocutors', *Critical Inquiry*, 15, pp. 205–20.

—— (1994), *Culture and Imperialism,* London: Vintage, 1994.

Perse, Saint-John (1953), *Vents/Winds*, trans. Hugh Chisholm, New York: Pantheon Books.

—— (1956), *Eloges and Other Poems*, trans. Louise Varèse, New York: Pantheon Books.

—— (1958), *Amers/Seamarks*, trans. Wallace Fowlie, NewYork: Pantheon Books.

—— (1972), *Oeuvres complètes*, Paris: Gallimard (Pléiade).

—— (1992), *Exil*, trans. Denis Devlin, in Roger Little, ed., *Translations into English*, Dublin: Dedalus Press.

Saint-Pierre, Madeleine (1972), 'Créole ou français? Les cheminements

Bibliography

d'un choix linguistique', in Jean Benoit, ed., *L'Archipel inachevé*, Montreal: Montreal UP, pp. 251–66.

Sartre, Jean-Paul (1948), 'Orphée noir', in Léopold Sédar Senghor, ed., *Anthologie de la nouvelle poésie nègre et malgache*, Paris: Presses Universitaires de France, pp. ix–xliii.

Sartre, Jean-Paul (1963), *Black Orpheus*, trans. Samuel Allen, Paris: Présence Africaine.

Scharfmann, Ronnie (1992), 'Rewriting the Césaires', in Maryse Condé, ed., *L'Héritage de Caliban*, Paris: Jasor, pp. 233–46.

Schnepel, Ellen (1993), 'The Creole movement in Guadeloupe', *International Journal of Society and Language*, 102, pp. 117–34.

—— (1993) 'The other tongue, the other voice: language and gender in the French Caribbean', *Ethnic Groups*, 10, pp. 243–68.

Schwarz-Bart, André (1972), *La Mulâtresse Solitude,* Paris: Seuil.

—— and Schwarz-Bart, Simone (1967), *Un plat de porc aux bananes vertes,* Paris: Seuil.

Schwarz-Bart, Simone (1972), *Pluie et vent sur Télumée miracle*, Paris: Seuil.

—— (1974), *The Bridge of Beyond,* trans. Barbara Bray, London: Heinemann. Re-edition published 1982 with an introduction by Bridget Jones.

—— (1979), *Ti Jean L'horizon,* Paris: Seuil.

—— (1987), *Ton beau capitaine*, Paris: Seuil.

Senghor, Léopold Sédar (1971), 'Problématique de la Négritude', *Présence Africaine,* 78, pp. 3–26.

Shapiro, Norman R. (1970), *Négritude: Black Poetry from Africa and the Caribbean*, New York: October House.

Sieger, Jacqueline (1961), 'Entretien avec Aimé Césaire', *Afrique*, 5, pp. 64–7.

Smith, Robert P. (1974), 'Michèle Lacrosil, novelist with a color complex', *The French Review*, 47, pp. 783–90.

Soyinka, Wole (1976), *Myth, Literature and the African World*, Cambridge: Cambridge University Press.

Spear, Thomas. 1993, 'Individual quests and collective history', *World Literature Today*, 67:4, pp. 723–30.

Taylor, Patrick (1989), *The Narrative of Liberation*, Ithaca and London: Cornell University Press.

Théâtre du Cyclone (1975), *Nuit blanch, Siklòn*, Pointe-à-Pitre: Imprimerie guadeloupéenne des éditions sociales.

Toumson, Roger (1989), *La Transgression des couleurs: Littérature et langage des Antilles, 18e, 19e, 20e siècles*, 2 vols, Paris: Editions Caribéennes.

Bibliography

Trouillot, Michel-Rolph (1995), *Silencing the Past: Power and the Reproduction of History*, Boston: Beacon Press.

Ventresque, Renée (1995), *Le Songe antillais de Saint-John Perse*, Paris: L'Harmattan.

Verderosa, Constantin (1994), *Scènes créoles,* Paris/Schoelcher: L'Harmattan/GEREC.

Victor, Gary (1996), 'Haiti (overview)', in Don Rubin, ed., *World Encyclopedia of Contemporary Theatre*, London and New York: Routledge, pp. 297–303.

Walcott, Derek (1979), *The Star-Apple Kingdom*, London: Cape.

—— (1986), *Collected Poems: 1948–1984,* New York: Farrar, Straus & Giroux.

—— (1990), *Omeros*, London: Faber and Faber.

—— (1992), *The Antilles: Fragments of Epic Memory*, The Nobel Lecture, London: Faber and Faber.

—— (1993), *The Odyssey*, London: Faber and Faber.

Webb, Barbara (1992), *Myth and History in Caribbean Fiction*, Amherst: University of Massachusetts Press.

Wichmann Bailey, Marianne (1992), *The Ritual Theater of Aimé Césaire*, Tübingen: Narr.

Williams, Patrick and Chrisman, Laura, eds (1993), *Colonial Discourse and Post-colonial Theory: A Reader*, Hemel Hempstead: Harvester Wheatsheaf.

Wilson, Elizabeth (1990), 'Le voyage et l'espace clos', in Carole Boyce Davies and Elaine Savory Fido, eds, *Out of the Kumbla: Caribbean Women and Literature*, Trenton, New Jersey: Africa World Press, pp. 45–58.

Wing, Nathaniel (1992), 'Ecriture et relation dans les romans d'Edouard Glissant', in Yves-Alain Favre, ed., *Horizons d'Edouard Glissant*, Biarritz: J & D Editeurs, pp. 295–302.

Warner-Vieyra, Myriam (1982), *Juletane*, Paris: Présence Africaine.

Wynter, Sylvia (1968), 'We must learn to sit down and discuss a little culture: reflections on West Indian writing and criticism', *Jamaica Journal*, 2:4, pp. 23–32.

—— (1990), 'Beyond's Miranda's meanings: un/silencing the "demonic ground" of Caliban's woman', in Carole Boyce Davies and Elaine Savory Fido, eds, *Out of the Kumbla: Caribbean Women and Literature*, Trenton, New Jersey: Africa World Press, pp. 355–71.

Young, Robert (1990), *White Mythologies*, London Routledge.

Yoyo, Emile (1969), *Saint-John Perse et le conteur,* Paris: Bordas.

Ziller, Jacques (1991), *Les DOM-TOM*, Paris: Librairie Générale de Droit.

Zimra, Clarisse (1977), 'Patterns of liberation in contemporary women writers', *L'Esprit créateur*, 17:2, pp. 103–14.

—— (1987), 'Tracées césairiennes dans *L'Isolé Soleil*', in Jacqueline Leiner, ed., *Aimé Césaire ou L'athanor des cultures*, Paris: Présence du livre caribéen, pp. 347–67.

Zobel, Joseph (1950), *La Rue Cases-Nègres*, Paris: Présence Africaine

Notes on Contributors

Régis Antoine is Emeritus Professor at the University of Nantes, France, and teaches Antillean and Haitian literature in the Centre International d'Etudes Francophones, at the Sorbonne (Paris IV). He has published numerous books and articles on francophone Caribbean writing, most notably *Les Ecrivains français et les Antilles* (1978) and *La Littérature franco-antillaise: Haïti, Guadeloupe et Martinique* (1992). He is currently working on an anthology entitled *Rayonnants écrivains de la Caraïbe* (Editions Maisonneuve et Larose).

Roger Baines teaches and researches French language at the University of East Anglia. He recently obtained his PhD on the work of Pierre Mac Orlan, and holds the Institute of Linguists' Diploma in Translation.

Celia Britton is Carnegie Professor of French and Director of the Francophone Studies Centre at Aberdeen University. She has published a number of articles on Edouard Glissant and other French Caribbean writers and has just completed a book on Glissant: *Edouard Glissant and Postcolonial Theory: Strategies of Language and Resistance* (University Press of Virginia, 1999).

Jane Brooks is currently working on a thesis entitled 'The figuring of the narrator, language and identity in a selection of novels by Patrick Chamoiseau and Raphaël Confiant'. She also teaches English as a Foreign Language and English for Academic Purposes at the University of Sussex.

Angela Chambers is Senior Lecturer in French and Director of the Centre for Applied Language Studies at the University of Limerick, Ireland. She is currently Vice-President of the European Language Council. In addition to the poetry of Césaire, on which she has published, her current research interests include literary translation in colonial and post-colonial contexts.

Suzanne Crosta is an Associate Professor of French at McMaster University, Canada, where she teaches francophone African and Caribbean literatures. She is the author of *Le Marronnage créateur: dynamique* *textuelle chez Edouard Glissant* (1991) and of numerous essays on French West Indian writers (Mayotte Capécia, Patrick Chamoiseau, Maryse Condé, Xavier Orville, Gisèle Pineau). Her current research focuses on childhood and life narratives in the Caribbean.

Joan Dayan is Professor of English at the University of Arizona. As well as numerous articles on romance and race in the Caribbean, she is the author of *A Rainbow for the Christian West: Introducing René Depestre's Poetry* (1977); *Fables of the Mind: An Inquiry into Poe's Fiction* (1987) and, most recently, *Haiti, History and the Gods* (1998). She is currently working on a book entitled *Held in the Body of the State: Chai, Codes of Deterrence and the Death Penalty in an Arizona Prison*.

Mary Gallagher teaches in the Department of French at University College Dublin. Her teaching and research interests are principally in the area of francophone writing and twentieth-century writing by women. She has published on Saint-John Perse and on Edouard Glissant and is editor of the Association for the Study of Caribbean and African Literature in French (ASCALF) Bulletin.

Sam Haigh is a lecturer in the Department of French Studies at the University of Warwick, where she teaches French and francophone litera-ture. Her main research interest is in francophone Caribbean writing, and she has published on French and Antillean women's writing. She has recently completed a book entitled *Mapping a Tradition: Francophone Women's Writing from Guadeloupe*, and is co-editing the *Routledge Reader in Francophone Literatures*.

Bridget Jones is currently a Senior Research Fellow in the Modern Languages Department at the Roehampton Institute, London, and taught French at the Mona campus of the University of the West Indies from 1964 to 1982. She has co-edited a book entitled *Francophonie: Mythes, masques et réalités* (1996) and has published a wide range of articles on numerous aspects of Caribbean literature. She recently published *Paradoxes of French Caribbean Theatre: An Annotated Checklist* (1997), which is part of an ongoing, collaborative project to establish a computer database on French Caribbean theatre.

Lise Morel is currently doing research at Aberdeen University on contemporary francophone and anglophone Caribbean literature. She has published an article on the *carnavalesque* in the work of Patrick

Notes on Contributors

Chamoiseau and Raphaël Confiant, and has also worked on the issue of the 'consumption' of Caribbean literature.

Beverley Ormerod, born in Jamaica, introduced French Caribbean literature courses at the University of the West Indies (Mona), where she lectured in the 1960s. She is now Associate Professor of French at the University of Western Australia, specializing in francophone literature and Renaissance poetry. She is author of *An Introduction to the French Caribbean Novel* (1985) and co-author, with Jean-Marie Volet, of *Romancières africaines d'expression française* (1994).

Patrick Williams is Reader in Critical and Cultural Theory at Nottingham Trent University. His publications include: (with Laura Chrisman) *Colonial Discourse and Post-colonial Theory* (1993); (with Peter Childs) *An Introduction to Post-colonial Theory* (1996), and *Ngugi wa Thiong'o* (1998).

Clarisse Zimra holds degrees in literary studies and the humanities from the Université d'Aix-en-Provence, Cambridge University and the University of Washington. She currently teaches English and Comparative Literature at Southern Illinois University – Carbondale (SIUC), as well as participating in the Research Faculty Seminar on colonial, post-colonial and migration studies of the Irish Studies Center – SIUC. She has published in scholarly journals in France, the USA and Canada, coordinated and edited the American translation of Daniel Maximin's *L'Isolé Soleil*, as well as Assia Djébar's *Femmes d'Alger dans leur appartement* for the CARAF series of the University of Virginia.

Index

Index

Index

Index

Index